Priestly Formation in the Human Virtues

The Priest as a Man of Justice

Priestly Formation in the Human Virtues

Volume I

The Priest as a Man of Justice

Angel Perez-Lopez

TAN Books
Gastonia, North Carolina

Nihil Obstat: Reverend Matthew Kauth, STD
Censor Deputatus

Imprimatur: Most Reverend Peter J. Jugis, JCD
Bishop of Charlotte
July 5, 2017

The nihil obstat and imprimatur are official declarations that a book is free from doctrinal or moral error. No implication is contained therein that those who grant the nihil obstat or imprimatur agree with the contents, opinions, or statements expressed.

ISBN: 978-1-5051-0703-6

Published in the United States by
TAN Books
PO Box 269
Gastonia, NC 28053
www.TANBooks.com

Printed in India

"What shall I render to the Lord
for all his bounty to me?
I will lift up the cup of salvation
and call on the name of the Lord" (Psalm 116:12–13).

—With gratitude to those responsible for my priestly formation.

CONTENTS

FOREWORD

WHEN I was in my sophomore year at Iowa State University, the power of the Catholic faith in which I was raised came alive for me in a way I had never experienced. Quite suddenly I was amazed and captivated by what I read and heard in Scripture. I experienced the Real Presence of Christ in the Eucharist and longed to spend time in his presence. I felt freedom and the lifting of burdens when my sins were absolved in the sacrament of Reconciliation. I began to pray in a relational way, opening my heart to God. I came to know that God had a plan for my life, that his plan would bring me real happiness and fulfillment, and that I had never asked him what that plan was. The switch was thrown, my faith had come to life, and this has made all the difference. That was 1992. Eight years later, I was ordained a priest for the Diocese of Sioux Falls, and thirteen years later still, I was appointed rector of Saint John Vianney Theological Seminary in Denver, Colorado, tasked with leading the formation of priests for the New Evangelization.

Over the years, I have met many practicing Catholics for whom that switch has not yet been thrown. At Saint John Vianney, we form the seminarians in something I call "The Transmission for the New Evangelization." That's "transmission" in the sense of a car or truck, the combination of parts that bring the power of the vehicle's engine to where the rubber hits the road. We form our seminarians in eight interlocking elements that facilitate the power of God being brought to bear where "the rubber hits the road"; that is, in the concrete circumstances of people's lives. These elements include relational prayer, discernment of spirits, proclamation of the kerygma, servant leadership, the gifts of the Holy Spirit, and healing and deliverance in Christ. Additionally, the evangelistic priest needs an unflagging interest in a person's experience of God coupled with a desire to engage that person relationally, creating a favorable environment for them to take the next step in relationship with Christ and the Church.

And, of course, that relational engagement calls for well-formed human virtues. It was want of a systematic, substantial, and practical resource for formation in human virtue specially tailored to the priest and future priest that led me to ask Fr. Angel Pérez-López to undertake the labor that has matured and borne fruit in the form of this series. And so I am delighted and full of gratitude to be able to present *Priestly Formation in the Human Virtues, Volume 1: The Priest as a Man of Justice.*

John Paul II's exhortation on priestly formation speaks of the aim of human formation in seminary:

> In order that his ministry may be humanly as credible and acceptable as possible, it is important that the priest should mold his human personality in such a way that it becomes a bridge and not an obstacle for others in their meeting with Jesus Christ the Redeemer of humanity. (*Pastores Dabo Vobis*, no. 43)

Those involved in seminary formation today know the particular challenges present in this realm of the formation effort. Fr. Angel's extensive research and writing on formation in the human virtues is a tremendous gift to help meet these challenges. This volume and the ones that follow draw on his deep expertise in philosophy and moral theology, an expertise seasoned by his experience in seminary formation. St. Thomas is the main guide throughout the project, but he is not the only one. Fr. Angel brings out the best of what is old and what is new, to offer an eminently practical resource to both understand these virtues in-depth and form them through effective practices and applications.

Each chapter presents a different virtue and, uniquely, offers a concrete guide consisting of a variety of practices that promote growth in the virtue and eliminate obstacles to that virtue. The guide is a kind of workout plan, offering a set of spiritual exercises to strengthen the virtue and weaken its opposing vices. The in-depth understanding of the virtue presented allows formators and seminarians alike to see clearly how these various practices specifically target the needed growth in particular aspects of the virtue considered.

This program of priestly formation in the human virtues is organized around the cardinal virtues viewed through a very particular and important lens. The author calls it the perspective of charity. This specific focus informs the entire project beginning with the premise that spiritual formation is the integrating factor of all other aspects of seminary formation (Program for Priestly Formation, no. 119 and *Pastores Dabo Vobis,* no. 45). Charity, as human and divine friendship, is the essence of spiritual formation. Consequently, formation in human virtue with candidates for Holy Orders should not be approached as if seminary were the Aristotelian *Lyceum*. Rather, supernatural grace and one's personal relationship with God must be a continual point of reference for the formation of these human virtues. Charity is like the "soul" (*anima*) of every aspect of priestly formation. It is like the "soul" of one's intellectual formation. It is like the "soul" of one's pastoral activity. It is also like the "soul" of human formation. Human virtues are to be fostered within the context of our personal relationship with God, within the context of our friendship with him. This friendship is what most effectively animates our growth in virtue.

Viewing growth in human virtues in the context of one's relationship with God leads the author to begin this series by treating the virtues related to justice, with the significant starting point of the virtue of gratitude.

I am deeply grateful for Fr. Angel's devoted research and labor to author this outstanding resource for priestly formation in the human virtues. His teaching has proved so very fruitful for our seminarians! I sincerely pray that this series will assist seminaries far and wide in forming future priests whose human personality can serve as bridge for others in their meeting with Jesus Christ, the redeemer of humanity.

Fr. Scott Traynor
Rector, Saint John Vianney Theological Seminary 2013–2017
Denver, Colorado

Acknowledgments

MANY more people than I can list here have contributed to this book in one way or another. Yet, I would like to acknowledge first those who have been responsible for my own priestly formation. I owe them an enormous debt of gratitude, which will last unto eternity. To them I dedicate this work. I would also like to offer a special word of appreciation to my brother Fr. Israel Pérez-López, with whom I have had the pleasure to discuss in much detail the entire content of this book. He has helped me greatly with his reassuring insights and critical reading of the original manuscript. I want to thank Archbishop Samuel J. Aquila and Fr. Timothy Gallagher as well for their endorsements and encouragements throughout this project. Moreover, I am grateful to Fr. Scott Traynor for having the vision, for taking the initiative of asking me to work on a program on priestly formation in the human virtues for Saint John Vianney Seminary in Denver, and for writing the foreword. To Mary Justice, I am thankful for patiently proofreading the entire book more than once. I am also grateful to Fr. Gary Selin and Fr. Andreas Hoeck for reading and/or discussing with me some of its contents. Last but not least, I would like to express my deep gratitude to the seminarians that I have had the honor of forming and teaching during my years at Saint John Vianney. Their contribution to this book is of paramount importance. Of course, despite the assistance of all these people, none of them can be held accountable for the defects of my argument or presentation. They remain entirely my own.

Abbreviations

All Scripture quotes are from the Revised Standard Version Catholic Edition (RSV-CE), unless otherwise noted. All the magisterial documents cited have been accessed at the Vatican website (w2. Vatican.va). For Plato, Aristotle, and Thomas Aquinas, unless otherwise indicated, I have followed the translations referenced in the bibliography. I have also used the English translations indicated for Augustine and other Church Fathers. Occasionally, I had to consult the *Patrologia Latina*. In those instances, the translations are mine.

AL	Francis, *Amoris Laetitia.*
CA	John Paul II, *Centesimus Annus.*
CCC	*Catechism of the Catholic Church.*
De Civitate Dei	Augustine, *The City of God.*
DH	Vatican II, *Dignitatis Humanae.*
De Malo	Thomas Aquinas, *Quaestiones Disputatae de Malo.*
De Moribus Ecclesiae	Augustine, *Of the Morals of the Catholic Church.*
De Perfectione	Thomas Aquinas, *De Perfectione Spiritualis Vitae.*
De Potentia	Thomas Aquinas, *Quaestiones Disputatae de Potentia Dei.*
De Principis Naturae	Thomas Aquinas, *De Principis Naturae Ad Fratrem Sylvestrum.*
De Trinitate	Augustine, *The Trinity.*

De Veritate	Thomas Aquinas, *Quaestiones Disputatae de Veritate.*
De Virtutibus	Thomas Aquinas, *Quaestiones Disputatae de Virtutibus.*
EG	Francis, *Evangelii Gaudium.*
FC	John Paul II, *Familaris Consortio.*
FR	John Paul II, *Fides et Ratio.*
GS	Vatican II, *Gaudium et Spes.*
In Duo Praec.	Thomas Aquinas, *In Duo Praecepta Caritatis et in Decem Legis Praecepta Exposition.*
In Ethic.	Thomas Aquinas, *Sententia Libri Ethicorum.*
In Meta.	Thomas Aquinas, *In libros Metaphysicorum expositio.*
In Sent.	Thomas Aquinas, *Scriptum Super Libros Sententiarum.*
LG	Vatican II, *Lumen Gentium.*
MD	John Paul II, *Mulieris Dignitatem.*
OT	Vatican II, *Optatam Totius.*
PDV	John Paul II, *Pastores Dabo Vobis.*
PL	*Patrologia Latina.*
PO	Vatican II, *Presbyterorum Ordinis.*
RH	John Paul II, *Redemptor Hominis.*
RMis	John Paul II, *Redemptoris Missio.*
ST	Thomas Aquinas, *Summa Theologiae.*
SCG	Thomas Aquinas, *Summa Contra Gentiles.*
Super De Trinitate	Thomas Aquinas, *Super Boethium De Trinitate.*
Super Eph.	Thomas Aquinas, *Super Epistolam ad Ephesios Lectura.*

Super Ga.	Thomas Aquinas, *Super Epistolam ad Galatas Lectura.*
Super Heb.	Thomas Aquinas, *Super Epistolam ad Hebraeos Lectura.*
Super I Cor.	Thomas Aquinas, *Super Primam Epistolam ad Corinthios Lectura.*
Super II Cor.	Thomas Aquinas, *Super Secundam Epistolam ad Corinthios Lectura.*
Super Io.	Thomas Aquinas, *Super Evangelium S. Ioannis Lectura.*
Super I Tim.	Thomas Aquinas, *Super Primam Epistolam ad Timotheum Lectura.*
Super Matt.	Thomas Aquinas, *Super Evangelium S. Matthaei Lectura.*
Super Phil.	Thomas Aquinas, *Super Epistolam ad Philipenses Lectura.*
Super Rom.	Thomas Aquinas, *Super Epistolam ad Romanos Lectura.*
TOB	John Paul II, *Man and Woman He Created Them.*
VS	John Paul II, *Veritatis Splendor.*

A Word To Those Responsible For Priestly Formation

BLESSED Paul VI spoke quite forcefully about the need for priestly formation to focus on all the virtues. He viewed them as part of a sound priestly asceticism, which is demanding but not suffocating.[1] He further noted that in priestly formation, education in the natural or acquired virtues should be harmonized with the supernatural ones. The pope was quite explicit in noting the individual importance or value of some of these virtues. It is worth quoting the full list:

> Self-denial in the highest degree—an essential condition if one would follow Christ; humility and obedience as expressions of internal truth and of an ordered liberty; prudence, justice, courage, and temperance—virtues without which it is impossible for true and profound religious life to exist; a sense of responsibility, fidelity, and loyalty in the acceptance of one's obligations; a balance between contemplation and action; detachment and a spirit of poverty, which will give tone and vigor to evangelical freedom; chastity, the result of a persevering struggle, *harmonized with all the other natural and supernatural virtues*; a serene and secure contact with the world to whose service the young man will dedicate himself for Christ and for His kingdom.[2]

---

1 For the need to rediscover asceticism in priestly formation, see Linacre Institute, *After Asceticism: Sex, Prayer, and Deviant Priests* (Bloomington, IN: AuthorHouse, 2006).

2 Paul VI, *Sacerdotalis Coelibatus*, 70. Emphasis added.

Pius XI also explained that "all Christian virtues should flourish in the soul of the priest."[3] Such a flourishing is also foundational for the priest's teaching office: "The priest must teach the truths of faith; but the truths of religion are never so worthily and effectively taught *as when taught by virtue*; as reflected in the common saying: 'Deeds speak louder than words.'"[4] Those responsible for priestly formation should, in fact, also be examples of virtue. The same pope said to bishops:

> Give the best of your clergy to your seminaries; do not fear to take them from other positions. These positions may seem of greater moment, but in reality their importance is not to be compared with that of the seminaries, which is capital and indispensable. Seek also from elsewhere, wherever you can find them, men really fitted for this noble task. *Let them be such as teach priestly virtues, rather by example than by words, men who are capable of imparting, together with learning, a solid, manly and apostolic spirit.*[5]

These and other documents of the Church's magisterial teaching require that priestly formation, especially human formation, involves a formation in the virtues.

A Practical Difficulty

Yet there seems to be a practical difficulty. Today, a good number of rectors, formation advisors, and spiritual directors find a certain lack of the resources that could aid them in translating these magisterial teachings into concrete practice. Many did not use any such resources in their own seminary training. So the task of effectively forming future priests in concrete virtues can be truly daunting and intricate.

---

3 Pius XI, *Ad Catholici Sacerdotii*, 39. Emphasis added. See also PO, 3, 15; PDV, 26–28, 30, 55.

4 Pius XI, *Ad Catholici Sacerdotii*, 36. Emphasis added.

5 Ibid., 66. Emphasis added.

When I myself first approached this task, as a formation advisor at St. John Vianney Seminary in Denver, I was haunted by questions such as these:

- Which precise virtues are to be fostered? In which order are they to be taught?
- How is priestly formation in the moral virtues different from the classes that seminarians take in moral or spiritual theology?
- What is the correct balance between intellectual information about the virtue in question and practical advice in order to grow in it?
- How can we overcome the false impression that formation in the virtues is a narcissistic and Pelagian project of independence and autonomy?
- Which concrete actions promote the growth of a given virtue? Which concrete actions remove the obstacles and vices that hinder its full development?
- How does priestly human formation in the acquired virtues relate to the spiritual life and our call to supernatural charity?
- What sort of spiritual exercises can a seminarian adopt in order to grow in each specific virtue?

At first, I must confess, even though I am both a philosopher and a theologian, I was a bit lost. I certainly knew where to go in order to learn more about the virtues. However, when I searched for resources that answered these questions in particular, I could not find what I was looking for.

For this reason, I decided to begin the serious endeavor of finding the correct answers. The four books in this series, entitled *Priestly Formation in the Human Virtues,* are the fruit of wanting to share this work with priests and seminarians. Every chapter in this series attempts to offer a service to those involved in priestly formation by addressing these precise and practical points when dealing with particular virtues.

I hope that my scholarly expertise as a philosopher and a moral theologian, combined with my experience as a practicing Catholic, seminarian, priest, spiritual director, and seminary formation advisor, can enable me to offer a service to those involved in the formation of future priests. Perhaps this is what Fr. Scott Traynor, then rector at Saint John Vianney Seminary in Denver when I began this project, had in mind when he asked me to work on a program of human formation in the virtues, as part of a larger vision oriented to the formation of priests for the New Evangelization. I am grateful to him because the contents of this book, as well as the idea of a series of books on priestly formation in the human virtues, came about as an answer to his request.

My goal is to show that by growing in virtue, seminarians will freely affirm and bring to perfection their own human and male identities, as ultimately revealed in Christ.[6] As a result, they will be more authentic priests by sharing more intimately in Jesus's priesthood. Never is a man more himself than when he fulfills his own unique and personal vocation in salvation history.

Those who want to exercise physically in an effective manner usually consult with a professional trainer. The trainer's knowledge and experience allows him to identify with precision the exact series of exercises needed, the required times for rest, the kind of diet to be followed, and so on.

Following this kind of advice is essential to avoid wasting time. Anyone can show up at the gym and spend some time there doing whatever exercises come to mind. Some people may even have some knowledge of what they are doing. Nevertheless, nothing

---

6 For a philosophical treatment of this idea, see Antonio Millán-Puelles, *La Libre Afirmación de Nuestro Ser: Una Fundamentación de La ética Realista* (Madrid: Ediciones Rialp, 1994).

compares, in terms of effectiveness and success, to the guidance of a personal trainer. For this reason, professional athletes usually have recourse to the aid of such trainers in order to achieve marked success in their careers.

Something analogous happens when we want to "exercise" spiritually in the virtues.[7] To do so effectively, and with the limited amount of time available in seminary, seminarians need help in singling out with precision the virtues to work on and the correct order in which to do so.

This task is not as easy as it may seem. To name virtues, we must know something of their essence and proper acts.[8] Moreover, not every good action is a virtue or good operative habit. Unfortunately, our contemporary culture is not a friend of distinctions. Nonetheless, they are quite important for the task at hand. They have enormous practical consequences.

For instance, today many people talk about kindness as a virtue. To be sure, being nice, kind, and pleasing to other people, is a good thing. It can be a good act. However, as we will see in great detail in this book, this good act springs from the virtue of affability. Yet kindness and affability should not be confused.

This is not simply a matter of terminology. Consider, for example, how sometimes the very virtue of affability requires us to be *unkind and displeasing to others*.[9] If we call affability "kindness," this important point will escape our attention.

But there is more. A man can injure himself at the gym while having the good intention to work out but lacking the precise knowledge of what he is doing. In a similar way, if we keep confusing affability with kindness, we may end up fostering not a good action, but a harmful vice.

---

7 The expression is inspired by *ST* I–II, q. 65, a. 1, ad 1.

8 See *De Veritate*, q. 10, a. 9, c.

9 See *ST* I–II, q. 115, a. 1, c.

Indeed, flattery is precisely the vice that belongs to people who are always nice and kind no matter what, who do not have the virtue of affability, and who are unable to displease others when necessary. Remember: King Saul was rejected by God precisely because he disobeyed him out of fear of displeasing his soldiers (see 1 Sm 15:24). Certainly, no seminary formation program wants to promote vices.

Virtues are all interconnected. Although they may be chiefly in one power or faculty of the soul, they extend to others in their synergy.[10] Thus, virtues form a sort of "organism."[11]

It is critical to choose well the order of the virtues in which we will spiritually exercise, so as to grow in them. Also, it is vital to identify exactly the concrete actions that promote the growth of a certain virtue, and to explain to the person who is being formed why these actions do so. Moreover, it is imperative to single out and eradicate the exact obstacles or vices that impede the growth in this same virtue, being able, once again, to explain why these particular behaviors are obstacles that need to be removed, and which positive actions need to be utilized for this removal.

Some of these vices are difficult to recognize, because they look very much like virtues. For instance, prodigality can look like generosity; flattery may be easily mistaken for affability; insensibility has a semblance of temperance; servility resembles humility. Other vices, instead, are so opposed to the virtues that

---

10 See *ST* I–II, q. 56, a. 2, c.

11 See Aristotle, *Nichomachean Ethics*, VI. 13. 1144b3; Reginald Garrigou-Lagrange, *The Three Ages of the Interior Life: Prelude of Eternal Life*, *vol.* 1, trans. Timothea Doyle (Rockford, IL: TAN Books and Publishers, 1989), 48–96; Martin Rhonheimer, *The Perspective of Morality: Philosophical Foundations of Thomistic Virtue Ethics*, trans. Gerald Malsbary (Washington, DC: Catholic University of America Press, 2011), 244–48; Julia Annas, *The Morality of Happiness* (New York: Oxford University Press, 1993), 73–84.

they are easily identifiable, but are quite difficult to eradicate. So what is the best strategy to follow?

Finally, we also need to understand what kind of supernatural aids God offers in order to grow into each of the virtues, and how to access them for our spiritual life. All these things constitute the material, as it were, for the precise series of spiritual exercises that we need to practice so as to grow into a particular virtue.

In the Footsteps of Thomas Aquinas and John Paul II

Priestly Formation in the Human Virtues is deeply informed by the philosophy and theology of St. Thomas Aquinas. In a sense, I would like to propose herein a journey in his footsteps, keeping up with this great master as much as possible.

The great Canadian Thomist philosopher Fr. Lawrence Dewan prompted me to a profound reflection on the saint's insights into human formation when I was trying to create this program for the seminary in Denver. He proposed in seed form what these books aim to offer to seminarians and priests:

> Not all can be theologians and philosophers, but all deserve the benefits of the centuries-long experience the Church has in these areas. I wish to stress the lifelong use of St. Thomas's *Summa theologiae secunda secundae*. Moral education, self-help in spirituality, requires that we make such a book, such a treatise on human living, a constant stimulus of our reflection.[12]

Now, I am a student of Aquinas, thanks to the mediation of Pope St. John Paul II. So this work reflects his influence as well. On some occasions, I have tried to enrich Thomas's teachings, not necessarily

---

12 Lawrence Dewan, *Wisdom and Law: Essays in Thomistic Ethics* (New York: Fordham University Press, 2008), 362.

with new content, but with some practical applications to priestly life in light of the philosophy and theology of the Polish pope.

I have emphasized in my reading of Aquinas two particular points from Wojtyła's theology. In light of the pope's emphasis on the Vatican II document *Gaudium et Spes* (nos. 22, 24), I have underlined the christocentrism of the virtues and their connection with the gift of self. Even before his election to the papacy, Wojtyła argued that "this gift of self, which man can and should make in order to fully find himself, is realized through particular virtues and through each of them."[13] The future pope thought that this emphasis would bring about "a new and perhaps more personalistic *grasp of the entire aretology* [theory of the virtues]."[14] I have followed that indication to the best of my abilities.

The texts I will quote throughout this book will show that neither of these points is absent in Aquinas's theology of the virtues. However, I must grant that they are not easily seen by someone who does not know his biblical commentaries, and who has only a partial knowledge of some of his major works. Indeed, when reading the Angelic Doctor, sometimes the trees do not allow us to see the forest.

Other authors have helped me in different chapters. Yet it is to Thomas and John Paul II that these books are most indebted. I like to think that they are the true teachers in these pages, as I would consider myself only their assistant. I have simply tried to let their voices be heard and to explain their wisdom concerning formation in the virtues.

As Dewan said, not everybody can be a professional philosopher and theologian. Yet every priest or seminarian, as a

---

13 Karol Wojtyła, "On the Meaning of Spousal Love," in *Love and Responsibility*, trans. Grzegorz Ignatik (Boston: Pauline Books & Media, 2013), 284.

14 Ibid.

student and teacher of virtue, must have some knowledge about philosophy and theology, even if knowledge is not actually enough to become virtuous. Consider a useful analogy.

Education in virtue is similar to the art of music. Theoretical knowledge is necessary but insufficient. For example, we do not learn how to play the classical guitar simply by reading books about it. We actually need to practice and eventually play the instrument.

In the same way, we learn virtue by both intellectual knowledge and practice. The art of gaining the knowledge about virtue necessary to become truly virtuous, and not just learned, belongs to what the ancients understood as philosophy. As Pope Benedict explains, the ancients were teachers of human formation: "Philosophy at that time was not generally seen as a difficult academic discipline, as it is today. Rather, the philosopher was someone who knew how to teach the essential art: *the art of being authentically human*—the art of living and dying."[15]

Along these same lines, Aristotle explained that people too young in age, and above all, in character, were not suitable candidates to hear his lectures on the virtues. They were not eligible, precisely because Aristotle's lectures were not meant simply to convey information, but rather to lead his students to the state of virtue. The Greek philosopher was quite insistent:

> A young man is not a proper hearer of lectures on political science; for he is inexperienced in the actions that occur in life, but its discussions start from these and are about these; and, further, *since he tends to follow his passions, his study will be vain and unprofitable, because the end aimed at is not knowledge but action.*[16]

---

15 Benedict XVI, *Spe Salvi*, 6. Emphasis added.

16 *Nichomachean Ethics*, I. 3.1094b29-1095a12. Emphasis added. See Ignacio Yarza, *La Racionalidad de La ética de Aristóteles: Un Estudio Sobre Ética a Nicómaco I* (Pamplona: EUNSA, 2001).

Aristotle thought that being young, in this sense, is not a matter of years. Mainly, it is all about character. To be admitted into his school, the candidate had to have received a minimum formation in his family and in his village (*polis*).[17] For this reason, the text continues:

> It makes no difference whether he is young in years or youthful in character; the defect does not depend on time, but on his living, and pursuing each successive object, as passion directs. *For to such persons, as to the incontinent, knowledge brings no profit*; but to those who desire and act in accordance with rational principle, knowledge about such matters will be of great benefit.[18]

According to Aristotle, then, *a certain level of maturity* is necessary, with three aspects: 1) experience in the actions that occur in life, 2) power to integrate our passions, and 3) desire to act in accordance with reason. In fact, "it is among people who are already trying to live virtuous lives that the study of the virtues will have some point."[19] These three characteristics could be considered the prerequisites for being admitted as an ethics student in the Aristotelian gymnasium near Athens known as the Lyceum.

In a sense, and with the additional supernatural advantages afforded to us by God's revelation in Jesus Christ, we are doing something quite similar in this book. We are not only concerned about knowledge; we are, above all, concerned about becoming virtuous, which empowers us to be happy and to lead others to happiness. As Dewan says again, "The study and cultivation of virtuousness is precisely the production of responsible liberty."[20]

---

17 See Dewan, *Wisdom and Law*, 360.

18 *Nichomachean Ethics*, I. 3.1094b29-1095a12. Emphasis added.

19 Dewan, *Wisdom and Law*, 361.

20 Ibid., 359. Emphasis added.

How to Use This Book

These four books have been forged within the experience of my role as a formation advisor at Denver's Saint John Vianney Seminary. They are meant primarily for seminarians, but they can also be used by ordained priests, as part of their ongoing priestly formation.[21] If that is the case, I recommend that the priest's spiritual director accompany him throughout the process.

Each chapter of these books deals with one virtue. Each one has been previously delivered under the format of a formation conference or catechesis for the seminarians. So formation advisors or those responsible for priestly human formation can use them as a sort of script or schema to be adapted to the unique circumstances of each seminary community.

No book can really replace this key role. Those responsible for priestly formation have an indispensable awareness about the unique circumstances of a given seminary, diocese, and its seminarians. One, two, or even three conferences could be offered per chapter, depending on how they are arranged.

A few words about the common structure of the chapters will facilitate the use of this book. The opening section always deals with the value or *importance* of the virtue at hand for priestly formation, priestly life, and future ministry. I have often invoked magisterial documents, as well as spiritual authors and other theological and philosophical authorities, explaining why the virtue treated is important.

This first section always concludes with a set of questions. They are meant to be discussed in small groups and to be meditated upon privately in prayer. The answers should be realistic and sincere.

By nature, the human will is always attracted to what is perceived as good and averse to what is perceived as evil. Therefore,

21 See PDV, 9, 70–81.

the purpose of this sort of questionnaire is to *motivate* future priests to engage in the task of growing in that particular virtue.

To this end, the questionnaire about the value of the virtue under consideration always follows a fixed pedagogical pattern. At first, it aims to bring to the seminarian's awareness the need he has to grow in the virtue treated, by pointing out what its lack does to his personal life. Moreover, since the future priest is part of the seminary community, to whose common good he is to contribute with his own virtues, I direct his attention to the impact that the lack of this virtue always has for the seminary.

Next, I aim to move the seminarian's awareness forward in time. Priests are to be both virtuous themselves and teachers of virtue by word and example. So I ask seminarians to imagine what lack of this virtue will mean for their future life as a priest, and for the life of their spiritual children.

Finally, I conclude by asking them to imagine the opposite: How will the presence of this virtue be truly enriching, not only for their own lives, but also for the particular community whose common good they will be fostering in their priestly ministry? In most cases, we are talking about their future parish. (Other questions could be added, depending on circumstances.)

The remainder of the chapter is always a succinct selection of the most essential *traits* of the virtue. The goal is not only to convey information but, above all, to explain which and why particular acts promote growth in that virtue, and which and why particular acts remove the main obstacles that hinder such growth. In this sense, my treatment of the virtues in these volumes does not exactly correspond with the scientific perspective found in moral theology books.

I do not offer here, properly speaking, a philosophical and theological theory of virtue. Neither do I study, in depth and with rigor, the virtues in general or each one individually in light of all their causes. Rather, I have a very specific practical goal in mind.

I have chosen what I deem essential information to practice and teach the precise list of spiritual exercises with which each chapter concludes.[22] Thus, every exercise listed in each chapter finds its raison d'être in the previous treatment of the virtue.

Even so, the list of exercises is not exhaustive. Adaptation to particular circumstances may be needed here as well. For instance, for those familiar with Ignatian spirituality, these exercises could be used within the context of the Examen prayer.[23]

Clearly, no talk or conference, and certainly no book, can make someone virtuous. It does not matter how competent the speaker or the author is. To become virtuous, we need spiritual practice in the virtue. As a result, the initial conference given on the virtue is only the beginning of a practical and spiritual process.

In my view, these exercises should take a month or more. In this manner, seminarians will have time to exercise spiritually and to revisit the parts of the text most pertinent to their own lives at that particular time. In this way they will move back and forth between the spiritual exercises and their explanation in the text.

A Tool of Encouragement and Training

These spiritual exercises and their explanation provide a teaching tool, not only for the seminarian, but also for the formation advisor and the spiritual director. It should be a tool of encouragement and training. This instrument should not be understood in a mechanical way. Growing in virtue is not like repairing a car.

Contrary to popular belief, virtues are neither mechanisms nor routines. They are much more complex. They are, rather, creative

22 See *ST* I–II, q. 63, a. 2.

23 For a great treatment of this topic, see Timothy M. Gallagher, *The Examen Prayer* (New York: Crossroad, 2006).

ways of expanding and conquering, as it were, the good use of our freedom.

Adopting the perspective of charity, these spiritual exercises harmonize natural acts with prayer, the sacraments, the gifts of the Holy Spirit, and other supernatural aids. Although these exercises are meant primarily to foster good actions and behaviors, they also constitute an instrument of discernment in a threefold manner.[24]

First, they bring to our awareness many forgotten elements of the moral and spiritual life. Second, they aid the seminarian in understanding and accepting good motions and inspirations, which come from his own virtues (natural or supernatural), his guardian angel, or God himself. Third, these spiritual exercises also assist the seminarian to understand and reject temptations, and to correct bad habits or customs he may have picked up along the way.

This threefold discernment should take place at different levels: in the conscience of the seminarian and in his relationships with his confessor, his spiritual director, and his formation advisor. Without confusing these different levels, it is imperative to remember that we need the help of others. God's help is always needed. The assistance of the confessor, the spiritual director, and the formation advisor is also part of the deal.

Of course, the degree to which the seminarian needs their help as instrumental agents of his formation varies, depending on the virtue and the circumstances of the individual seminarian. Yet I would like to emphasize that neither these exercises nor these books are meant to be sheer self-help. Thomas makes the following applicable analogy:

> We acquire knowledge not only by discovering it but also through teaching, that is, through someone else's agency. Likewise, we find

---

24 For an elucidating treatment of discernment of spirits in St. Ignatius, see Timothy M. Gallagher, *The Discernment of Spirits: An Ignatian Guide for Everyday Living* (New York: Crossroad, 2005).

> help in acquiring virtues through correction and training, that is, through someone else's agency. The more we are disposed to virtue of our own accord, the less we need correction and training, just as the sharper our natural intellectual talent, the less we need others to teach us.[25]

Nonetheless, just as we need the help of our teachers of philosophy and theology in order to grow in our intellectual formation, we also need the help of our confessor, spiritual director, and formation advisor in order to grow in virtue.

Since many spiritual directors and formation advisors treasure St. Ignatius's *Spiritual Exercises* as a gift for the entire Church, it is important to note that growth in virtue has its own important place, not only in the Examen prayer, but also in the rules of discernment for the first week of the Exercises. We read in the fourteenth rule that the enemy "conducts himself as a leader, intent upon conquering and robbing what he desires."[26] He surrounds us like a besieging force surrounds a city. He "looks in turn at all our theological, cardinal, and moral virtues; and where he finds us weakest and most in need for our eternal salvation, there he attacks us and attempts to take us."[27] It is wise, therefore, to strengthen those weak points within us. It is especially important to do so, while in spiritual consolation, and in conjunction with God's grace. In the pages that follow, I intend to offer a practical way of doing so.

The Ordering of Virtues to be Considered

Pedagogical studies in the genetical sequence—that is, in how to

---

25 *De Virtutibus*, q. un., a. 9, ad 9.

26 Gallagher, "The Text of the Rules," in *The Discernment of Spirits: An Ignatian Guide for Everyday Living*, 10.

27 Ibid.

educate someone in the virtues—show that we should alter the order in which Thomas Aquinas deals with the virtues in the *Secunda secundae*. The Angelic Doctor seems to be concerned there with the best order for the teaching of theology, not necessarily with the best pedagogical order for the genesis of the virtues in the spiritual development of the human person.

Thus, Roqueñí proposes that, within the context of the family, we should begin teaching children the virtues in the province of temperance, then move to those in the province of fortitude, and from there, go to the ones in justice, then prudence.[28] Since seminarians are not infants but young adults, I have altered this order. I propose to begin with the virtues in the province of justice; then move to the ones that belong to temperance; then to the ones associated with fortitude; and finally, prudence. Of course, this order is not set in stone as the best order. It is only a proposal, which I think has its own important benefits.

Nevertheless, I should emphasize that it would be highly convenient to work through all the materials of these books during a seminarian's priestly formation. To do it twice would be optimal. However, we all know that seminarians' time is limited, and not everything in this regard can be completed in the years of seminary formation.

For this reason, ongoing priestly formation is necessary. As I already mentioned, these books can be useful in that regard, as well as in conjunction with the priest's spiritual director. Yet it is essential to exercise in the virtues as a whole and not to isolate just one or two.

In fact, explaining the connection between the virtues and replying to an objector who argues that we could exercise and

---

28 See José Manuel Roqueñí, *Educación En La Afectividad: Una Propuesta Desde El Pensamiento de Santo Tomás de Aquino* (Pamplona: EUNSA, 2005).

develop one virtue without the others, Aquinas clarifies that "man needs to exercise himself at the same time in the matters of all moral virtues. And if he exercise himself, by good deeds, in all such matters, he will acquire the habits of all the moral virtues."[29]

Virtues go together. Thomas explains that attempts to exercise only one specific and isolated virtue will fail. He says that if someone were to "exercise himself by good deeds in regard to one matter, but not in regard to another, for instance, by behaving well in matters of anger, but not in matters of concupiscence; he will indeed acquire a certain habit of restraining his anger; *but this habit will lack the nature of virtue*, through the absence of prudence, which is wanting in matters of concupiscence."[30]

Dealing first with the priest as a man of justice has the advantage of beginning with the acquired virtues that are most evidently *relational*, avoiding the risk of viewing formation in the virtues as a narcissistic project of autonomous independence. Another advantage is that, at the same time we deal with these virtues, we also come to important conclusions as to how to organize the seminary community in order to create the best context to grow in virtue.

Additionally, the virtues in the province of justice have a very positive impact on the subculture of the seminary and on the seminarians. They promote attitudes of authentic participation in the community, in view of the common good of forming men to the priesthood. Furthermore, the virtues in the province of justice are also foundational, in my view, to foster other virtues related to the provinces of temperance, fortitude, and prudence.

For instance, promoting veracity (or living in the light of truth) in the seminarian's relationship with his confessor, spiritual director, and formation advisor seems fundamental to foster priestly chastity and many other virtues as well. What is more, beginning with the

---

29 *ST* I–II, q. 65, a. 1, ad 1.

30 Ibid. Emphasis added.

province of justice also provides an opportunity to take the virtue of gratitude as the starting point of our spiritual exercises. Such a virtue, in my view, is the best way of commencing to exercise the human virtues from the perspective of charity.[31] Virtue is learnt in community and within the logic of the gift of self, wherein gratitude is the first response to being loved by God and others.

31 For the close relationship between the virtues within the province of justice and charity, see Rhonheimer, *The Perspective of Morality*, 232–33.

King David's Testament: An Introduction

"BE strong, and show yourself a man and keep the charge of the Lord your God, walking in his ways and keeping his statutes, his commandments, his ordinances, and his testimonies, as it is written in the Law of Moses" (1 Kgs 2:2–3).

These are King David's last words to his son Solomon, right before his death. They serve as his last will and spiritual testament. After all his accomplishments and failures as king of Israel, David offers these words of wisdom as his legacy to his son and future heir to the throne.

This testament conveys two precious principles or moral maxims. First, for his son to be a good king, he needs to follow God's law. Second, to follow this law amounts to presenting himself as a man, growing in his humanity. Thus, while the first principle connects God's law to the morally good exercise of kingship, the second relates this same law to a much broader phenomenon: namely, human identity, the true meaning and vocation of being a man who flourishes in his masculinity. The Latin Vulgate *emphatically* evinces this last point by using the direct imperative "*esto vir*"—be a man!

The Promise of a Future King

Solomon failed to follow his father's instructions. The First Book of Kings recounts how his predilection for foreign women led him to disobey God's law. He had seven hundred wives and an additional three hundred concubines (see 1 Kgs 11:3). Influenced by them, Solomon turned to false gods or idols. He even disobeyed God himself, who appeared to him *twice*, in order to correct him (see 1 Kgs 11:9–10).

To be sure, his father David had sinned and had not behaved impeccably during his reign. However, David was humble and sincere. By contrast, Solomon's "heart was not wholly true to the Lord his God, as was the heart of David his father" (1 Kgs 11:4).

As a result, God foretold Israel's ruin because of Solomon's infidelity and idolatry. Yet the Lord's paternal corrections would always keep David in mind: "I will for this afflict the descendants of David, *but not for ever*" (1 Kgs 11:39; emphasis added. See 1 Kgs 11:11–13, 33–34).

This affliction, God declares, will finally end when the Messiah, descending from David's regal line, comes at last. He "will be great, and will be called the Son of the Most High; and the Lord God will give to him the throne of his father David" (Lk 1:32). Indeed, Jesus will inherit David's throne and will bring his testament to a perfect and *unexpected* fulfillment.

With respect to the first principle of David's testament, the incarnate Son of God will be the King of the Jews and the King of kings, because of his obedience and perfect fulfillment of God's law (see Mt 5:17, 27:37; Phil 2:8–11). In turn, with respect to the second principle of that testament, Jesus will be not just any man, but the God-Man, who "reveals man to man himself and makes his supreme calling clear."[1] What is more, the Lord will bring to fulfillment both principles of David's testament in exercising his priesthood, by means of his sacrificial gift of self for the Church (see Eph 5:25). For this reason, I think that we can find in David's testament an important indication for priestly formation in the human virtues.

---

1 GS, 22.

THE NATURE OF CHRIST'S AUTHORITY

David's words to Solomon, as future king of Israel, imply that following God's law is indispensable in order to rule over others. To rule others, a future priest must learn to rule himself.[2] To reign over the people, he needs to reign over his desires. The Second Vatican Council understands this kind of kingship, through obedience to God's law, as a participation in Christ's pastoral governance, his *munus regendi*.[3]

Christ's royal authority or power (*exousia*), fully displayed on the mount of mission, where he commissioned the Apostles (see Mt 28:16–20), stands in clear contrast to the power promised by the devil if Jesus would prostrate himself and worship him, on the mount of temptation (see Mt 4:8–9). At this last mount, the devil claims to be the ruler of the world, capable of delegating power to Christ. He presents to Jesus the splendor of that power, the same power we renounce during the baptismal promises and at their renewal.

Joseph Cardinal Ratzinger (later Pope Benedict XVI) explains that the devil's *exousia*, authority, or power, "signifies being able to do what you want, enjoying what you want, having everything at your disposal and being able to choose the place of honor."[4] This *exousia* is an empty promise. It is a cheap forgery of God's real authority and power. It is based on terror, fear, selfishness, and the idolization of oneself.

David learned from his own experience and failures that the kind of power and authority the devil is proposing does not make a good king of the Jews. As a result, in his testament to Solomon, he advises his son to *rule by being obedient to God*. Jesus will fulfill this testament completely on the cross at Mount Calvary. There, his regal power and

---

2 See *Super Heb.*, cap. 5, no. 259.

3 See LG, 36; CCC 1592.

4 LG, 39.

authority are revealed as the fulfillment of David's testament, as a kingly power that comes from obedience to God's will.

Mount Calvary stands, therefore, as the necessary path to the mountain of mission, where we find the risen Christ receiving all power in heaven and on earth. On the cross, Christ fulfills the first principle of David's testament through the exercise of his priesthood. Because of his priestly obedience and gift of self, God exalts him and gives him the name above every other name (see Phil 2:9–11). God makes him not only the King of the Jews, but also the King of kings.

Becoming More Human by Doing What is Good

David's last words to his son Solomon, as they are ultimately fulfilled in Christ, must resound once again in Catholic seminaries around the world. We can find in them great wisdom for engaging in human priestly formation in the virtues. Within the context of seminary life, these fatherly words reflect the desire that every seminary priest responsible for priestly formation has for his seminarians.

The seminarians and priests who follow in Christ's priestly footsteps should configure their formation so as to be animated always by this first principle of David's testament: to be head in the Church and to rule, they should be the first to serve by discerning and obeying God's law.

On the other hand, David's testament relates God's law to human identity, flourishing in their masculinity. To be a man, to show oneself a man, implies following God's law. There is an interesting play on words here for the entire Latin tradition. This passage relates being a man (*esto vir*) to being *virtuous*, with having the strength (*virtus*) of character needed in order to do freely what is right and just, as prescribed by God's law. As a result, Solomon's male identity is both a *fact* and a *moral adventure* with a final destiny in self-fulfillment.

In this regard, David's testament brings to mind the rich man's question to Jesus about the secret of happiness: "Good Teacher, what must I do to inherit eternal life?" (see Mk 10:17). The Lord's answer matches David's: "You know the commandments" (Mk 10: 19). As the Greek poet Pindar once said, Solomon, or anyone who is to be happy, needs *to become who he is*. He is to work on his character formation. He is to acquire all sorts of "states of character that prepare us for acting rightly as human beings."[5]

Now, to become ever more human by doing what is good, by following God's law, is what formation or *education* in the virtues is all about.[6] Aquinas defines human formation or education as "the conducting and promoting [of the human person] to the perfect state of man *inasmuch as he is man*, that is to say, to the state of *virtue*."[7] In truth, growth in our human identity should never be opposed to the moral law or to growth in virtue.

As Thomas says, "All moral matters are reduced to the consideration of the virtues."[8] God's commandments, therefore, are not opposed to them. David's testament is absolutely right in identifying the following of God's law with growing in our humanity.[9] But we are also justified in identifying such growth with the acquisition of the virtues. To be a man (*vir*), to reach the perfection of our humanity by following the commandments

---

5 Dewan, *Wisdom and Law*, 359.

6 See Jacques Maritain, *Education at the Crossroads* (New Haven: Yale University Press, 1943), 1.

7 *In IV Sent.*, d. 26, q. 1, a. 1, c. Emphasis added. See Antonio Millán-Puelles, "La Formación de La Personalidad Humana," in *Obras Completas*, vol. III (Madrid: Ediciones Rialp, 2013), 193–366. This definition has been adopted by the Magisterium. See Pius XI, *Divini Illius Magistri*, 33.

8 *ST* II–II, prologue.

9 See *ST* I–II, q. 94, a. 3, c.

and receiving human formation—all these things really mean to become virtuous.

In fact, all God's commandments promote the virtues. They do so *directly*, when they command a good action. For instance, to honor father and mother promotes the virtue of piety; to keep the Sabbath holy fosters the virtue of religion. In turn, the commandments also promote the virtues *indirectly*, by removing obstacles for their growth. For example, the commandments against lying or stealing indirectly promote the virtues of truthfulness and justice, respectively.

Christ's Gift of Self Fulfilled David's Testament

These brief considerations help us to understand better how Christ fulfilled the second principle of David's testament in his priestly sacrifice on the cross. There, he reveals the great dignity of our moral vocation to flourish in our humanity. He reveals the truth about man. He provides the exemplar to which our actions should conform in order truly to promote our human identity by the acquisition of the virtues.

As Thomas explains, "An example of *every virtue* is found in the Cross," because "the Cross was not only the altar on which he suffered, but also the *chair from which he taught*."[10] For this reason, the crucifixion of Christ *the* priest is the best "school" in which to form seminarians in their humanity. Priestly human formation should adopt this very model.

This book is meant to be read within this precise context, by spiritually placing ourselves at the foot of Christ's cross and his gift of self. It is there that we will see most perfectly demonstrated the core virtue of the priest: I mean, of course, the virtue of *charity*.

---

10 *Super Heb.*, cap. 12, lect. 1, no. 667. Emphasis added.

The Core Virtue of Charity

Pope St. John Paul II once spoke of "the priest as a man of charity." This is, in fact, the very title given to his general audience on July 7, 1993.[11] These words provide the right perspective for priestly formation in the acquired virtues. The single most important idea proposed throughout the four volumes of this series, *Priestly Formation in the Human Virtues*, is that the priest is a man of justice, temperance, fortitude, and prudence, precisely because he aims to be a man of charity.

This insight is the basis on which priestly formation in the human virtues should develop in its integration into the spiritual life. So this perspective is like the overarching thesis for this entire project. Consider briefly the various reasons why it is imperative.

The first reason concerns the proper relationship between human and spiritual formation for the priest, as explained by magisterial teaching. The fathers of the Second Vatican Council observe that charity is the essence of priestly spiritual formation.[12] This observation should not be surprising to anyone because, as St. Thomas also says, "the perfection of the Christian life consists radically in charity."[13]

Keeping this truth in mind, John Paul explains that "for every priest, his spiritual formation is *the core which unifies and gives life* to his being a priest and his acting as a priest."[14] According to the language of this text, spiritual formation can be compared to the

11 One can also find a development of this idea in Samuel J. Aquila, "The Priest as a Man of Charity: Integrating Human and Spiritual Priestly Formation," in *Christ as the Foundation of Seminary Formation*, ed. James Keating (Omaha: IPF Publications, 2016), 35–57.

12 See OT, 8; PDV, 45–46; *ST* II–II, q. 23, a. 1.

13 *ST* II–II, q. 184, a. 1, c.

14 PDV, 45. Emphasis added.

human soul in this regard: our one rational soul is the best example of a core reality that unifies and gives life to the whole.[15]

We can press this analogy even farther: spiritual formation is like the soul of priestly formation. Considering God's image in man as regards its accidental qualities, Aquinas affirms that "the whole human soul is in the whole body, and again, in every part, as God is in regard to the whole world."[16]

In other words, the whole soul is in the nose, but also in the brain, or in the eyes, or in the hands. Analogously, insofar as spiritual formation is the soul or the core that unifies and gives life to the priest's being and acting, it must also be *entirely* present in *every* aspect or part of priestly formation.

No one would deny that charity is the core that unifies and gives life, for instance, to the intellectual life of the seminarian.[17] Moreover, charity is also the core that unifies and gives life to priestly pastoral activity. Thus John Paul II speaks unrelentingly about *pastoral* charity (about fifty times in *Pastores Dabo Vobis* alone).[18] In the same way, charity must be the core that unifies and gives life to priestly human formation in the virtues.

We attribute the spiritual life to faith, because it "makes its first appearance in the act of faith, although its completion comes from charity, which is the *form of the virtues*."[19] We find here another key reason why the perspective of the priest as a man of charity must be

---

15 See *ST* I, q. 75, a. 1, c; q. 76, a. 6, ad 1; q. 77, a. 4, c; *SCG* IV. 81.

16 *ST* I, q. 93, a. 3, c.

17 See PDV, 53; Antonin-Gilbert Sertillanges, *The Intellectual Life: Its Spirit, Conditions, Methods*, trans. Mary Ryan (Washington, DC: Catholic University of America Press, 1998).

18 See, for instance, PDV, 21–26.

19 *De Veritate*, q. 14, a. 5, ad 12. Emphasis added. See also *In III Sent.*, d. 27, q. 2, a. 4, qc. 3, c.; Livio Melina et al., *Caminar a La Luz Del Amor. Los Fundamentos de La Moral Cristiana* (Madrid: Ediciones Palabra, 2007), 444–54.

adopted for priestly formation in the acquired virtues: charity is the form, the end, the mover, the mother, and the root of the acquired virtues.[20] Let us explore the meaning of this classical doctrine.

Form of the Virtues

To understand how charity is the *form of the acquired virtues*, we need to consider our moral life as the artistic formation of our own personality. Such a formation could be envisioned as the sculpting of virtues out of the "material" that I find in myself. I am both the one sculpting and the material being sculpted, because "human acts can be considered in both ways [as actions and passions], since man moves himself, and is moved by himself."[21]

As a result, my desires for food and drink are like the material for sculpting the virtue of temperance; my sexual inclination and desires are like the material for the formation of the virtue of chastity. My feelings of anger are like the material out of which I can be the creator of the virtue of meekness; my fear and daring are like the material for the creation of the virtue of fortitude. My feelings of hope are like the material for the formation of the virtue of humility, and so on.[22]

In all of these instances, we shape our own personality by imprinting, as it were, a *form* into some material. In the cases described, the form imprinted is an order of reason.

Now, the virtues themselves can become materials for my moral formation. They can also be imprinted with a formal aspect. In voluntary actions, the contribution of the end is also formal.

---

20 See *De Caritate*, a. 3, c.

21 *ST* I–II, q. 1, a. 3, c.

22 See Karol Wojtyła, *The Acting Person*, ed. Anna-Teresa Tymieniecka (Dordrecht: D. Reidel, 1979), 83; *SCG* III. 23; *ST* I–II, q. 6, a. 5, ad 2; *ST* III, q. 13, a. 1, c.; *De Potentia*, q. 5, a. 5, c.

For instance, if someone steals a gun in order to commit murder, he is materially a thief, but formally a murderer. That is what he willfully intended when he stole the gun. Similarly, if a seminarian obeys his superior and cleans the halls, but he does it out of love for God, he is materially obeying, but formally loving God. His virtue of obedience is like the material out of which he sculpts an act of charity by willing this particular end.

In this sense, St. Thérèse of Lisieux discovered that her deepest vocation in the Church consisted in "not allowing one little sacrifice to escape, not one look, one word, *profiting by all the smallest things and doing them through love*."[23] She discovered that the acquired moral virtues, and all other human acts, need to receive this formal impact from charity.

In fact, the acquired virtues concern created goods. In that sense, they are imperfect: they do not lead to our supernatural end; in and of themselves, they do not bring about meritorious actions. Therefore, created goods need to be directed to the Uncreated Good. And this is exactly what charity does, as the form of the acquired virtues: it directs them to God.

End and Mover of the Virtues

Closely related to this idea is charity's role as *their end*. As we already explained, the acts of the precepts of God's law promote the virtues. But St. Paul clearly states that, "love is the fulfilling of the law" (Rom 13:10; see Gal 5:14; Col 3:14).[24] All of the acts of God's commandments and consequently, all of the acts of the acquired virtues, find their end or completion in charity. As a result,

---

23 Thérèse of Lisieux, *Story of a Soul: The Autobiography of Saint Thérèse of Lisieux*, trans. John Clarke (Washington, DC: ICS Publications, 1996), 196. Emphasis added.

24 See *De Caritate*, a. 3, c; *Super Rom.,* cap. 13, lect. 2, nos. 1058–59.

charity is not only the form but also the end of the acquired virtues. The latter are, at the same time, ends in themselves and a means to charity. Charity is also *their mover* because, in a particular way, it commands and governs their acts.

In order to illustrate this point, perhaps it would be useful to contrast pride and charity. The vice of pride is the king of sins, insofar as in all of them, we find a certain disordered love for one's own excellence. Correspondingly, charity is the queen of all virtues, because in them, inasmuch as they are oriented towards our eternal salvation, we find a certain love for God. For this reason, Augustine says that, "the love of self to the point of despising God gave rise to the earthly city. In turn, the love for God to the point of despising oneself has risen to the heavenly city."[25]

Thomas explains this Augustinian thesis in a very Aristotelian way. Charity leads to heaven; it is the perfection of Christian life. As such, it moves and commands the other virtues analogously to the way in which a higher art commands and governs a lower one.[26] For example, the art of architecture commands and governs the art of the bricklayer and that of the plumber, or the art of building ships is governed by the art of navigating them. Likewise, charity is the supreme art that governs the arts of all the other virtues.

As a result, the art of loving God moves, rules, and governs the art of being prudent, just, temperate, or courageous. Charity moves the priest to become a man of justice, temperance, fortitude, and prudence. In this way, charity is "common to all the virtues by reason of the diffusion of its governance."[27]

---

25 *De Civitate Dei*, XIV. 28. The translation is mine.

26 See Aristotle, *Nichomachean Ethics*, I. 2.1094a24–26. See Aquinas's commentary, *In I Ethic.*, lect. 2, no. 25.

27 *De Malo*, q. 8, a. 2, c.

Mother and Root of the Virtues

Charity is also the *mother and root* of the acquired virtues. Being a mother involves conceiving within oneself an offspring. Charity is a mother since it engenders in her womb the acquired virtues. Precisely because we will to love God, we conceive and perform acts of justice, obedience, veracity, religion, prudence, temperance, meekness, and so on.

In this sense, Thomas says that "it is necessary for habits in the lower powers to be formed through the habits which are in the higher ones. Thus, the formation of the lower virtues should come from some higher virtue."[28] Since there is no higher virtue than charity, the formation of the lower acquired virtues should take place through charity's motherhood.

Given that charity is the form, end, mover, mother, and root of the acquired virtues, it is clearer now why the priest is a man of justice, temperance, fortitude, and prudence because he aims to be a man of charity. For this reason, life in the seminary presupposes participation in the Church's sacramental life, and it fosters the life of grace in the seminarian. Consequently, it would be neither wise nor prudent to adopt a different perspective from that of charity in order to promote the acquired virtues.

In fact, without this adequate perspective, we risk not promoting any virtue at all. As Thomas says, "In one who has charity there can be no act of virtue not formed by charity. For, either the act will be directed to the proper end, and this can be only through charity in one who has charity, or the act is not directed to the proper end, and so is not an act of virtue."[29]

---

28 *De Veritate*, q. 14, a. 5, c.

29 *De Veritate*, q. 14, a. 5, ad 13. Emphasis added.

The Seminary is Not the Lyceum

To adopt our perspective does not deny that a pagan could acquire true but imperfect virtues.[30] Every acquired human virtue, which aims at an honest and genuine good, is a true and authentic virtue in some sense. Yet, it remains essentially imperfect and human, as long as it is not elevated and directed by grace and charity towards our supernatural end.[31]

Our question is not the theoretical possibility or impossibility of the existence of true virtues among the pagans.[32] That is not really the seminary's *Sitz im Leben* or its *de facto* situation. Rather, our pressing question is whether or not seminaries should look at priestly human formation as pagan virtue, as if seminary were the Aristotelian Lyceum.

In my opinion, the answer must be no; we should not view the process that way. Human priestly formation must take place within an integral view of the human person or an adequate anthropology of the gift of self that is inherent in charity.[33] Human formation must receive its unity and ultimate end from the spiritual dimension of priestly formation, whose core is friendship with God.

Thus, John Paul II unequivocally says that "human formation, when it is carried out in the context of an anthropology which is open to the full truth regarding the human person, *leads to and finds its completion in spiritual formation.*"[34] We cannot pursue priestly human formation in the human virtues *etsi gratia non daretur*—as if grace were not given.

---

30 See *ST* II–II, q. 23, a. 7; I–II, q. 63, a. 2, ad 2; q. 65, a. 2, c.

31 See *ST* I–II, q. 109, a. 4, c; *De Virtutibus*, q. un., a. 9, c.

32 For an excellent scientific study of this question, see David Decomiso, *Ethics as a Work of Charity. Thomas Aquinas and Pagan Virtue* (Stanford: Stanford University Press, 2014).

33 See GS, 24.

34 PDV, 45. Emphasis added.

In fact, we know that God often provides even for those things that we could do by nature that are needed for salvation, but few could successfully attain. For example, it is possible for human nature to know through reason alone that God exists. Yet, "even as regards those truths about God which human reason could have discovered, it was *necessary* that man should be taught by a divine revelation; because the truth about God such as reason could discover, would *only be known by a few*, and that *after a long time, and with the admixture of many errors*."[35] Similarly, God offers us the grace to grow in the human virtues, so that they are not accessible only to the few, after a long time, and with the admixture of many errors. No seminary would want their seminarians to exercise virtue without this great help.

Overcoming False Optimism

As a result, to adopt the perspective of charity allows us to overcome a sort of false optimism, which shuns the opportunities afforded by God's grace to the future priest. As the *Catechism* explains, within the context of human virtues, "it is not easy for man, wounded by sin, to maintain moral balance. Christ's gift of salvation offers us the *grace* necessary to *persevere in the pursuit of the virtues*."[36]

Aquinas admits of this difficulty as well when he explains how to move out of the situation of incontinence, that is, out of the situation of knowing what to do, but lacking the willpower to do it: "Mere knowledge does not suffice to cure the incontinent man, for he needs the inward assistance of grace which quenches concupiscence, besides the application of the external remedy of admonishment and correction, which induce him to begin to resist

---

35 *ST* I, q. 1, a. 1, c. Emphasis added.

36 CCC 1811. Emphasis added.

his desires, so that concupiscence is weakened."[37] As we said, it would be neither prudent nor wise to attempt to grow in virtue at the seminary without all the resources we have at our disposal. Human formation would be rather soulless without the spiritual life.

Moreover, to adopt the perspective of charity also allows us to emphasize the relational dimension of the education in virtue. Human virtue cannot be understood as merely growing in independence: virtue is an acknowledged dependence on others.[38] We grow in virtue by acting together with others and in union with God. All of our virtues are meant for the good of the community and for God's glory.

Additionally, the perspective of charity emphasizes the christocentric nature of growth in the virtues as well as the gift of self. To grow in true virtue is to perfect our being created in God's image and likeness, by resembling Christ more and more, as sons in the Son.[39] It is to follow in his footsteps in the ultimate fulfillment of David's testament.

The Order of Love

This same perspective of charity also rediscovers a sort of forgotten dimension of virtues. We find it not only in the classical theology of Augustine and Aquinas, but also in the phenomenology of Max

---

37 *ST* II–II, q. 156, a. 3, ad 2. Emphasis added.

38 This is one of the main theses found in Alasdair MacIntyre, *Dependent Rational Animals: Why Human Beings Need the Virtues* (Chicago: Open Court, 2001), especially chapters 7–10.

39 See *ST* I, q. 93, a. 9; VS, 64; Fernando Ocáriz Braña, *Hijos de Dios En Cristo. Introducción a Una Teología de La Participación Sobrenatural* (Pamplona: EUNSA, 1972); José H. Gomez, *Men of Brave Heart: The Virtue of Courage in the Priestly Life* (Huntington, IN: Our Sunday Visitor, 2009), 18.

Scheler.[40] In my opinion, this perspective actually corresponds to that personalistic dimension of the gift of self in the theory of the virtues mentioned by Wojtyła.

Thus, the cardinal virtues are seen as an *ordinata dilectio* or as an *ordo amoris*, that is to say, as an order of love: "Temperance is love giving itself entirely to that which is loved; fortitude is love readily bearing all things for the sake of the loved object; justice is love serving only the loved object, and therefore ruling rightly; prudence is love distinguishing with sagacity between what hinders it and what helps it."[41]

In this way, charity elevates all these virtues toward God as our ultimate end: "Temperance is love keeping itself entire and incorrupt for God; fortitude is love bearing everything readily for the sake of God; justice is love serving God only, and therefore ruling well all else, as subject to man; prudence is love making a right distinction between what helps it towards God and what might hinder it."[42]

In conclusion, the integrating role of the spiritual dimension of priestly formation urges us to look at education in the human virtues from this exact perspective, considering the entire supernatural organism of grace given to us by God. How do we attain that love for God, which animates our entire being incorrupt for God, so as to give ourselves to him (temperance), bear everything readily for his sake (fortitude), serve him and others by ruling rightly over all else (justice), and make a right distinction between what helps and hinders the other virtues and our union with the Lord (prudence)?

---

40 See *ST* I–II, q. 55, a. 1, ad 4; q. 56, a. 3, ad 1; Max Scheler, "*Ordo Amoris*," in *Selected Philosophical Essays*, trans. David Lachterman (Evanston, IL: Northwestern University Press, 1973), 98–135.

41 *De Moribus Ecclesiae*, 15, 25.

42 Ibid.

CHAPTER 1

GRATITUDE AND MERCY

THE VALUE OF GRATITUDE

THE importance of the virtue of gratitude has been underlined by spiritual authors and philosophers alike. It is the very first step that St. Ignatius of Loyola assigns in the *Spiritual Exercises* to the Examen prayer: "To give thanks to God our Lord for the favors received."[1]

According to Dietrich von Hildebrand, gratitude inserts the human person into the logic of the gift of self. He would say that the grateful seminarian "emerges from immanence, from the confines of ego-relatedness and *enters into the blissful giving of himself to God.*"[2] A grateful priest grows in interior freedom; he "becomes great and expansive. Blessed and victorious freedom blooms in his soul."[3]

Søren Kierkegaard has also described gratitude's spiritual enrichment for the human person. He says that a man's "riches indeed increase with every time he prays and gives thanks."[4] By

---

1 Ignatius of Loyola, *The Spiritual Exercises of St. Ignatius*, trans. Louis J. Puhl (New York: Vintage Books, 2000), no. 43. On the Examen prayer, see Gallagher, *The Examen Prayer*.

2 Dietrich von Hildebrand, *The Art of Living* (Manchester, NH: Sophia Institute Press, 1994), 107. Emphasis added.

3 Ibid.

4 Søren Kierkegaard, *Christian Discourses*, trans. Walter Lowrie (Princeton: Princeton University Press, 1971), 20.

contrast, a future priest who is enslaved by the vice of ingratitude is impoverished: "How poor not to be able to pray; how poor not to be able to give thanks; how poor to have to receive everything with ingratitude."[5]

Likewise, St. Thérèse of Lisieux offers quite a vivid personal testimony of the value of this virtue. She points to its importance in her own spiritual growth: "Gratitude is the thing that *brings us the most grace* . . . I have learnt this from experience; *try it and you will see*."[6]

In my view, priestly formation in the human virtues should begin right here, with this precise spiritual exercise or virtuous experiment recommended by St. Thérèse. Following her advice, we want to experience, within the life of our seminary community, how many graces gratitude will bring about. To exercise in this virtue opens a path to fall in love and to remain in love with God.

There cannot be a better starting point to priestly formation in the human virtues than the consideration of God's great gifts as a sure testimony of his love. The precise goal of priestly formation in the virtues is none other than the art of loving (*ars amandi*). And the best way of learning how to love is by being truly loved: "We love, because he first loved us" (1 Jn 4:19).

Christ loved us to the end (see Jn 13:1). His self-gift out of love for every member of the Church clearly shows that his is the gratuitous initiative; ours is the responsibility (see Eph 5:25). Hence, the first response or answer to such a radical love and gift of self must be *gratitude*.

---

5 Kierkegaard, *Christian Discourses*, 20.

6 Christopher O'Mahoney, ed. *St. Thérèse of Lisieux by Those Who Knew Her: Testimonies from the Process of Beatification* (Huntington, IN: Our Sunday Visitor, 1975), 138. Emphasis added. See Gallagher, *The Examen Prayer*, 178–79.

Gratitude and Giving

Gratitude is closely related with the phenomenon of giving. The imposition of names often provides a direct contact with what is most evident in the human experience of a given phenomenon. For this reason, the Scholastics used to begin their treatises dealing with nominal definitions, thereby acquiring an initial "phenomenological contact" with the reality under scrutiny.

Following their lead, we can note that the English word "gratitude" is a transliteration from the Latin *gratitudo*, which in turn is rooted in the word *gratia* (grace). *Gratia* is a vast term. Among its various meanings, three are most important for our purposes.

First, *gratia* could mean the spontaneous act of love for another person's good. In this sense, we say, "I am in his good graces." Second, *gratia* could also refer to a gift freely given to another as the fulfillment of that kind of love previously mentioned.

Third, *gratia* could refer to the *effect* that the giver's love and his gifts have *in the recipient*. They engender in him a sort of disposition to make a return of the gifts and of the love received. This last meaning of *gratia*, as it relates to the other two, corresponds most appropriately to the phenomenon of gratitude.[7]

Our etymological considerations show that gift and gratitude are like two sides of one coin. A gift is a gratuitous donation. It

---

7 See John Richardson, "The Virtue of Gratitude According to the Mind of Saint Thomas Aquinas" (Washington, DC: Pontificium Institutum Angelicum de Urbe, 1954), 22–23. Moreover, one could distinguish a stricter meaning of gratitude reduced to a benefactor that is not God, one's parents, or any superior. In this way, the gratitude that is often *materially* included, as it were, in the virtues of religion, piety, and observance, would not be part of the specifically distinct virtue of gratitude. However, in our first spiritual exercise within the province of justice, we are not targeting that exact and precise goal only; rather, we will include it in a broader context more suitable for our pedagogical purposes.

consists in handing something over *without the intent of reward.* But why would anyone give something to others *without expecting anything in return*? Love, as the first meaning of *gratia*, is the answer.

We freely give valuable good things to people because we love them. In so doing, we will their good for their own sake. We experience a kind of love for them that goes beyond the realm of emotions and that enters into the sphere of the human will and free choice.

For instance, a priest may choose to offer prayers in secret for his parishioners, without any intent of recompense from them. He is giving them a "good thing." He is gracing them with his prayers. Simultaneously, he is also freely choosing to will (*velle*) their good (*bonum*).

Hence, traditionally, this kind of love is called *benevolentia* (goodwill, benevolence). The priest of our example offers prayers for his parishioners *because* he wills their good, *because* he has benevolence toward them. For this reason, benevolence is a kind of love which has a foundational role in any authentic gift given to another human person.

Thomas Aquinas explains this phenomenon by saying that "the reason of donation being gratuitous is love; since therefore do we give something to anyone gratuitously forasmuch as we wish him well. So what we first give him is the love whereby we wish him well. Hence it is manifest that love has the nature of a first gift, through which all free gifts are given."[8]

Go back to our example to reveal the complete meaning of this important text. The reason for the priest's offering prayers for his parishioners, without intent of being paid back, is his love for them.

8 *ST* I, q. 38, a. 2, c. See also the more extensive text of *In I Sent.*, d. 18, q. 1, a. 2, c. For a superb commentary on this text, see Jacobus Ramírez, *Los Dones Del Espíritu Santo* (Madrid: Editorial San Esteban, 1978), 28–30.

When he prays, he is making *two* simultaneous gifts. Both of them are, at the same time, the object of his free choice: the offering of his prayers and the gift of his love for them.

The second gift is more radical than the first. His love for the parishioners is the motive force, what drives the priest to offer prayers. His love for them radically affects the description of his action.

Consider another example. When someone washes dishes out of charity, as we know, the full description of his action is that he is doing an act of love. Granting a compatibility between what one does and why he does it, the end of the action intimately determines its essence.

Coming back to the example of the priest, we could certainly describe his action simply as "praying," just as we could say that the other person is "washing dishes." Nonetheless, there is a fuller description of the priest's action: "He is freely loving his people by praying for them." Since the reason for freely offering prayers for his parishioners is his love for them, and since the motive force is his willing their good for their own sake, we can conclude with Aquinas that the most primordial and essential gift given to the parishioners is the gift of the priest's love.

We can corroborate this conclusion in the experience of forgiveness. Notice that in English, as well as in other languages, the word "forgiveness" is closely connected with gift. To "for-give" someone is to offer him an undeserved gift. The reason for that kind of gift is either love for the person forgiven, love for God, or both. Consequently, love is the first gift herein, by which all other gifts—such as the gift of forgiveness—are given gratuitously.[9]

---

9 For a philosophy of forgiveness, see Mariano Crespo, *El Perdón. Una Investigación Filosófica* (Madrid: Ediciones Encuentro, 2004).

Responsibility in Justice

Gratitude is the other side of the coin of the phenomenon of giving. It has to do with one's response to this kind of primordial love. It is *responsibility for the gift*. It is the first answer that should be elicited in our will through the mediation of our awareness of God's gift (see Jn 4:10).

Gratitude is a responsibility in justice toward someone who has made a gift to us. It is the just and right answer to that primordial love and those other gifts. Yet as Thomas noted, one of these two takes priority: the primordial love, by which other things are given, has precedence. For this reason, von Hildebrand rightly notes that, above all, "gratitude primarily refers *to the loving disposition of the other toward me*."[10]

Conversely, ingratitude is a kind of injustice. It neither recognizes nor responds to the love of the giving person or to his other gifts. In the worst case, a seminarian could be ungrateful by actually repaying evil for good. Then, the love of the donor is unjustly answered with hate.

Immanuel Kant has described this kind of ingratitude as *inhuman*: "It is inhuman to hate and persecute one from whom we have reaped a benefit, and if such conduct were the rule it would cause untold harm. Men would then be afraid to do good to anyone lest they should receive evil in return for their good."[11] Hence, Kant concludes, this kind of ingratitude is the essence of vileness.

Ignatius of Loyola also expresses with great force the evil of ingratitude. He argues that, in light of God's goodness, "Ingratitude is one of the things most worthy of detestation before our Creator and Lord, and before all creatures capable of His

---

10 Von Hildebrand, *The Art of Living*, 130. Emphasis added.

11 Immanuel Kant, *Lectures on Ethics*, trans. Louis Infield (Indianapolis: Hackett, 1984), 219.

divine and everlasting glory, out of all the evils and sins which can be imagined. For it is a failure to recognize the good things, the graces, and the gifts received. As such, it is *the cause, beginning, and origin of all evils and sins*."[12]

Although sins are specifically distinct from each other, Thomas similarly admits that "in every sin there is *material ingratitude to God*."[13] Conversely, the evil of this vice underlines the great value of its opposite virtue: "Recognition and gratitude for the good things and gifts received is greatly loved and esteemed both in heaven and on earth."[14]

Gratitude, Mercy, and Joy

From the perspective of charity, gratitude is closely connected with divine mercy. God's mercy is basically the shape that his divine love adopts when confronted by our misery. God is merciful because, out of love, he wills good things for us that destroy or alleviate what makes us most miserable, that which hinders our eternal salvation.

Since we all have an experience of God's mercy, it seems appropriate to take as the starting point for our growth in the virtue of gratitude the awareness of God's forgiving and regenerating love. "We love, because he first loved us" (1 Jn 4:19). "But God

---

12 Ignatius of Loyola, *Letter to Simón Rodriguez, March 18, 1542*, cited in Gallagher, *The Examen Prayer*, 59. Emphasis added.

13 *ST* II–II, q. 107, a. 2, ad 1. Emphasis added. Richardson explains that Thomas opposed in his time some theologians for whom "ingratitude is equal to the gravity of all previous sins. For St. Thomas the gravity of ingratitude as a circumstance of sin cannot be greater than the gravity of the sin to which it is attached" (Richardson, "The Virtue of Gratitude," 20).

14 Ignatius of Loyola, *Letter to Simón Rodriguez, March 18, 1542*, cited in Gallagher, *The Examen Prayer*, 59.

shows his love for us in that *while we were yet sinners* Christ died for us" (Rom 5:8; emphasis added).

As Pope Francis has rightly noted, this is the heart of the Gospel; this is the *kerygma.* For every Christian, seminarian, or priest, every moral demand should be seen in this light.[15] Hence, although I will not develop here the philosophy and theology of mercy, I have entitled this chapter "Gratitude and Mercy," because their interconnection seems to be the optimal and most Christian way for a future priest to grow in gratitude.[16]

Additionally, this same interconnection best explains why *grateful priests are joyful priests*: "The essence of gratitude includes joy."[17] A grateful seminarian or priest rejoices in the possession of a great good; namely, the gift of love inherent in the liberal gift of something good for him. A grateful priest is joyful, above all, because of his constant awareness of God's gift of self in Christ's redemptive and spousal love for his Church. In this manner, the words of the psalmist always find an actual or habitual echo in his prayer and pastoral activity: "What shall I render to the Lord / for all his bounty to me?" (Ps 116:12).

These brief remarks on the virtue of gratitude should be enough to show its importance for priestly formation. As Christians and (future) priests, we want to grow in this virtue not only for our own sake, but also for the sake of others. As priests, and within the context of our spiritual paternity, we need to have the virtue of gratitude in our own lives, we need to teach it to others with

15 See EG, 34–39.

16 One could continue to disclose this interconnection by considering that gratitude toward God for his forgiving and regenerative love elicits compassion for others. Most importantly, it also elicits that kind of willing good things for them, out of love, which truly eliminates or alleviates their misery; that is, whatever obstacle is hindering their true happiness and union with God.

17 Von Hildebrand, *The Art of Living*, 115.

our example, and we need to empower others who will be future teachers of this same virtue with what is necessary for their mission.

Additionally, these introductory comments are meant to initiate our reflection on gratitude by motivating each one of us to devote ourselves to the spiritual exercises needed to grow in this virtue. Let us briefly pause, then, and reflect on the following questions:

(1) What does lack of gratitude do to my life?
(2) What does lack of gratitude do to the life of the seminary?
(3) What will lack of gratitude do in my future life as a priest?
(4) What will my incapacity to be an example of gratitude mean for the life of my spiritual children?
(5) How will my growth in the virtue of gratitude impact my life as a seminarian and as a future priest, as well as the life of those around me in the seminary, and in my future parish?
(6) Have I experienced the joy of being grateful?
(7) Has God opened my eyes to the depth of his forgiving and regenerative love for me in my life?

Simon and the Woman

Luke 7:36–50 tells us about a woman who approached Jesus while he was dining at the house of a Pharisee. The encounter between Jesus, Simon, and this woman offers a paradigm, as it were, for the virtue of gratitude in its connection with mercy. It gives us the right perspective to inquire into its essence.

While we know that Simon was the Pharisee's name, the only thing we know about this woman is that she was a public sinner (see Lk 7:37). Simon was perplexed at the fact that Jesus would allow her to touch him. Then, Jesus told him a parable about the essence of gratitude.

This parable unlocks what is really going on between Jesus and the woman. The Lord directly connects her gratitude with her experience of God's mercy, pointing in this way to their intimate connection. The parable entails the following scenario:

[Jesus said:] "A certain creditor had two debtors; one owed five hundred denarii, and the other fifty. When they could not pay, he forgave them both. Now which of them will love him more?" Simon answered, "The one, I suppose, to whom he forgave more." And he said to him, "You have judged rightly" (Lk 7:41–44).

The creditor did not have the legal obligation to forgive the debt of those two debtors. They had no legal right to be excused from paying. In forgiving their debt, he made a gratuitous gift to them.

We are not told in the parable the reason why the creditor did so, whether it was out of love for the debtors, out of love for God, or for both reasons. What we are told, however, is that this kind of gift engenders love in its recipients. Although the word is not used, we can reasonably suspect that gratitude is part of this picture.

Moreover, there seems to be a certain law of proportionality: the greater the debt, the greater the gift received in its forgiveness, and consequently, the greater the love (and gratitude) in the debtor. The application of the parable seems clear.

Jesus is like the creditor. He brings forgiveness to both Simon and to the woman, who are like the two debtors. Yet only the woman really welcomes *both* Jesus *and* God's forgiveness.

Simon thinks that he is righteous, at least more so than the woman. Although Christ is eating at his house, he has not really welcomed him. Apparently, this Pharisee does not welcome Christ's forgiveness for the same reasons the chief priests and the elders did not believe in John's baptism for the repentance of sins (see Mt 21: 23–27). They thought they were healthy, and that they did not need God's healing. In this way, Simon's invitation to Christ sharply contrasts with the centurion's attitude, who, unlike this Pharisee, acknowledged that he was not worthy that Jesus should enter under his roof (see Mt 8:8).

Our Lord's point does not seem to be who is a greater sinner, but rather who has a greater awareness of God's gift, who has better understood his own sins in light of God's gratuitous forgiveness. As noted, this awareness determines who really welcomes and receives Christ. Unlike the Pharisee, the woman at Christ's feet is aware of how much God has forgiven her. Her own sins, insofar as they have been forgiven by God, are a clear testimony of divine love and mercy.

Love engenders love. The way to learn how to love is to be loved. As a result, this woman's experience of love and forgiveness generates in her a response of love through the mediation of gratitude. Thus, Jesus concludes: "He who is forgiven little, loves little" (Lk 7:47).

Unlike Simon, the woman has truly welcomed Jesus into her life. For this reason, the Lord reproaches the Pharisee: "I entered your house, you gave me no water for my feet, but she has wet my feet with her tears and wiped them with her hair. You gave me no kiss, but from the time I came in she has not ceased to kiss my feet. You did not anoint my head with oil, but she has anointed my feet with ointment" (Lk 7:44–46).

Simon seems to have a harder time acknowledging his sinful condition. He apparently has had a harder time experiencing God's love. At least, we could conclude that Simon lacked the awareness of God's gift in preserving him from the same sins this woman had committed.

In contrast, since this woman could not deny her sinful condition as it was publicly known, she was well-disposed to receive God's mercy. The disparity between Simon and the woman also calls to mind Jesus's words to the chief priests and the scribes: "The tax collectors and the harlots go into the kingdom of God before you" (Mt 21:31).

The woman in the story has received the gift of the Messiah, who did not come for those who are healthy, but for those who are sick (see Mk 2:17; Lk 5:31; Mt 9:12). She humbly acknowledges this gift. Moreover, she expresses her appreciation and thanks with her loving affection toward the Lord.

In addition, she is moved to action. She washes his feet with tears of contrition and love. She wipes them with her hair. And she anoints Christ's feet. We can even suspect that this woman was moved to further actions. It is possible that she served Christ and followed him during the rest of his public ministry.

This Gospel passage offers a paradigm for the connection between gratitude and mercy. It also shows three main acts of gratitude: humble acceptance of the gift, expressing a loving appreciation and thankfulness, and being moved to action in repayment of the debt of gratitude. Therefore, this Gospel passage invites us to go deeper into the essence of gratitude by understanding its relationship with justice, as well as the acts that belong to this particular virtue.

Annexed to Justice

The nature of gratitude as a virtue annexed to justice further explains the elements in Jesus's parable of similarity and dissimilarity between the two debtors' initial debt to the creditor and the debt of love and gratitude resulting in them from the creditor's forgiveness. To explain this point, we need the help of philosophy and theology.

Although Aristotle did not explicitly study the virtue of gratitude, he included its content in his treatment of friendship and justice. Aquinas advances the thought of the Stagirite in this regard, in light of Roman and Christian sources.[18] Much like Aristotle, Thomas places gratitude within the province of the cardinal virtue of justice.

Gratitude perfects the human will in order to act in accordance

---

18 See Richardson, "The Virtue of Gratitude," 2–21.

with right reason in its relationship with another's good. Obviously, gratitude presupposes some acts of the intellect. As can be seen in the Scriptures, gratitude entails the intellectual recognition and estimation of the goods received from another. Simon lacked in these two acts.

In addition, the Scriptures point to the importance of intellectual memory or recollection of God's deeds in salvation history. "Then, take heed lest you forget the Lord, who brought you out of the land of Egypt, out of the house of bondage" (Dt 6:12). This memory or intellectual recollection is imperative even in times of trial.

Judith says in this regard: "In spite of everything let us *give thanks* to the Lord our God, who is putting us to the test as he did our forefathers. *Remember* what he did with Abraham, and how he tested Isaac, and what happened to Jacob in Mesopotamia in Syria, while he was keeping the sheep of Laban, his mother's brother" (Jdt 8:25–26; emphasis added).

Still, gratitude entails another intellectual act: the rational determination of the proper way of repaying one's debt of love. In the story of Simon, we are not told when the woman met Christ's forgiveness. But we can presume that she did before she came into the Pharisee's home. She considered her entrance into the house as a proper way to manifest her gratitude.

Now, despite these intellectual acts presupposed by gratitude, the latter is not an intellectual but a moral virtue. It primarily resides in the will. Gratitude is one of justice's potential parts, or one of its annexed virtues.

This means that gratitude is not one kind of justice, or a species of justice, like an apple is one kind of fruit. Rather, gratitude is a virtue that is somewhat similar to and somewhat different from justice.[19] Although annexed virtues "have something in common with the principal virtue," in some respect, they "fall short of the

---

19 See *ST* II–II, q. 106, a. 5, ad 2.

perfection of that virtue."[20]

The perfections mentioned by Thomas have to do with the *equality* that is characteristic of justice. In this last virtue, there is a debt required by law, a true obligation to give to another, and a stipulation according to which the returned is as much as is owed.[21] Any virtue that does not fulfill any of these three conditions falls short of the equality or perfection of justice.

Both justice and gratitude imply a sort of debt to be paid. However, the nature of the debt varies in each case. Whereas justice implies a "legal debt," gratitude implies only a "moral debt." A debt is something to which another has a right. A *legal* debt corresponds to a positive right, that is to say, to a positive law.

For instance, when a valid and signed contract stipulates that a kind of work deserves a specific kind of compensation, an employer should fulfill his contract and the amount agreed per hour to his employee, provided the latter has done his part. This is a matter of justice in the strict and proper sense. Were the employer not to fulfill his contract, he could face a lawsuit.

The best examples of this kind of debt are found in what is traditionally called *commutative* or *strict* justice, that is, the kind of justice that regulates legal exchanges among individuals, such as buying and selling. In Jesus's parable, the creditor did not have this kind of legal debt toward his debtors. On the contrary, the debtors were the ones who had a legal debt of commutative justice toward the creditor. They were legally bound to pay the creditor.

In turn, a *moral* debt corresponds to a natural right, to a law imparted to the human mind by nature. For instance, consider the scenario in which someone has made a donation to the seminary. The seminary has a moral debt to that person to show its

---

20 *ST* II–II, q. 80, a .1, c.

21 See *In III Sent.*, d. 33, q. 3, a. 4, qc. 1, c.

appreciation and thankfulness.[22]

This debt arises from the consideration of the honesty or goodness of the very virtue of gratitude. In that sense, it is "a moral debt required by virtue."[23] But no one would sue the seminary in a court of law for not sending a note of thanks, or for not holding an appreciation dinner.

Although gratitude governs the return of a debt, even in accordance with a certain equality, this return is not required by law. Rather, it springs "from a certain moral goodness [*honestate*], by which it happens that one gives thanks for a benefit though he cannot be forced to do so in a court of law."[24] Acts of gratitude are binding because of our understanding of the goodness of its virtue. The debt that belongs to gratitude gushes forth out of wanting to repay that primordial love inherent in any gratuitous donation.

For this reason, Aquinas says that "the debt of gratitude flows from the debt of love [*debitum gratitudinis ex debito amoris derivatur*]."[25] Although the benefactor has no intention of obliging the recipient to make any payment, nevertheless, the recipient experiences a moral obligation and responsibility toward the very person of the benefactor. It is a distinctive kind of obligation. It requires the same gratuitous love that is contained in its cause. When we consider God as *the* benefactor and donor of love, we can certainly speak here with John Paul II about the freedom of the gift.[26]

The existence of the debt of gratitude is explained by the metaphysical principle according to which every effect reverts to its cause. The effect in question is the gift. The cause is

---

22 See *In V Ethic.*, lect. 12, nos. 1016–17; *ST* II–II, q. 106, a. 1, ad 2 & a. 4, ad 1.

23 *ST* II–II, q. 107, a. 1, c.

24 *In III Sent.*, d. 33, q. 3, a. 4, qc. 1, c.

25 *ST* II–II, q. 107, a. 1, ad 3.

26 See TOB, 13:2–22:7.

the benefactor.

The reception of the gift entails a relationship to its cause, a relationship between the benefactor and the recipient. In turn, the essence or nature of the debt of gratitude is explained by the gift's gratuity, especially by the love that moves us to offer other gifts as primordial gift. The gratuitous and loving intention of the benefactor resonates in our conscience, demanding a rational return.[27]

This rational return should be equal in nature to the gift received; that is, it should also be gratuitous and loving. Yet gratitude's rational return should aim to go beyond equality with respect to the intensity of benevolence.[28]

This is an important difference between justice and gratitude. Commutative or strict justice looks to repay the exact amount received. For example, when we borrow fifty dollars, we should pay back fifty dollars, no more and no less. Instead, in gratitude we always aim at surpassing the benevolence with which the benefactor has bestowed his gifts on the recipient. Since benevolence is not a physically measureable thing, this surpassing is a metaphorical way of signifying a greater degree of intensity.

This last phenomenon unveils another difference between justice and gratitude. Justice is based more on the distinction between one man and another. In turn, insofar as gratitude fosters mutual benevolence, it aims at the communion of persons in a never-ending reciprocal giving and loving.

This never-ending virtuous circle makes Thomas say that "the debt of gratitude flows from charity, which the more it is paid the more it is due."[29] Thus, we can never be too grateful insofar as we

---

27 See *ST* II–II, q. 106, a. 3, c.

28 See *ST* II–II, q. 106, a. 6, c.

29 *ST* II–II, q. 106, a. 6, ad 2.

can never have too much benevolence toward a benefactor.[30]

Three Key Acts of Gratitude

The story of Simon and the woman has already indicated the main acts of the virtue of gratitude. Aquinas further identifies them with precision. We will go through his exposition, addressing some potential obstacles to these acts as well. As a result, we will obtain efficient and fruitful spiritual exercises in this virtue.

Thomas talks about three main acts needed to foster gratitude. First, we need to recognize the favors received, overcoming the obstacles of entitlement and pride. Second, we need to learn how to express our appreciation and thanks. Third, we are to acquire the ability to repay favors received with prudence.

Humbly Recognizing the Gift

To recognize the gifts received, a seminarian needs to overcome the obstacle of entitlement; he needs to take nothing for granted. Von Hildebrand emphasizes the happiness inherent in gratitude by contrasting two different kinds of men. "We only need to distinguish clearly between *the man who takes for granted* his existence as a person, the gifts that God has bestowed on him, as well as the love and friendship of others which have been given to him, and *the man who takes nothing for granted, but who acknowledges that everything is an unmerited gift*."[31]

The contrast is quite sharp. The man who lives in gratitude "stands within the truth, while the former is blindly imprisoned in his obtuse indifference."[32] The future priest who takes things for granted is marked by desolation. He is unable to see "the

30 See Richardson, "The Virtue of Gratitude," 62.

31 Von Hildebrand, *The Art of Living*, 112–13. Emphasis added.

32 Ibid.

abundance and value of the gifts he has received, nor knows that they are unmerited gifts, nor recognizes that in them shines the goodness, mercy, and love of God!"[33]

We can corroborate the truth of von Hildebrand's observations by looking back to Simon and the woman in the Gospel account. Unlike the Pharisee, the woman at Christ's feet was able to recognize the gift inherent in the forgiveness of her sins.

To recognize a favor (*gratia*) as such, a seminarian needs to acknowledge that he is receiving something good from another. In addition, the future priest needs to realize that this gift is unmerited, that he is not entitled to it. But this is harder than it seems. The Pharisees fall into this trap because pride is one of the greatest obstacles in the way of this twofold recognition.

Consequently, the spiritual exercises in gratitude imply indirectly a certain growth in the virtue of humility. We will look at humility within the province of temperance. Yet some important considerations on pride as an obstacle to gratitude are now in order.

Gregory the Great distinguishes different ways of being proud, different ways of disorderedly desiring our own excellence.[34] Excellence comes from a good actually being possessed in reality. But the real possession of a good can be considered in itself, in its cause, and in its mode.

Considered in itself, the greater the good really possessed, the greater the excellence. Considered in its cause, it entails a greater excellence to possess a good from ourselves, rather than from another. Considered in the mode or the way in which a good is possessed, the more this good is possessed, the greater excellence there is for the possessor.

Different species of pride result from these different

33 Von Hildebrand, *The Art of Living*, 113. Emphasis added.

34 See *ST* II–II, q. 162, a. 4, c.

considerations of excellence as the real possession of a good. I will not consider all of them now, but only the ones most related to the virtue of gratitude and the vice of ingratitude.

The consideration of the real possession of a good in itself correlates with the kind of pride that consists in boasting about what we do not have. The consideration of the real possession of a good in its cause correlates with two other forms of pride: to believe that the good we have actually comes from ourselves and not from another, and to believe that the gifts received from another (including God) are not really gifts, but somehow merited by ourselves. These forms of pride create a serious obstacle because, as Thomas says, "the ungrateful man ascribes to himself what he has from another."[35]

One may think that this problem is quite easy to solve, that it is enough to point out the things we receive as gifts in our daily life. Unfortunately, to consider these things in their universality is not the whole solution, because actions are in the particular.

Consider another example: A married man may give talks about the evil of adultery. He might be utterly convinced that, in the universal, adultery is a mortal sin, something that is evil and despicable. But the same person may judge very differently in the particular situation. Affected by his own emotions, he may judge that, in this particular situation, with this particular wife of his and that other particular woman, and the experiences he is enduring, adultery is really what he wants for himself here and now.[36]

Similarly, we may say in the abstract universal that everything

---

35 *ST* II–II, q. 162, a. 4, ad 3. Gregory's order, mentioned here by Aquinas, is not the same as ours. Gregory's first two species correspond to our second and third.

36 See *ST* II–II, q. 162, a. 4, ad 1.

we have is a gift, that we are not entitled to all these many things. But when we move from "talking the talk" to "walking the walk," it may be proven that our *practical convictions* are quite otherwise. For this reason, if we truly want to remove the obstacles for the virtue of gratitude in an effective manner, we need to trust the popular saying, "Actions speak louder than words." We need to examine, in search of these forms of pride, not so much the content of our thoughts but *our actions*, not so much what we think about something, but how we act in that regard.[37]

Aquinas says that those who fall into this kind of ingratitude, not wanting to acknowledge the gifts received or feeling entitled to them, are accustomed to "find fault with the favor received."[38] This situation is particularly interesting for priestly life and for life in the seminary. Such an attitude plunges its roots into egoism and disordered self-love.

We may easily fall into the obstacle of ingratitude if we quickly complain about the parish assignment, the pastor with whom we are working as priests, our bishop, the rector in the seminary, the teachers, formators, other seminarians, and so on. Instead of experiencing our priestly life or our years in the seminary as an unmerited gift and an opportunity, we will blindly go through the motions with a bitter and ungrateful spirit, self-centered, and unable to live in the freedom of the gift.

Sometimes it may be the case that someone does an *apparent* favor to us with not-so-good "strings attached" to it. In this scenario, the gift being offered is not truly a gift, because it is not *gratis*. Through it, the giver may intend to abuse the dependency of gratitude, expecting in repayment something not morally good.

---

37 This need is even more urgent when one realizes how hidden pride can be. See *ST* II–II, q. 162, a. 6, ad 1.

38 *ST* II–II, q. 107, a. 2, c.

Sometimes we encounter similar situations in parish life.[39] In this case, in the measure that is possible, we are obliged to refuse the favor. "If this is impossible, then we may accept the favor, but we must not concede any sort of power to him that would induce us to do something against our conscience."[40]

Out of pride, a seminarian may grow *accustomed* to taking things for granted. This taking things for granted may give rise to an illogical situation. A future priest may be ungrateful in the face of great things that have become a sort of routine, while developing a sense of gratitude for smaller things that are out of the ordinary.

The situation is truly paradoxical. It would be like listening to a whispering voice, while being unable to hear the thunder of a hundred cannon firing at the same time. Kierkegaard uses this same image to warn us against the force of routine. He says: "Let the thunder of a hundred cannon remind you three times daily to resist the force of habit."[41]

Kierkegaard does not mean by habit what we mean by virtues as operative habits. Rather, he is using the word in the sense of "fixed custom or routine." Thus, he continues by pointing out that we must "be careful that this also does not become a habit [routine]! For you can become accustomed to hearing the thunder of a hundred cannon so that you can sit at table and hear the most trivial, insignificant things far more clearly than the thunder of the hundred cannon—which you have become accustomed to hearing."[42]

Following this advice, candidates to the priesthood need to resist the force of routine in seminary life. We need to be on guard

---

39 See Richardson, "The Virtue of Gratitude," 43–44.

40 Von Hildebrand, *The Art of Living*, 128.

41 Søren Kierkegaard, *Works of Love*, trans. Howard Hong (New York: Harper Torchbooks, 1962), 51.

42 Ibid.

against the kind of negligence that makes us fall into forgetfulness and leads to ingratitude.[43]

Expressing Our Appreciation and Thanks

It is impossible to express meaningfully our appreciation and thanks to another when we do not recognize the favors received. This second act presupposes the first, as well as the removal of the obstacle of pride. When someone confers a favor upon us, two things must be considered.

First and foremost, one is to consider, in the measure that is possible, his intention; that is, the love with which he makes the gift. Secondly, one is also to look at the gift in question.[44] Obviously, "God alone sees man's disposition in itself: but in so far as it is shown by certain signs, man also can know it."[45] To do so, we need to be well-disposed.

Here we may find another potential obstacle for gratitude. A seminarian may be judgmental about the intention of others; he may not presuppose the best in them. Hence, a future priest may not appreciate the gifts that are being given to him as such, as gifts. The candidate to the priesthood may judge that others are doing something for him with some ulterior motive in mind.

Instead, Aquinas teaches that "it is the mark of a happy disposition to see good rather than evil."[46] Therefore, "when the manner of giving leads the recipient to doubt the motives of the giver, he should not for this reason dismiss his obligation of gratitude. Though the manner of giving can make a gift less

---

43 See *ST* II–II, q. 107, a. 1, ad 2.

44 See *ST* II–II, q. 106, a. 4, c.

45 *ST* II–II, q. 106, a. 5, ad 3.

46 *ST* II–II, q. 106, a. 3, ad 2.

acceptable, the benefactor should always receive the benefit of the doubt."[47] In order to be grateful, we should not require from the giver that the gift entails a loss for him.

Gratitude commands that a repayment with respect to the affection of the heart of the giver be made at once. This immediate repayment consists in receiving the gift graciously, namely, *expressing* our appreciation and thanks. Thomas explains that "since gratitude regards the favor inasmuch as it is bestowed gratis, and this regards the disposition of the giver, it follows again that repayment of a favor depends more on the disposition of the giver than on the effect."[48]

The immediate expression of our appreciation and thanks should go beyond simply saying thank you. Other words could be used. What is determinant, however, is that the words used truthfully convey an internal and humble state of mind: an "acknowledgement of indebtedness and even a feeling of respectful submission."[49] Such acknowledgement honors the benefactor and could even take place in public as a token of appreciation.

Often we receive gifts that we will never be able to match. But as we have noted, gratitude looks not so much for the equality of external things, but for a certain equality of wills.[50] No matter how poor a seminarian or a priest may be, he can always match the liberal and generous disposition of the heart of the benefactor, who in giving things gratis is giving, above all, the primordial gift of his love.

This happens, for instance, between children and parents, and between those who play a key role in the formation and integral education of the human person. We may give to our father only

---

47 Richardson, "The Virtue of Gratitude," 44.

48 *ST* II–II, q. 106, a. 5, c.

49 Richardson, "The Virtue of Gratitude," 56.

50 See *ST* II–II, q. 106, a. 6, ad 3.

lesser things than what we received from him, but these lesser things could be given with greater love. For this reason, Thomas argues that "in repaying favors we must consider the disposition rather than the deed. Accordingly, if we consider the effect of beneficence, which a son receives from his parents, namely, to be and to live, the son cannot make an equal repayment. . . . But if we consider the will of the giver and of the repayer, then it is possible for the son to pay back something greater to his father."[51]

Repaying the Favor with Prudence

That we need to consider, most of all, the disposition of the giver does not imply that we ought to ignore the deed done. To grow in the virtue of gratitude, a seminarian or priest needs actually to repay the favor received with prudence. The latter is foundational for all human virtues. Without it, there cannot be gratitude.

Prudence is affected by the inclination of the other virtues, which are like a dispositive material cause. Yet for all the cardinal virtues to be such, and for all the virtues within their particular province to be virtuous, they all need prudence. Consider the following example.

A seminarian may have the inclination to drink alcohol without drinking to excess. He may desire to be temperate. Nonetheless, this material disposition is not enough. Additionally, he needs to determine, rationally and according to circumstances, how much alcohol he can drink without violating temperance. Hence, prudence causes the other moral virtues to be such, at the level of determination and specification of their concrete ends.

For this reason, Thomas says: "A right judgment in any matter requires two things. The first is the virtue itself that pronounces judgment: and in this way, judgment is an act of reason [an act of

51 See *ST* II–II, q. 106, a. 6, ad 1.

prudence], because it belongs to the reason to pronounce or define. The other is the disposition of the one who judges, on which depends his aptness for judging aright. In this way, in matters of justice, judgment proceeds from justice, even as in matters of fortitude, it proceeds from fortitude. Accordingly, judgment is an act of justice in so far as justice inclines one to judge aright, and of prudence in so far as prudence pronounces judgment."[52] Likewise, even if we have the inclination or desire to be grateful, without prudence, we would not be able to determine and specify the concrete acts of gratitude to be done in order to repay the favors received.

Even though the intention of the giver or benefactor should be matched *immediately* and with equality, the virtue of gratitude does *not* require repayment for the gift received as soon as possible and with equality, that is, matching in repayment the gift that has been conferred on the recipient. The virtue of gratitude, instead, commands to repay the favor (1) at a suitable place and time; (2) according to one's means; and (3) trying, in a measure that is possible, to surpass the gift of love received.

With respect to the first point, the worst scenario would be the one in which a seminarian not only fails to repay a favor, but returns evil for good. Another scenario of ingratitude would consist in not returning the favor because the future priest quickly finds fault with the favor received, or because, being judgmental, he esteems the kindness of the giver as though it were unkindness.[53] For example, someone may help us do something that was our duty and we conclude, "He just wanted to show off" or "He just wanted to humiliate me."

There are also candidates for the priesthood too eager to pay back a favor received. Some may think that such earnestness is

52 *ST* II–II, q. 60, a. 1, ad 1.

53 See *ST* II–II, q. 107, a. 2, c.

something good. In reality, Aquinas notes, following Seneca, that this is not a virtue: "If instead of choosing a convenient time, one wished to repay at once, favor for favor, it would not seem to be a virtuous, but a constraint, repayment."[54]

Here, we see another difference between justice and gratitude. While the debt of justice is to be paid as soon as we can, this is not so with the debt of gratitude. We should wait for the proper time. Such a delay is oriented to making visible both the acceptance of the gift received and our deep affection and love for the giver.

For this reason, Thomas adds, "An unwilling debtor is ungrateful."[55] Indeed, out of pride, a seminarian may hate being dependent on others. He may hate to experience for a while the debt of gratitude.[56] In fact, von Hildebrand notes, "A man who is reluctant to be grateful to others, feeling this to be a burdensome dependence, is still a slave of his pride."[57] This person's "insensitivity to the generosity contained in every gift, also shows that he himself has not yet fully entered into the kingdom of goodness."[58]

Out of pride, a future priest may hate to feel lower than the gratuitous giver. The moral obligation to repay the debt of gratitude may be interpreted as a restriction of his freedom. Thus, von Hildebrand concludes very acutely that it is "deeply characteristic of pride that the beauty of the helper's generosity is ignored and only resentment against formal superiority is felt."[59]

---

54 *ST* II–II, q. 106, a. 4, c. As Thomas later explains, in ad 2, not every earnestness of the will is virtuous, but only the one regulated by right reason or prudence.

55 Ibid.

56 See Richardson, "The Virtue of Gratitude," 45.

57 Von Hildebrand, *The Art of Living*, 124.

58 Ibid.

59 Ibid., 126.

From another angle, what are we to do when a seminarian or a parishioner persists in being ungrateful? Besides letting this person know of his ungratefulness in an appropriate manner, one of the most effective strategies is found in the *Summa Theologiae*. There, Thomas explains that someone who "bestows a favor on an ungrateful person affords him an occasion not of sin but of gratitude and love . . . He that bestows a favor must not at once act the part of a punisher of ingratitude, but rather that of a kindly physician, by healing the ingratitude with repeated favors."[60] Aquinas's advice echoes Jesus's words to his disciples: "Love your enemies, and do good, and lend, *expecting nothing in return*; and your reward will be great, and you will be sons of the Most High; for he is *kind to the ungrateful* and the selfish" (Lk 6:35; emphasis added).

The second requirement for the prudent repayment of the debt of gratitude is that the repayment *must* be according to our means. If a seminarian has nothing else or cannot do anything else, a little thing done with great love would suffice. In this sense, "no man is excused from ingratitude through inability to repay, for the very reason that the mere will suffices for the repayment of the debt of gratitude."[61]

The third and last requirement for the prudent repayment of the debt of gratitude establishes that, in the measure that we can, we need to try to surpass the gift received. In other words, since we have received something gratis, we are to give something gratis. But if a seminarian tries to match only the quantity of the gift of the benefactor, he is not giving something gratis, but only returning what he received.[62]

Clearly, in many instances, we are to look at the disposition of the giver and try to be even more benevolent in ours. Moreover, it is also important to remember that gratitude moves us to

60 *ST* II–II, q. 107, a. 4, ad 2–3.

61 *ST* II–II, q. 107, a. 1, ad 2. See also II–II, q. 106, a. 6, ad 1.

62 See *ST* II–II, q. 106, a. 6, c.

acknowledge that the benefactor deserves praise and honor for having donated something with liberality, without being bound to do so, and without intention of being repaid. There could be a sort of material excess in this last requirement, if prudence is not governing and leading the act. By way of excess, a future priest could give to another something that is not truly good, or he could assist or cooperate in a sinful behavior. In these instances, the virtue of gratitude is falsified.

Ingratitude

As we already noted, ingratitude is a kind of injustice. It is explicitly condemned in Sacred Scripture (see 2 Tm 3:2). It opposes the virtue of gratitude by neither recognizing nor responding to the love of the giving person or to his other gifts.

Ingratitude could take the shape of an omission or the shape of a positive action directly opposed to the benefactor. Accordingly, there is a distinction between *privative* ingratitude and *positive* ingratitude.[63]

Thomas establishes degrees of privative ingratitude, which correspond (in reverse order) to the key acts of gratitude previously treated: "The first degree of ingratitude is when a man fails to repay a favor, the second when he declines to notice or indicate that he has received a favor, while the third and supreme degree is when a man fails to recognize the reception of a favor, whether by forgetting it or in any other way."[64] Aquinas also identifies acts of positive ingratitude corresponding to the same acts: "It belongs to the first degree of ingratitude to return evil for good, to the second to find fault with a favor received, and to the third to esteem kindness as though it were unkindness."[65]

---

63 See Richardson, "The Virtue of Gratitude," 63.

64 *ST* II–II, q. 107, a. 2, c.

65 Ibid.

As we noted, in a sense, every sin entails some material ingratitude. However, the specific and full-fledged formal sin of ingratitude entails a certain willful contempt for the gift received: "Formal ingratitude is when a favor is actually contemned."[66]

This contempt entails a denial of both our dependence on the benefactor and our moral debt of gratitude. It usually belittles the gift or suggests that the benefactor was obliged to give it. In this manner, a seminarian may lack gratitude towards his superiors or teachers, justifying himself with the idea that they are doing only what they are supposed to do as part of their job.

Additionally, when the benefactor is targeted by sins of detraction, for instance, and he is the object of such sins precisely because he is a benefactor, we are also faced with formal ingratitude. This kind of contempt is a serious matter. It has the capacity not only to oppose gratitude, but also the charity with which one ought to love his benefactor.

Gratitude Toward God

Gratitude does not belong to God insofar as he is no man's debtor. Although we all owe gratitude to God, strictly speaking, God owes gratitude to no one: "Who has given a gift to him that he might be repaid? For from him and through him and to him are all things" (Rom 11:35–36).

That God has no moral obligation of gratitude does not belittle his goodness. On the contrary, it only emphasizes even more the gratuitousness of his divine love for the human person. He gave us himself in giving us his Son and the Holy Spirit. Without any obligation whatsoever, "God so loved the world that he gave his only Son, that whoever believes in him should not perish but have eternal life" (Jn 3:16).

---

66 *ST* II–II, q. 107, a. 2, ad 1.

Nevertheless, gratitude toward God is essential in our formation in the virtues. To be sure, gratitude is not a theological virtue. Its object is not God himself, but rather the moral debt of love and virtue that has arisen as a result of his favors.[67]

Of course, we are speaking of gratitude in a wide sense here, since at this point, we have begun to cross into the realm of religion, which moves the human person to perform acts of worship and thanksgiving to God. Yet the intimate interconnection between the virtues allows us to make this crossing over, as it were, which will be further developed in our treatment of religion. The reason is quite practical. Without denying the exact distinction of the virtues, from the perspective of charity, spiritual exercises in gratitude indirectly exercise the virtue of religion as well.

We have many prayers of gratitude in our daily life. Above all, consider the Eucharist. Looking at the Liturgy of the Hours, we can refer to the Benedictus, the Magnificat, or the Nunc Dimittis. Of course, our gratitude to God implies that we believe him to be a benevolent God.[68]

It is often the case that our growth in gratitude entails a preliminary growth into our conscious awareness of God's goodness in our lives. This growth needs to take place not only in the universal, but also in the concrete and singular, in which we come to realize that in *all* the events of our lives, God is at work *for the good* of those who love him (see Rom 8:28).

Just as pride is an obstacle for gratitude, humility is a predispositive virtue that combats the danger of entitlement before God: "The thankful person is conscious of the fact that he is a beggar before God and possesses no right in relation to God on which he can insist, that all is a gift of the goodness of God and that

---

67 See Richardson, "The Virtue of Gratitude," 26–27.

68 See von Hildebrand, *The Art of Living*, 104.

he can make no claim against God."[69] A seminarian who achieves this state of gratefulness toward God leads a life of recollection, an interior life of praise in which his eyes are truly opened. He avoids being apathetic, obtuse, and superficial.[70]

All of us should be grateful to God for many things. However, let us point out two main realities that will help us to grow in gratitude and in love: the forgiveness of our sins and the preservation from sinning in any other way through God's grace. Whether our lives resemble that of Thérèse or that of Augustine, we are to be grateful to God.

In fact, in Augustine's *Confessions*, we find a beautiful meditation in this regard:

> What man who reflects upon his own weakness can dare to claim that his own efforts have made him chaste and free from sin, as though this entitled him to love you the less, on the ground that he had less need of the mercy by which you forgive the sins of the penitent? There are some who have been called by you and because they have listened to your voice they have avoided the sins which I here record and confess for them to read. But let them not deride me for having been cured by the same Doctor who preserved them from sickness, or at least from such grave sickness as mine. Let them love you just as much, or even more, than I do, for they can see that the same healing hand which rid me of the great fever of my sins protects them from falling sick of the same disease.[71]

We may be too enthusiastic after this presentation and attempt to see the need for gratitude in absolutely everything, even in the "crosses" that God sends us. Yet this is not completely accurate.

---

69 Von Hildebrand, *The Art of Living*, 107.

70 See ibid., 108.

71 Augustine of Hippo, *Confessions*, trans. R. S. Pine-Coffin (New York: Penguin Books, 1961), II. 7. For a greater set of distinctions on this topic, see *ST* II–II, q. 106, a. 2, c.

The proper response for an evil allowed by God for our own good or the good of others is not gratitude, but humble acceptance.

Jesus *accepted* his Father's will in Gethsemane. Obviously, there was no sin whatsoever in Christ's petition to be freed from death. But neither was there gratitude in that prayer of petition. That prayer is a sublime example of humble acceptance.

Aquinas explains that the first part of Christ's prayer—that if it were possible this chalice might pass from him—expresses the simple and natural desire of Christ's human will to live (*voluntas ut natura*).[72] On the other hand, the second part—that God's will would be done and not his—expresses the free choice (*voluntas ut ratio*) by which Jesus freely *obeys* the Father and adheres his human will to the Divine Will.[73] Hence, we have to affirm with von Hildebrand that "gratitude is the response to all the *positive* gifts and submissive, *loving acceptance* is the response to *the crosses*."[74]

Spiritual Exercises in Gratitude

We have provided the knowledge essential to understanding the virtue of gratitude, a knowledge needed not only to grow better in this virtue but also to teach others and equip those who will teach about gratitude. Now we will conclude our reflections by offering some spiritual exercises in gratitude. Their context could be the Examen prayer.

For these exercises to be fruitful, we are not to work through the Examen and conclude what we are supposed to say or to do, as if looking for the correct answer. Instead, we are to find—honestly, realistically, and humbly—the acts and areas in which we have the opportunity to exercise spiritually in this virtue. These

---

72 See *ST* III, q. 21, a. 3, c.

73 See *ST* III, q. 21, a. 4, c.

74 Von Hildebrand, *The Art of Living*, 119. Emphasis added.

spiritual exercises should be carried out on different levels: in our conscience at prayer, with our confessor if there is a need for the sacrament of reconciliation, with our spiritual director, and with our formation advisor.

Consider which of the following statements are true, and which are not.

	I often pray the Examen prayer, giving thanks to God for the gifts received from him.
	I have experienced how gratitude has helped me to live not for myself, but for Christ (cf. 2 Cor 5:15).
	I have experienced how gratitude enriches me by increasing my interior freedom.
	I have experienced how gratitude has been the channel God has used to give me many other graces.
	The virtue of gratitude has helped me to fall in love and to stay in love with God.
	I want to respond to Christ's sacrificial and spousal gift of self for his Church.
	I have found that ingratitude is the cause, beginning, and origin of many of my sins.
	I view every moral demand of the Gospel in light of the *kerygma*.
	I have experienced great joy when I have been grateful.
	In my daily actions, I often meditate on Ps 116:12: "What shall I render to the Lord / for all his bounty to me?"
	I would like to acquire the virtue of gratitude not only for my sake, but also for the sake of my future ministry as a priest.
	I have been praying with Lk 7:36–50, asking God to help me truly to welcome him and his mercy into my life, acknowledging that I am not healthy but sick.
	In my practical convictions, I humbly recognize the many unmerited gifts I receive in my daily life at the seminary.

	In my practical convictions, I struggle with entitlement and with taking things for granted.
	I often boast of good qualities or things that I do not really have.
	In my daily actions, I sometimes believe that the good qualities or things that I truly have come from myself and not from another.
	My daily actions manifest my internal conviction that the gifts received from others are merited by me, and that I deserve them.
	I have a tendency to find fault with the gifts that I receive, which results in complaining and detraction.
	I experience my own selfishness as an impediment to my growth in gratitude.
	The routine of my life has made me accustomed to great gifts, to the point of being blind to them.
	Instead of giving benefactors the benefit of the doubt, I have a tendency to presuppose a bad intention in people who give me gifts.
	When I receive a gift from others, I experience within myself a benevolent desire toward them that is expressed in words such as "Thank you."
	When I receive a gift from others, I pay more attention to their benevolent disposition toward me than to the other gifts given.
	When I receive a gift from others, I experience within myself an acknowledgement of indebtedness and a feeling of respectful submission toward them.
	When I receive a gift from others that I cannot match, I strive to give them in return a greater love.
	When I receive a gift from others, I usually repay the favor received at a suitable time.
	When I receive a gift from others, I tend to repay the favor as soon as possible because I do not like the feeling that I get when I owe something to someone.

	When I receive a gift from others, I usually repay the favor received according to my means.
	When I receive a gift from others, I sometimes end up doing things for them I should not have done, collaborating in morally questionable actions.
	When I receive a gift from others, I usually fail to repay the favor.
	When I receive a gift from others, I usually decline to notice or indicate that I have received a gift.
	When I receive a gift from others, I tend to ignore it, not acknowledging it as a gift or easily forgetting about it.
	When I receive a gift from others, I return evil for good.
	When I receive a gift from others, I usually esteem their kindness as unkindness.
	When I receive a gift from others, I tend to belittle the gift by pointing out that it was the obligation of my benefactors to give such things.
	I tend to detract from the people I resent for giving things to me, because I judge that they feel superior to me.
	To grow in gratitude, I need to realize that God has always been acting in my life for my good, especially in moments of suffering.
	I am consciously aware of being a beggar before God.
	I feel entitled to what God gives me because of the difficulties that I have experienced in my life.
	I am deeply grateful to God for having preserved me from other sins.
	I am deeply grateful to God for the forgiveness of my sins.
	I am aware that even though my sins deserve eternal damnation, God offers me his mercy, love, and eternal salvation in Christ.

CHAPTER 2

JUSTICE IN THE SEMINARY COMMUNITY

THE VALUE OF JUSTICE

KEEP justice, and do righteousness" (Is 56:1). *The Catechism of the Catholic Church* defines justice as "the moral virtue that consists in the constant and firm will to give their due to God and neighbor."[1] It also explains that "justice toward men disposes one to respect the rights of each and to establish in human relationships the harmony that promotes equity with regard to persons and to the common good."[2]

Justice was highly valued in Greek philosophy. Plato thought of it as the foundational virtue from which other virtues spring. Justice constitutes their ordering. It is the harmonizing principle of the virtues that determines their field of action.[3] Aristotle also recognized the great importance of justice as the expression of perfect virtue.[4]

The Fathers of the Church highlighted its great value as well. For instance, Ambrose of Milan called justice the fruitful *genetrix* of other virtues, and John Chrysostom thought of it as the observance

---

1 CCC 1807.

2 Ibid.

3 See Plato, *Republic*, IV. 433a; *Phaedo*, 82a.

4 See Aristotle, *Rhetoric*, I. 9; *Nichomachean Ethics*, V. 3.1129b.30.

of the commandments.[5] As we know, Augustine defined this virtue from the perspective of charity as "love serving only the loved object, and therefore ruling rightly," and "love serving God only, and therefore ruling well all else, as subject to man."[6]

Nevertheless, despite this great tradition, justice has been undervalued in the spiritual life. As Garrigou-Lagrange says, "Among the four cardinal virtues of prudence, justice, fortitude, and temperance, there is one, namely justice, which pious people do not consider sufficiently."[7] Overcoming this limitation, Pieper argues that "the demands of justice beset man at his spiritual core."[8]

The splendor of the value of justice for priestly formation is particularly evident in its role in the life of the seminary community. Justice overcomes selfishness and disordered self-love. It allows acting and redirecting all virtues for the common good of the seminary, namely, the formation of future priests.

The virtue of justice perfects the human will with respect to the good of others. As it is a *relational* virtue, it belongs in the arena of inter-personality and life in community. Hence, neither priestly

---

5 See Ambrose of Milan, "On the Duties of the Clergy" in *St. Ambrose: Select Works and Letters*, vol. 10, eds. Philip Schaff and Henry Wace, trans. H. De Romestin and H. Duckworth (New York: Christian Literature, 1896), I. 27. 126; I. 28. 10–136; Istvan P. Bejczy, *The Cardinal Virtues in the Middle Ages: A Study in Moral Thought from the Fourth to the Fourteenth Century*, ed. by Han Van Ruler (Boston: Brill, 2011), 12–22.

6 *De Moribus Ecclesiae*, 15. 25.

7 Reginald Garrigou-Lagrange, *The Three Ages of the Interior Life: Prelude of Eternal Life*, trans. Timothea Doyle, vol. 2 (Rockford, IL: TAN Books and Publishers, 1989), 90. Emphasis added.

8 Josef Pieper, *The Four Cardinal Virtues: Prudence, Justice, Fortitude, Temperance* (Notre Dame, IN: University of Notre Dame Press, 1966), 66.

formation nor the virtuous life in general should be conceived as an autonomous narcissistic project.

"The virtue of justice in all its forms seems to single out a truth most evident, which nevertheless our society is in danger of forgetting, namely, that *the human good is not isolated but is had in union with others*."[9] Thus, we can rise above the common objection that "Thomist virtue theory runs the un-Christian risk of portraying the virtuous individual as one concerned principally with himself or herself."[10]

Traditionally, a distinction is recognized between general and particular justice. The first is identified with legal or political justice.[11] Within the second, we find a further subdivision between commutative and distributive justice. These distinctions already point to justice's relational character, as it can be seen through their application to priestly formation.

Legal or political justice regulates the *I–we* dimension of the seminary, that is, the order between the part and the whole (*ordo partium ad totum*), between the individual members and the seminary community. Alternatively, commutative justice concerns the *I–thou* dimension of seminary life, or the order of one part to another (*ordo partium ad partes*), that is, the relationship between each individual member of the seminary community to each of the others.

---

9 Steven Jensen, *Living the Good Life: A Beginner's Thomistic Ethics* (Washington, DC: Catholic University of America Press, 2013), 108. Emphasis added.

10 Romanus Cessario, *The Moral Virtues and Theological Ethics* (Notre Dame, IN: University of Notre Dame Press, 2013), 20–21.

11 With this terminology, I am following Steven Jensen who explains: "It is perhaps better called political justice, to avoid the notion that this kind of justice merely concerns following human laws. According to Thomas, political justice is an overarching virtue, directing all other virtues. All that we do must be directed to the common good, for we are like parts of a whole, whose good arises from its order to the whole" (Jensen, *Living the Good Life*, 107).

In turn, distributive or ministering justice regulates the *I–we* dimension, the order of the whole to the part (*ordo totius ad partes*), the relationship between those governing the seminary community and each of its individual members.[12] Additionally, within the context of priestly formation in justice, we could also look ahead and consider the peculiar *I–we* relationship, which future priests will have in their exercise of authority, while governing a parish through a participation in Christ's *munus regendi*.

Explaining the value of justice among other virtues, Aquinas argues that legal or political justice "stands foremost among all the moral virtues, for as much as the common good transcends the individual good of one person."[13] General, legal, or political justice is able to assume and elevate any act of another virtue: "The good of any virtue, whether such virtue directs man in relation to himself, or in relation to certain other individual persons, is referable to the common good, to which justice directs: so that *all acts of virtue can pertain to justice, in so far as it directs man to the common good*."[14]

Hence, at the seminary or in a parish, it becomes a matter of justice toward the community and toward others to have fortitude and to be temperate, prudent, chaste, humble, meek, studious, patient, and so on. None of these virtues are just for ourselves. They are for the good of all. Justice demands their growth because they benefit both myself and others. Conversely, if I do not grow in them, I am committing an injustice toward the common good, toward the parish community, and toward the seminary. I owe this growth in virtue to them.

---

12 Pieper, *The Four Cardinal Virtues*, 71–72.

13 *ST* II–II, q. 58, a. 12, c.

14 *ST* II–II, q. 58, a. 5, c. Emphasis added. See also *ST* I–II, q. 60, a. 3, ad 2.

Particular justice also shines among the moral virtues because it resides in the highest part of the soul, in the spirit or *mens*, in the part that comprises the intellect and the will. Its object is also relational: "The other virtues are commendable in respect of the sole good of the virtuous person himself, whereas justice is praiseworthy in respect of the virtuous person being well-disposed toward another, so that justice is somewhat the good of another person."[15]

In fact, *every external act* directed to another belongs to the province of justice.[16] Consider the following example. A seminarian may get inordinately angry and strike another person. In this scenario, the sin committed is not only one of anger, but also one against justice.

Thomas says that "in such cases *justice is destroyed in so far as the due measure of the external act is destroyed*: while some other virtue is destroyed in so far as the internal passions exceed their due measure."[17] Striking the other seminarian was directly against the virtues of meekness, commutative justice, and political justice.

Let us reflect on another example, one from the realm of human sexuality. Sexual sins that do not involve another person are often viewed as something completely private, with no effect whatsoever on the community. However, as we know, chastity can be assumed and elevated by political justice.

For this reason, a future priest who sins against chastity harms himself as well as the common good of the seminary. Pieper explains that "the whole field of sexual aberration, not adultery and

---

15 *ST* II–II, q. 58, a. 12, c.

16 See Pieper, *The Four Cardinal Virtues*, 61.

17 *ST* I–II, q. 60, a. 2, c.

rape only, contains an element of injustice."[18] These are acts that have a negative impact not only upon ourselves and our neighbor, but also upon the common good of the seminary community.

The value of justice also shines when we consider that it inheres in the will, so as to exile from it selfishness or disordered self-love.[19] As we know, Augustine distinguishes two kinds of foundational loves, but only one of them gives rise to the citizenship of heaven: "The love of self to the point of despising God gave rise to the earthly city. The love for God to the point of despising oneself has risen to the heavenly city."[20]

The bishop of Hippo continues to contrast these two loves by pointing out that "the first boasts about itself, while the second boasts in the Lord. The first requires glory from men, while for the second, the greatest glory is God in the witness of conscience. The one lifts up its head in its own boasting; the other says to God: 'You are my glory, You lift up my head.'"[21]

Augustine is not contrasting two cities but rather two citizenships. He is really contrasting two foundational moral attitudes, which belong either to the citizens of the heavenly city or to the citizens of the earthly city. Here, the virtue of justice plays a foundational role. It combats disordered self-love within the context of acting together with others.

Thus, the one who loves God and belongs to the heavenly city is willing to despise himself in a certain way (*secundum quid*). He is willing to despise *in himself everything that separates him from God.* Anyone can already see that such a capacity is most valuable

---

18 Pieper, *The Four Cardinal Virtues*, 61.

19 See Garrigou-Lagrange, *The Three Ages,* vol. 2, 90.

20 *De Civitate Dei*, XIV. 28. The translation is mine. See *De Malo*, q. 8, a. 2, c.

21 Ibid.

for a future priest. Still, its value is evidenced even more when we go deeper into the meaning of proper self-love.

Thomas Aquinas takes up precisely this Augustinian and Pauline theme. He interprets it in an Aristotelian way, thanks to the philosophy of friendship. Judging aright about his own relationship with God and his personal identity, the future priest who loves himself with proper self-love becomes "friends," as it were, with his *interior* or *inward* man.

Seminarians who have that kind of love for themselves share in the self-love of the citizens of the heavenly city. Since they are friends with their interior man, they "wish the preservation thereof in its integrity, they desire good things for him, namely spiritual goods, indeed they do their best to obtain them, and they take *pleasure in entering into their own hearts*, because they find there good thoughts in the present, the memory of past good, and the hope of future good, all of which are sources of pleasure. Likewise, they experience no clashing of wills, since their whole soul tends to one thing."[22]

Future priests who love themselves in this way love others aright as well. They can love others as they love themselves.

Instead, the disordered love of self, proper to the citizens of the earthly city, entails loving ourselves against the truth about the human person, regarding what is inferior within the human person as if it were superior. For this reason, "the wicked have no wish to be preserved in the integrity of the inward man, nor do they desire spiritual goods for him, *nor do they work for that end, nor do they take pleasure in their own company by entering into their own hearts*, because whatever they find there, present, past and future, is evil and horrible; nor do they agree with themselves, on account of the gnawings of conscience."[23]

---

22 *ST* II–II, q. 25, a. 7, c.

23 Ibid.

The citizens of the earthly city, not *knowing* themselves aright, cannot *love* themselves aright. Seminarians trapped in this disorder lack that recollection proper to the man of prayer. They have a difficulty with silence and with being in their own company. They constantly need entertainment for precisely that reason.

Since they do not love themselves properly, they cannot love others appropriately. They will love them the way they love non-spiritual beings or spiritual qualities (accidents), namely, with sheer love of concupiscence.[24] Furthermore, future priests who do not love themselves aright cannot put their own virtues at the service of the common good.

These brief remarks on the virtue of justice should be enough to show its importance for priestly formation. They are meant to initiate our reflection by motivating us to devote ourselves to its spiritual exercises. Now, let us briefly pause and reflect on the following questions. Keep in mind the key role of justice in our life together with others, in directing all of our virtues for the common good.

(1) What does lack of justice do to my life?
(2) What does lack of justice do to the life of the seminary?
(3) What will lack of justice do in my future life as a priest?
(4) What will my incapacity to be an example of justice mean for the life of my spiritual children?
(5) How will my growth in the virtue of justice impact my life as a seminarian and as a future priest, as well as the life of those around me in the seminary, and in my future parish?

---

24 See Jesús García López, *Virtud y Personalidad según Tomás de Aquino* (Pamplona: EUNSA, 2003), 80–84; Jesús García López, "El Amor Humano," *Persona y Derecho 1* (1974): 267–82.

Acquired Responsible Freedom and the Truth of Life

Anyone involved in priestly formation has heard about responsible freedom. However, few are able to explain with precision what it means. It is closely linked with our virtue for this chapter. Justice can be understood in a very broad sense as "a certain rectitude of the mind, *whereby a man does what he ought in any matters*."[25] Thus conceived, justice is not specifically distinguished from the other virtues, but belongs to them all.[26]

This broad meaning of justice corresponds with both its biblical sense as *adjusting* to the Divine Will in the freedom of God's children, and with the patristic notion of the "truth of life" (*veritas vitae*).[27] Now, "since man, *by his natural reason, is inclined to justice*, while sin is contrary to natural reason, it follows that *freedom from sin is true freedom which is united to the servitude to justice*, since they both incline man to what is becoming to him."[28]

Without ever alluding to this text explicitly, Wojtyła unfolds this notion when he affirms: "Human freedom is not fulfilled by subordinating truth to itself but *by subordinating itself to truth*."[29] Acquired responsible freedom results from the use of one's freedom of choice.[30] The latter is innate or natural to the human person.

---

25 *ST* I–II, q. 61, a. 4, c. Emphasis added.

26 See Angel Rodríguez Luño, *Scelti in Cristo Per Essere Santi: Morale Speciale*, vol. 3 of Sussidi Di Teologia (Roma: EDUSC, 2008), 47–54.

27 See Bernardo Estrada, "La Giustizia in Matteo: Presenza Del Rengo." Rivista Biblica, no. 59 (2011) 373–403.

28 *ST* II–II, q. 183, a. 4, c.

29 Wojtyła, *The Acting Person*, 154. Emphasis added. I have altered the English translation in view of the original text. See Karol Wojtyła, *Osoba i Czyn-Persona e Atto,* ed. Tadeusz Styczen (Santarcangelo: Rusconi Libri, 1999), 330.

30 See Antonio Millán-Puelles, *El Valor de La Libertad* (Madrid: Ediciones Rialp, 1995).

In turn, acquired responsible freedom adds to our freedom of choice the *habit* of using the latter well by subordinating to the truth, that is to say, by being free from sin and by becoming a servant of justice. We are not talking about one particular habit or virtue in the strict and proper sense of the word. Rather, it is like an integral whole composed of different virtues, a whole that in itself shares in the essential characteristics of habits and that corresponds with the perfect state of man as man, that is, the state of virtue.

Acquired *responsible* freedom is strictly dependent on our capacity for the truth. It is a proper *response* to that exact capacity. Without our intellectual capacity for the truth, we would not have free choice. Our freedom is made possible by the intellect.[31]

Most importantly, our natural freedom is also conditioned by its reference to the truth. Its very nature points to its perfection, to *an objective condition for its fulfillment: the subordination to the truth about the good.* For this reason, John Paul II also calls this perfection *responsible* freedom. It is a freedom that *responds* to its own nature.[32] We acquire more freedom or grow in more freedom by choosing the *true* and not merely the apparent good.

Moral Freedom and the Royal Way

The human person has the active power to be the cause of his own obedience to God's commandments. In this way, he can reach the fulfillment of his vocation responsibly and in collaboration with the Creator.[33] To *subordinate* oneself to the truth about the good means to love one's self properly, being good friends with one's interior

31 See *De Veritate*, q. 24, a. 2, c; Wojtyła, *The Acting Person*, 140–41.

32 See PDV, 8, 10.

33 See ibid., 36.

man. As a result, acquired or moral freedom confers on the human person a royal way of self-possession and self-governance.

We already encountered this idea in David's testament. Augustine also hinted at the royal character of this freedom in connection with justice. *Serving* God means to *rule*. It means to become a king in God's kingdom, that is, in union with God, *the* King, as his adoptive children. For this reason, as was said, Augustine understood justice to mean "love *serving* only the loved object, and therefore *ruling* rightly," as "love *serving* God only, and therefore *ruling* well all else, as subject to man."[34]

Note his choice of verbs (serving and ruling) to describe what justice is when perfected by love. By serving God, the human person rules over everything else. This idea is highly theological. It evokes the threefold subordination present in the state of original justice: "God made man upright" (Eccl 7:29). Before original sin, "God bestowed this favor on man in his primitive state, that as long as his spirit [*mens*] was subject to God, the lower powers of his soul would be subject to his rational spirit [*mens*], and his body to his soul."[35]

This same idea has solid philosophical grounds. Different degrees of life reflect different degrees of self-possession. Human life manifests its greatest degree of self-possession in the acquisition of moral freedom. Subordinating our freedom of choice to the truth about the good entails a human perfection; it amounts to an authentic human way of living according to our rational nature.[36] Moral freedom perfects one's self-possession, thereby imparting a sort of kingship, a sort of regal freedom to be identified in the supernatural life with the freedom of God's children.

---

34 *De Moribus Ecclesiae*, 15. 25. Emphasis added.

35 *ST* II–II, q. 164, a. 1, c. Translation altered. See also *ST* I, q. 95, a. 1; q. 97, a. 1.

36 See Millán-Puelles, *El Valor de la Libertad*, 201–3.

John of the Cross teaches that this moral freedom consists in loving God with all our strength, that is, with all our powers: "The strength of the soul comprises the faculties, passions, and appetites. All this strength is ruled by the will. When the will directs these faculties, passions, appetites toward God, turning away from all that is not God, the soul preserves its strength for God, and comes to love him with all its might."[37] This is the true freedom that John of the Cross so beautifully describes as follows:

> All the sovereignty and freedom of the world compared to the freedom and sovereignty of the Spirit of God is utter slavery, anguish, and captivity. Those, then, who are attached to prelacies or to other such dignities and to freedom of their appetites will be considered and treated by God as base slaves and captives, not as offspring . . . Thus they will be unable to reach the royal freedom of spirit attained in divine union, for freedom has nothing to do with slavery. And freedom cannot abide in a heart dominated by desires, in a slave's heart. It abides in a liberated heart, in a child's heart.[38]

John of the Cross's views on royal freedom correspond with the acquired responsible freedom of God's children and with that servitude to justice which Thomas previously mentioned.[39] This freedom is also closely connected with the patristic and Thomistic notion of the truth of life (*veritas vitae*), also called the truth of justice (*veritas iustitiae*).

As is known, truth is defined as the conformity (*adequatio*) between reality and the mind.[40] The truth of life or the truth of

---

37 John of the Cross, *The Ascent of the Mount Carmel*, III. 16. 2. The following edition is utilized: John of the Cross, *The Collected Works of St. John of the Cross*, trans. Kieran Kavanaugh and Otilio Rodriguez (Washington, DC: ICS Publications, 1991).

38 John of the Cross, *The Ascent of Mount Carmel*, I. 4. 6.

39 This same idea is also present in PDV, 40, 74.

40 See *ST* I, q. 16, a. 1, c.

justice is a sort of general virtue that undergirds all other virtues, a virtue whereby we *conform* our life with the Divine Mind. It is "a certain kind of truth according to which man shows himself in deed and words as he really is. Particularly, the truth of 'life' refers to man *as he fulfills in his life that to which he is ordained by the Divine Intellect.*"[41]

Moreover, the "truth of life" is related to the Book of Life, wherein are written the good works we are to perform in order to conform to God's eternal plan.[42] John Paul II has quite often used this Thomistic idea. It corresponds to his beloved expression "the truth about man." This truth refers to the truth about every human being as contained in Christ as God's Logos and his redemptive gift of self for the Church. However, it also refers to the unique plan God has assigned in Christ to each one of us in the fulfillment of our personal vocation.

Perfected Freedom as Justice

The exercise of acquired freedom in relationship to the truth of justice is a core virtue needed in priestly formation. John Paul II explains it as follows: "Among the virtues most necessary for the priestly ministry must be named that disposition of soul by which priests are always ready to seek not their own will, but the will of him who sent them."[43]

This acquisition of perfected freedom as justice is quite important for many other virtues. It certainly impacts the entire

---

41 *ST* I, q. 16, a. 4, ad 3. Emphasis added. See also *ST* II–II, q. 109, a. 2, ad 3.

42 See *ST* I–II, q. 91, a. 1, ad 2; *De Veritate*, q. 7, aa. 1–7.

43 PDV, 28.

maturation of our affectivity. The latter "requires a clear and strong training in freedom, which expresses itself in convinced and heartfelt obedience to the 'truth of one's own being, to the 'meaning' of one's own existence, that is to the 'sincere gift of self' as the way and fundamental content of the authentic realization of self."[44]

In this context, the pope describes perfected freedom in terms of ruling over oneself, not being confined to selfishness and individualism. "Thus understood, freedom requires the person to be truly master of oneself, determined to fight and overcome the different forms of selfishness and individualism which threaten the life of each one, ready to open out to others, generous in dedication and service to one's neighbor."[45]

Acquired responsible freedom is a freedom gained while acting together with others. In the case of future priests, this is a freedom to be acquired in the community life of the seminary. For this reason, the pope clarifies that, "on this educational journey toward a mature, responsible freedom, the community life of the seminary can provide help."[46]

God does not want to rule over us as if we were irrational animals or robots. He wants our free collaboration. As Augustine says, "God made you without you. You did not, after all, give any consent to God making you. How were you to consent, if you did not yet exist? So while he made you without you, he does not justify you without you. So he made you without your knowing it, he justifies you with your willing consent to it."[47]

---

44 PDV, 44.

45 Ibid.

46 Ibid.

47 Augustine of Hippo, *Sermons 151–183 (III/5)*, ed. John E. Rotelle, trans. Edmund Hill (New York: New City Press, 1992), *Sermon* 169, 13.

For this very reason, the acquisition of servitude to justice as acquired responsible freedom is of the utmost importance for priestly formation. John Paul II has put it very forcefully: "The gift of the Spirit does not take away the freedom of the priest."[48] Hence, "the candidate himself is a necessary and irreplaceable agent in his own formation: All formation, priestly formation included, is ultimately a self formation. No one can replace us in the responsible freedom that we have as individual persons."[49]

Priestly formation is a responsible collaboration with the Holy Spirit. It demands the (future) priest's initiative and servitude to justice in order to experience acquired freedom. To be sure, "the agent par excellence of his formation is the Holy Spirit."[50] Yet, the Spirit's action must be freely welcomed. "To welcome this action implies also, on the part of the candidate, a welcome for the human 'mediating' forces which the Spirit employs. As a result, the actions of the different teachers become truly and fully effective *only if the future priest offers his own convinced and heartfelt cooperation to this work of formation.*"[51]

Utilitarianism and the Personalistic Norm

Our understanding of justice is closely connected to that of rights. Since justice gives to each person what is his own, it seems to be preceded by the act of something becoming one's due: "The act by which a thing becomes one's own property is prior to the act of justice."[52] But the human person has rights that do not spring from his actions but rather from his very nature, that is, from the very

48 PDV, 70.

49 Ibid., 69.

50 Ibid.

51 Ibid. Emphasis added.

52 *SCG* II. 28. 3.

fact that we have been created as this kind of being and in God's image and likeness. As Thomas says, "By the act of creation, a created thing first possesses something of its own."[53]

Consequently, the knowledge and practice of justice presupposes an adequate anthropology that gives a coherent account of *natural* rights. For the practical purposes of this book, it is enough to point out that every human being should be treated in accordance with his personal dignity, rooted in having been created in God's image. In other words, the proper knowledge a future priest has of himself should be transferred to other persons, so as to acknowledge and affirm in them the same dignity that he discovers in himself. Thus, the other can be treated as another *I*, as his neighbor.

To know and to willfully affirm the other person as another *I* is a matter of justice. But how exactly do we get to know others as another *I*? It may be helpful to delineate briefly the philosophical coordinates of how I get to know the personal dignity of another through an indirect apprehension based on lived experience.[54] This precise description may aid spiritual directors, formation advisors, or even psychologists in order to lead seminarians through this exact process, identifying the accurate steps in which they need to grow.

The whole thing "starts from the lived experience of one's own I."[55] To be sure, I cannot experience another's *I* with the

---

53 SCG II. 28. 3.

54 For this reason, Wojtyła says: "The reality of the other does not result principally from categorical knowledge, from humanity as the conceptualized essence 'human being,' but from an even richer lived experience, one in which I as though *transfer what is given to me as my own I beyond myself to one of the others*, who, as a result, appears primarily as a different *I*, another *I*, my neighbor" (Wojtyła, *Person and Community*, 200–1). Emphasis added.

55 Ibid., 201.

same immediacy as I experience my own self. Nevertheless, there is a way for me to "*understand* that the other is constituted in a *similar fashion*, that the other is also an *I*."[56] Without a syllogism or deduction, my particular reason (*vis cogitativa*) knows another's substance as the center of reference for the sensible qualities of his body, so that I can apprehend the meaning behind his bodily gestures. I apprehend his body as human, as informed by a rational soul like mine.

In this manner, "as human beings, we are capable of participating in the very humanity of other people, and because of this every human being can be our neighbor."[57] This peculiar conscious participation arises "from my awareness that this being is another *I*, which means also 'also an *I*'."[58]

Experiencing the other as my own self implies recognizing in the other all the elements I know about my personal dignity. In this way, "the *thou* stands before my self as a true and complete 'other self,' which, like my own self, is characterized not only by self-determination, but also and above all by self-possession and self-governance. In this subjective structure, the *thou* as 'another self' represents its own transcendence and its own tendency toward self-fulfillment."[59]

Personal Dignity and Justice Towards Others

Future priests often have a certain difficulty being just toward others because they have not discovered their own personal dignity. Since

---

56 Wojtyła, *Person and Community*, 200. Emphasis added.

57 Ibid.

58 Ibid.

59 Ibid., 245.

they do not know themselves aright, they do not love themselves properly. As a result, they cannot be just toward others in respecting their natural rights as a human person. Others are not our neighbor but only a sheer tool or instrument for our purposes.

This process continues moving in the direction that goes from knowing and affirming my personal identity to establishing a proper and just relationship with another.[60] I am not only aware of the other's dignity as expressed through his rational body, but I am also aware of how my experience of the other relates to my own self. Hence, "the *I–thou* relationship, far from leading me away from my subjectivity, in some sense more firmly grounds me in it."[61]

Through that same mediation of the body, the future priest experiences the *thou-I* relationship. I experience the other experiencing me. I experience that the other is able to experience my own ego in a similar way as I do. I face the other in such a way that we both experience each other.

In this new awareness, the other is revealed as a being with whom I can *dialogue*, a being with whom I can *freely collaborate in friendship or communion*. Thus, there can be an interpersonal encounter of dialogue and communication between us. There can be community among us because there can be *communio*, because there can be communication and partnership in the same *munus*.[62]

Often the seminarian's growth in the virtue of justice and in

---

60 See Antonio Malo, *Io e gli Altri: Dall'Identità alla Relazione* (Roma: EDUSC, 2010).

61 Wojtyła, *Person and Community*, 243.

62 Following Aristotle, Thomas Aquinas speaks of *communicatio* as an important factor specifying different kinds of friendship. See *In VIII Ethic.*, lect. 9, no. 1661. For a good clarification of *munus* and *communio*, see Andreas Hoeck, "Holy Communion: Sharing in the Threefold *Munus* of the Divine Gladiator," *Homeletic and Pastoral Review* (2013), in http://www.hprweb.com/2013/06/holy-communion-sharing-in-the-threefold-munus-of-the-divine-gladiator/.

authentic friendships are closely associated. If he is not capable of respecting the natural rights of others, he will always remain at the level of useful and utilitarian friendships. Thus, his spiritual paternity as a priest will not be able to be exercised properly.

In fact, the brief process previously described constitutes the basic anthropological grounds for the personalistic norm. Since the other is a rational being like me, with a nature capable of free self-determination and of acquired responsible freedom, it would be against his personal dignity and rational nature to treat him only as a means to an end, as I would treat a sheer tool.

Expressed negatively, the human person should *not* be treated only as a means to an end. Expressed positively, I should love another person *as another self*.[63] Both aspects of the personalistic norm are a matter of *justice*. To love God and to love my neighbor as myself "are the *first general principles of the natural law*, and are self-evident to human reason, either through nature or through faith."[64]

Since the personalistic norm is a matter of justice, I strongly agree with Jensen when he rightly notes that "the antithesis to the virtue of justice is probably realized in the modern ethical theory called utilitarianism, as well as its many offspring, which go by the name of consequentialism."[65]

Insofar as the utilitarian mindset violates personal dignity, it is a serious obstacle to growth in the virtue of justice. It is a very

---

63 See Wojtyła, *Love and Responsibility*, trans. H. T. Willets (San Francisco: Ignatius Press, 1993), 40–44. For a more extensive discussion of this topic, see Angel Pérez-López, *De La Experiencia de la Integración a la Visión Integral de la Persona: Estudio Histórico-Analítico de la Integración en "Persona y Acción" de Karol Wojtyła* (Valencia: Edicep, 2012), 367–98.

64 *ST* I–II, q. 100, a. 3, ad 1. Emphasis added.

65 Jensen, *Living the Good Life*, 97.

serious enemy to a sound priestly formation. While the just person shares in the common good and is well-disposed to experience the communion of persons, the future priest afflicted by the utilitarian mindset is submerged in a profound loneliness.

He may be surrounded all day long by many people. They may even like him. He may have some apparent friends. He may be affable. Yet a seminarian or a priest deeply afflicted by the utilitarian attitude is deeply alone.

When others are reduced to sheer tools, they cannot be authentic friends, equals with whom to share my life. For priests or seminarians afflicted in this way, "no one is a person, an equal with who they can share their lives; everyone is a servant, a slave, or even a thing."[66]

Treating people like that is a direct violation of justice. It is a direct violation of their natural rights. A just priest will never treat other people as sheer instruments for his own profit and gain. He would realize that no human person is a being that exists simply for another; all human persons have the same *natural* and inalienable dignity, that this dignity cannot be lost, and that it does not even depend on their moral quality.

Often, the solution to combat the utilitarian attitude is not only to convey these truths, but also to correct an exaggerated 'goal-oriented attitude' in priests and seminarians. Our true goal must always be charity. If that is the case, everything else falls into its proper place.

Virtuous Friendship and Happiness

Without justice, there cannot be authentic and virtuous friendship, and without friendship, we cannot be happy. Incapacity for friendship equals incapacity for charity and incapacity for priestly ministry.

---

66 Jensen, *Living the Good Life*, 108.

By nature, we are *dependent* rational animals.[67] We all know ourselves as beings that can be part of a manifested and reciprocal benevolence with another human being, a habitual benevolence that is founded upon the sharing of goods, especially the sharing of the *munus* received from God.[68] The human person needs friends, not only for his *natural* happiness as considered by Aristotle but also for his *supernatural* happiness on this earth.[69]

Thomas explains that "if we speak of the happiness of this life, the happy man needs friends . . . not, indeed, to make use of them, since he suffices himself; nor to delight in them, since he possesses perfect delight in the operation of virtue."[70] A priest needs human friends "for the purpose of a good operation, namely, that he may do good to them; that he may delight in seeing them do good; and again that he may be helped by them in his good work."[71]

For this reason, besides God, a priest also needs *human* friends to share with and to communicate in his God-given *munus*, in his good work. Since charity is defined as human and divine friendship, and grace builds on nature, to be incapable of friendship all together is a serious obstacle to growth in charity.[72] Furthermore, since paternity, filiation, and fraternity are forms of friendship, a future priest incapable of friendship will not be able to be a good father, a good son, or a good brother.[73]

---

67 See MacIntyre, *Dependent Rational Animals*.

68 See Jacobus Ramírez, *De Caritate: In II-II Summae Theologiae Divi Thomae Expositio (QQ. XXIII-XLIV)*, vol. 12 of Opera Omnia (Salamanca: Editorial San Esteban, 1998), 38–39.

69 See Ramírez, *De Hominis Beatitudine*, 459–64.

70 *ST* I–II, q. 4, a. 8, c.

71 Ibid.

72 See *ST* II–II, q. 23, a. 1, c.

73 For paternity as friendship see, for example, *In VIII Ethic.*, lect. 12, no. 1706; for filiation, *In VIII Ethic.*, lect. 12, no. 1715; for brotherhood, *In VIII Ethic.*, lect. 11, no. 1695.

Verbal Injustices

I am not interested here in all the possible violations of the virtue of justice. Many of them are very uncommon or simply inexistent in seminaries. However, besides the utilitarian attitude, there are also some other bad habits that unfortunately are quite prevalent in priestly and seminary life. I am particularly thinking about some forms of verbal injustices, that is, the kinds of injustices that are done through the use of our words.

I am convinced that we need to educate our conscience with respect to these sins. They are often not seen in their gravity. Yet, as Scripture says, this a very serious matter: "Death and life are in the power of the tongue" (Prv 18:21). Our spiritual exercises in the virtue of justice aim to remove this kind of obstacle. At the same time, our end is to promote good positive attitudes.

Hence, we need to overcome the verbal injustice of reviling by learning or improving in our speaking to others, in accordance with their dignity; we need to avoid backbiting by learning to overcome envy, rejoicing in the good others have; we need to avoid talebearing, by promoting friendship and communion, and we need to avoid derision by promoting a healthy humor that fosters a spirit of Christian cheerfulness.

The Injustice of Reviling

A seminarian or a priest reviles when he verbally abuses someone, when he speaks to somebody or about somebody in an insulting, hostile, and abusive way. Aquinas views it as speaking against our honor and dignity, as "the harm done [by one's words] to a man to the detriment of his honor, or of the respect due to him from others."[74]

---

74 *ST* II–II, q. 72, a. 1, ad 1.

By its own nature, this is a grave and serious offense.[75] It is a serious obstacle against justice. It directly harms the dignity of the human person.[76] It unswervingly violates commutative justice. It is also a danger to the proper exercise of distributive justice in the person who rules.

Hence, it is a temptation for both seminarians and priests. Of course, this is also a temptation for those charged with the formation of future priests. This is another instance in which we can find wisdom in the following practical principle: *treat seminarians the way they are to treat others in the future; love them, and they will learn how to love others.*

A person in charge of some responsibility, let him be a seminarian or a priest, may get angry quite quickly and end up speaking to others in a way that is against their dignity and honor. Since the immediate root cause of this sin against justice is anger, the virtues of meekness and clemency, of which we will speak in our second volume dedicated to the priest as a man of temperance, are a good ally against this obstacle.[77]

Moreover, the virtue of humility is also a great antidote, inasmuch as the remote root of reviling is pride. In fact, Aquinas explains that "pride disposes a man to revile, in so far as those who think themselves to excel, are more prone to despise others and inflict injuries on them, because they are more easily angered, through deeming it an affront to themselves whenever anything is done against their will."[78] If a seminarian or priest struggles in this exact area, his spiritual exercises should combine the elements discussed in volume one and two on the virtues of justice, meekness, and humility.

---

75 See Rodríguez Luño, *Scelti in Cristo Per Essere Santi: Morale Speciale*, 109.

76 See ibid., 109–10.

77 *ST* II–II, q. 72, a. 4, c.

78 *ST* II–II, q. 72, a. 4, ad 1.

Reviling another is a grave offense. Our Lord says that it can be a mortal sin (see Mt 5:22). Thomas explains that "this is a mortal sin no less than theft or robbery, since a man loves his honor [or dignity] no less than his possessions."[79] It would seem that from the side of the Christian who receives the offense, one should never speak up, always offering the other cheek (see Mt 5:39; Lk 6:29).

Although we should always be ready to do so, sometimes, when someone does something unjust to us, we need to follow Christ's own example. When he was unjustly struck by one of the officers of the high priest, Jesus did not remain silent. Instead, he rebuked the officer, saying, "If I have spoken wrongly, bear witness to the wrong; but if I have spoken rightly, why do you strike me?" (Jn 18:23).

Hence, it is true that sometimes "we are bound to hold our minds prepared to submit to be reviled, if it should be expedient."[80] Yet, other times, what is needed is to imitate Christ in his words to the officer. Sometimes, we are to oppose being reviled: "It sometimes behooves us to withstand against being reviled, and this chiefly for two reasons. First, for the good of the reviler; namely, that his daring may be checked, and that he may not repeat the attempt. . . . Secondly, for the good of many who would be prevented from progressing in virtue on account of our being reviled."[81]

Obviously, when we answer to another's reviling, this should be done out of charity. For this reason, it is even more convenient to reject the reviling against another than against ourselves.[82] In any instance, we need to overcome reviling by learning or improving in our speaking to others, in accordance with their dignity.

---

79 *ST* II–II, q. 72, a. 2, c.

80 *ST* II–II, q. 72, a. 3, c.

81 Ibid.

82 See *ST* II–II, q. 72, a. 3, ad 2.

The Injustice of Backbiting

A seminarian or a priest falls into backbiting when he speaks behind another's back, with the intent to damage the other's good name or reputation.[83] Most unfortunately, this sin is also quite common among clergymen. Gatherings of seminarians or of priests are often tainted by an atmosphere of backbiting.

This peculiar sin, "by its very nature, aims at blackening a man's good name. Wherefore, properly speaking, to backbite is to speak ill of an absent person in order to blacken his good name."[84] The seminarian or priest who commits this injustice "by uttering such words secretly, he, for his own part, causes his hearers to have a bad opinion of the person against whom he speaks."[85]

Considered in itself, the gravity of this sin is unquestionable (see Rom 1:30). For Aquinas, "backbiting according to its genus is a more grievous sin than theft."[86] No wonder the demon of backbiting is often a great obstacle to the whole common good of the seminary community. In backbiting against those who are responsible for the formation of future priests, some older seminarians close the soul's door of their brothers to God's action, by destroying docility and openness to "the human 'mediating' forces which the Spirit employs."[87]

This is a radical obstacle that may take a while to remove. It promotes a subculture in many seminaries, in which formation is not seen as ally but as an enemy, as a hoop that needs to be jumped through in order to be ordained a priest. However, backbiting is not only a sin by seminarians targeting formation advisors or teachers.

---

83 See CCC 2477–78.

84 *ST* II–II, q. 73, a. 2, c.

85 *ST* II–II, q. 73, a. 1, c.

86 *ST* II–II, q. 73, a. 3, c.

87 PDV, 69.

It is also common among seminarians themselves, among priests, and among teachers. For this reason, backbiting has the capacity to establish a sort of culture of death in a seminary community.

According to Gregory the Great, envy is one of the most common root causes of backbiting.[88] As is known, envy is a form of sadness before the good of another, which springs from vanity, and which should be combated with benevolence. "Envy represents a form of sadness and therefore a refusal of charity; the baptized person should struggle against it by exercising good will. Envy often comes from pride; the baptized person should train himself to live in humility."[89]

In our common language, we often refer to good and bad envy. Yet, when envy is understood with precision, it is always something morally bad. We need to distinguish admiration from envy.

To desire to have a good that another has is not always something sinful. I may admire the holiness or virtue of another without feeling envy. I may even feel sad about the fact that I do not have a good possessed by another and still not be envious. This is the case of the person who has zeal. St. Paul explicitly says in 1 Cor 14:1, "Desire the spiritual gifts." I may desire a spiritual good which I do not have, feel sad about the fact that I do not have it, and yet I may not be envious.[90]

In light of these clarifications, we should offer a more precise explanation of Damascene's definition of envy as *tristitia in alienis bonis*—sadness in the good of another.[91] The passion of sadness has to do with an evil present to us.[92] Another's good can be perceived

88 See *ST* II–II, q. 73, a. 3, ad 3.

89 CCC 2540.

90 See *ST* II–II, q. 36, a. 2, c.

91 John Damascene, *De Fide Orthodoxa*, cap. 14 (PG 94: 932), cited in *ST* II–II, q. 36, a. 1.

92 See *ST* I–II, q. 36, a. 1, c.

as something bad for us. But, why? This is the crucial question that leads to the exact essence of envy.

We can feel sadness about another's good without feeling envy, as when a man is sad that his enemy advances in life. He feels sad because he knows that the better the enemy does, the worse it will go for him. Envy, instead, is a very peculiar form of sadness regarding another's good *motivated by a desire for excellence.* When a future priest is envious, another's good makes him sad *because he judges the other's good as a diminishment of the glory and excellence that he desires for himself.*

Indeed, "another's good may be reckoned as being one's own evil, insofar as it conduces to the lessening of one's own good name or excellence. It is in this way that envy grieves for another's good: and consequently men are envious of those goods in which a good name consists, and about which men like to be honored and esteemed."[93] For this reason, I mentioned earlier that the form of pride that fuels envy is vanity: "those who love to be honored are more envious."[94]

The connection between envy and backbiting appears clearly when we remember that glory has to do with the acknowledgement or clarification of goodness—to glorify is to clarify (*glorificare est clarificare*).[95] Thus, priests and seminarians are most envious with respect to the goods that account for the most public recognition. When affected by envy, they are deeply saddened by another's good reputation and honor. As a result, they seek to diminish or to destroy it by speaking ill about him in his absence.

Backbiting is the way of surviving their sadness. It seems like a quick antidote. However, in reality, it only worsens their condition. The real way of coming out of this situation is to avoid backbiting

---

93 See *ST* I–II, q. 36, a. 1, c.

94 *ST* II–II, q. 36, a. 1, ad 3.

95 See *ST* II–II, q. 132, a. 1, c.

altogether. Envy is best overcome by benevolence toward the other combined with a growth in humility.

The Injustice of Talebearing

Like the backbiter, the priest or seminarian who is a talebearer secretly speaks evil of their neighbor. But he does it for a different purpose. While the end and intent of the backbiter is to deprive his neighbor of his good name, the talebearer "intends to sever friendship."[96] He wants to stir the minds of others against his neighbor. Sometimes he does so with two people at the same time, thereby showing a great deal of duplicity.

For this reason, Thomas calls the talebearer a double-tongued person (*bilinguis*). "Since friendship is between two, the talebearer strives to sever friendship on both sides. Hence, he employs a double tongue toward two persons by speaking ill of one to the other."[97]

Now, as we know, friendship is a key element for man's happiness and for the very possibility of developing virtue. Aristotle even said that, "without friends no one would choose to live, though he had all other goods."[98] For this very reason, the gravity of talebearing is serious. It even surpasses that of backbiting and derision.[99] The best way for a seminarian or priest to overcome talebearing is by being "a man of communion."[100]

---

96 *ST* II–II, q. 74, a. 1, c.

97 *ST* II–II, q. 74, a. 1, ad 3.

98 Aristotle, *Nichomachean Ethics* VIII. 1.

99 See *ST* II–II, q. 74, a. 2. Regarding the contemporary difficulty in understanding this concept, Pieper affirms: "It is obvious that today we can no longer (rather, never again) describe such an act as 'talebearing.' The fact that current adult speech has not maintained such a usage, that we actually do not have words for such things and many others like them, seems to me most disturbing, and thought-provoking" (Pieper, *The Four Cardinal Virtues*, 55–56). Pieper also refers to the same problem with regard to *derisio* (mockery).

100 PDV, 18, 43.

The Injustice of Derision

A priest or a seminarian falls into derision when he makes fun of someone, mocking him. This is not a form of morally acceptable humor. In its place, "the derider intends to shame the person he derides."[101] Derision picks on some privation found in someone, that is to say, on an evil or defect. Instead of taking seriously the evil or defect of another, the derider considers it to be slight, as he uses it as an occasion for mockery.

Aquinas explains two ways in which this can happen. One could make fun of an evil that in-and-of-itself is small or not serious. "When anyone makes game or fun of another's evil or defect, because it is a slight evil in itself, this is a venial sin by reason of its genus."[102]

Nonetheless, derision could be a very serious sin when the defect is considered as a slight evil in relation to the person. Then, "to make game or fun of a person, is to scorn him altogether, and to think him so despicable that his misfortune troubles us not one whit, but is held as an object of derision."[103] Done in this way, derision is even worse than reviling. It entails a greater dishonor of the other. The way to overcome this obstacle is by promoting a healthy humor that fosters a spirit of Christian cheerfulness.

Seminary Community and The Common Good

The Seminary as a "We" Community

The virtue of justice turns the seminary into an authentic community, where there can be authentic participation in view of its peculiar

---

101 *ST* II–II, q. 75, a. 1, c.

102 *ST* II–II, q. 75, a. 2, c.

103 Ibid.

common good. The personalistic norm and the recognition of the other as another *I* are of foundational importance. Without them, no community can be really human. Without a unity in nature and love, no community can foster authentic participation, that is to say, a way of acting together with others that promotes flourishing in the virtues.

A seminary in which the personal dignity of everyone is not respected cannot be considered as a community that promotes human fulfillment. On the contrary, it becomes an instrument of alienation. Nothing more alienates the future priests and those responsible for their formation than the incapacity to love and to be perfected by loving others.

A seminary not ruled by the personalistic norm "renders participation difficult or even impossible. It devastates the *I—other* relationship, weakens the ability to experience another human being as another I, and inhibits the possibility of friendship and the spontaneous powers of community (*communio personarum*)."[104] Not ruled by the virtue of justice, the seminary becomes a dehumanizing "community," ultimately destined to annihilation.[105]

Instead, when ruled by justice, the seminary can become a community based on the unity of nature and love. The common union of a seminary should be based, first of all, in the common dignity of being human persons (unity of nature). Moreover, it should also be based on the unity of love for each other and for its common good. In this manner, the seminary can become a community marked by a habitual abiding "in a mutual affirmation of the transcendent value of the person."[106]

---

104 Wojtyła, *Person and Community*, 206.

105 See Wojtyła, *The Acting Person*, 297–99.

106 Wojtyła, *Person and Community*, 246.

The Seminary as an "I–Thou" Community

The seminary, as a community based on the unity of nature and love, has a twofold dimension. First, it has an *I–thou* dimension. Within it, the members of the seminary community "should not only unveil themselves before one another in the truth of their personal reality, but they should also *accept and affirm one another in that truth.* Such acceptance and affirmation is an expression of the moral (ethical) meaning of interpersonal community."[107]

Additionally, the seminary, as a community based on this unity of nature and love, also has a *we* dimension. This other dimension is determined by the relation of each of its members to its specific common good.[108] This relationship determines the very *meaning* of the seminary community as such.

As we saw in the example of washing dishes out of love in our previous chapter, what is more final is, in a sense, more formal. Hence, the common good of the seminary, being more final, defines the very essence or intrinsic form of the seminary community. What is more, this same relationship to the common good also accounts for the communion of its members. The seminary community is a communion of persons because there is a common *munus* shared by all of them.

The Seminary Community and Its End as "Munus"

We know from our study of metaphysics that "the end is the cause of causes, because it is the cause of the causality in all causes."[109] The agents of priestly formation are the efficient causes of the

---

107 Wojtyła, *Person and Community*, 245. Emphasis added.

108 See *In IV Sent.*, d. 27, q. 1, a. 1, qc. 1, c.

109 *De Principis Naturae*, cap. 4.

seminary community's existence. They constitute the seminary community, insofar as they act together with each other in view of their common end, namely, the formation of future priests.

These same agents are also the cause of their end coming into existence. The formation of future priests will not happen without seminarians acting as agents of their formation, without formation advisors, spiritual directors, and teachers being instruments or human mediating forces of the Holy Spirit. However, these agents are *not* the cause of the seminary's end or common good being an end or a good.

The formation of future priests is something good and desirable as an end *independently* of the agents of formation's actions. It is a lovable end *in and of itself*, independently of what the agents of priestly formation know or do. Yet their active and conscious pursuing of this end intimately defines the very axial essence of their community of persons as a *seminary community*. Their end is the very cause of their acting together with each other united in a community, as a *we*.

The seminary's end is the *munus* that binds them and specifies their common union in its core essence. Consequently, the relation to the objective common good determines the community's specific and objective nature. Thus, the final cause or end of the seminary community is the cause of the causality of the seminary's formal cause. But it is so through the mediation of the efficient cause, that is, through the mediation of the agents of priestly formation.

Although the common good of the seminary is an objective end, it becomes a conscious and subjective purpose of the agents establishing the community, part of the subjective participant's awareness and aspirations: "By virtue of this relation [to their common good], the people involved in it [the seminary community], while experiencing their personal subjectivity—the factual multiciplicity of human *I*'s—are *aware that they form a specific we*, and they *experience themselves in this new dimension*."[110]

110 Wojtyła, *Person and Community*, 247. Emphasis added.

As a result, those involved in seminary formation are to rediscover their own identity and personal interrelations in light of this common relationship to the formation of future priests as their common good: "In this relation [to the common good] the *I* and the *thou* also find their mutual relationship in a new dimension: they find their *I–thou* through the common good, which establishes a new union between them."[111]

Something similar happens in marriage. Married people rediscover their own identity, as it were, in light of the family as their common good. They know each other again or they 're-cognize' each other as father and mother. Their being father and mother perfects their conjugal union.

Similarly, the seminary community's identity is perfected by this rediscovery of our identity in light of its common good. We recognize the others in their full identity as seminarians, formation advisors, spiritual directors, teachers, etc. Most importantly, we acknowledge that acting together with all of them is a good thing that is not foreign to my own good; it is actually a common good which best expresses and brings about my own good.

As Wojtyła explains, "The common good's superior character and the greater fullness of value it represents derive ultimately from the fact that *the good of each of the subjects* of a community that calls itself a *we* is *more fully expressed and more fully actualized in the common good.* Through the common good, therefore, the human I more fully and more profoundly discovers itself precisely as a human *we*."[112]

Inauthentic Participation

There are objective obstacles to the virtue of justice in the acting together with other members of the seminary community. These

111 Wojtyła, *Person and Community*, 247. Emphasis added.

112 Ibid., 250. Emphasis added.

obstacles, instead of fostering the communion of persons and the gift of self, promote alienation. Justice opposes them all, insofar as it directs all of the virtues of the members of the seminary community to the common good.[113]

As Thomas explains, "It belongs to general justice to do good in relation to the community or in relation to God, and to avoid the opposite evil."[114] Aquinas calls this *legal justice* because, *essentially*, any law that is such is directed toward the common good.[115] Legal justice is 'legal' not because it refers to the fulfillment of any law but because it directs our actions and the virtues wherefrom they spring to the common good.

Thus, legal or political justice makes the project of becoming virtuous a relational project purified from selfishness and individualism. But the crux of fostering this kind of justice in the seminary community consists, first of all, in clearly identifying the authentic and the inauthentic ways of acting together with others, which either promote flourishing in the virtues or not.

Utilitarian Participation

One of the inauthentic ways of participating in a seminary community is understanding and arranging participation in a *utilitarian* fashion. In this case, the seminary loses its authentic communitarian character. The members of the seminary are not viewed in their personal dignity. The personalistic norm is not the foundation for a unity in nature and love. Hence, the seminary becomes *an aggregate of people*, wherein members of the community are, for the most part, *only numbers*.[116]

---

113 See *ST* II–II, q. 58, a. 12, c.

114 *ST* II–II, q. 79, a. 1, c.

115 See *ST* I–II, q. 90, a. 4, c.

116 See Jensen, *Living the Good Life*, 105.

Obviously, this inauthentic way of participation is not present in its pure and full form in any seminary. However, there is always the temptation to lean toward that direction, especially when we are too concerned with accomplishing goals, with filling holes in parishes because of an objective need for more priests, when one is too concerned with numbers. Yet, when it comes to priests, I am sure that it is not a matter of quantity. Above all, it is a matter of persons in their natural dignity and of the moral quality of those who are actually ordained.

Individualism and Totalism

Other inauthentic ways of participating in the seminary community are individualism and totalism.[117] They are two other major forms of alienation. They hinder the fulfillment of legal or political justice. In reality, they are like two sides of one coin. Individualism and totalism are two sides of an improper love of self: selfishness and (false) altruism. Individualism results from considering the good of the individual as the principal good that is opposed to the good of others.

Within this mindset, the member of the seminary remains alienated from true participation. He retains a defensive attitude in acting together with other members of the community. The others are always perceived as a source of limitation: "Individualism limits participation, since it isolates the person from others by conceiving him solely as an individual who concentrates on himself and on his own good; this latter is also regarded in isolation from the good of others and of the community. The good of the individual is then treated as if it were opposed or in contradiction to other individuals and their good."[118]

---

117 See Wojtyła, *The Acting Person*, 272–76.

118 Ibid., 274.

This attitude springs from selfishness. When seminarians are affected by this negative attitude of individualism, the community of the seminary is not perceived as the natural place wherein to flourish and grow in priestly formation. On the contrary, the seminary is seen as an *enemy* to one's own interests, something from which one needs *protection*. Those affected by this inauthentic attitude do not really believe that there is such a thing as seminary community.

"Seminary community" becomes only a name, an empty word often tossed around, but without any real and existent referent. Hence, when the individualistic seminarian, for instance, is confronted with the reality of the seminary community, he thinks that he is being confronted by many other individuals. Justice is then reduced to commutative justice.[119]

Totalism is a reversed individualism. It ends up making true participation and legal justice impossible. Totalism consists in a wrong organization of the seminary community, such that it unconditionally subordinates the individual member of the community and his own good to the seminary.

This totalitarian attitude is also based on a wrong understanding of self-love. It is grounded on "altruism." Such altruism is *imposed* on the members of the seminary community in light of a tacit presupposition, which evidently rings false when it is made explicit and is exposed by a concrete formulation: the good of the individual is an enemy to the good of the seminary community. Thus, Wojtyła explains that "the dominant trait of totalism may be characterized as the need to find protection from the individual, who is seen as the chief enemy of society and of the common good."[120]

Totalism presupposes pure selfishness in the members of the seminary community. It assumes that participation is alien to them.

---

119 See Pieper, *The Four Cardinal Virtues*, 73.

120 Wojtyła, *The Acting Person*, 274.

As a result, totalism concludes "that the 'common good' can be attained only by limiting the individual."[121]

As Pieper has explained, totalism negates private relations among individual members of the community. It attempts to make their life totally public, as if the individual member of the seminary community could be defined only by his membership to the whole. Therefore, there is neither commutative nor distributive justice. Individual relations are negated.

The rights of the individual members of the seminary, in relation to the community, are also violated. In such a scenario, legal or political justice is unthinkable as well. Hence, totalism negates all forms of justice.[122]

Neither individualism nor totalism are capable of acknowledging how natural authentic participation is to the human person. The common good resonates in our social nature. We are naturally inclined to the virtue of justice. We just need to second that natural motion with our freedom.

In addition, at the risk of stating the obvious, both of these erroneous configurations of a seminary forget that the common good is common or communal. The forgetfulness of this evident truth is quite widespread in our current culture. For this reason, it easily enters into our own worldview. Both individualism and totalism establish an either/or between the good of the seminary and the good of its individual member.

However, there should be a both/and. Also, the good of the seminary is always a good for the individual member of this same community. Both individualism and totalism err, because neither of them understands that the common good is also mine, by best expressing and bringing about my own good.

---

121 Wojtyła, *The Acting Person*, 274.

122 See Pieper, *The Four Cardinal Virtues*, 74.

There are also other inauthentic ways of acting, which belong not to the community as a whole, but to its individual members. These are other obstacles to growth in the virtue of justice.

Conformism and Non-Involvement

The first one to be treated is conformism. It refers to an attitude in the individual members of the seminary community whereby one does not intentionally contribute to the seminary's common good with his virtues and talents. The person afflicted by conformism assimilates in the seminary community in an exterior and superficial way, 'flying under the radar,' as it is often said. He remains passive in such a way that he does not reach fulfillment together with others.

Conformist members of the seminary community share in totalism or anti-individualism. They let themselves be absorbed by the collectivity. They externally go through the motions.

Still, they internally remain indifferent to the common good. Their external adherence to the rules is mostly motivated by a desire to avoid conflict and troubles. This attitude, often present in seminarians but not exclusive to them, must be eradicated from our seminaries. It directly contradicts everything John Paul II said about the seminarian being the "necessary and irreplaceable agent in his own formation."[123]

Conformism is a way of not being really involved in our priestly formation, a way of not taking ownership of it. Conformism denotes compliance and resignation, but not authentic participation. As Wojtyła would say, the conformism that is often found in seminarians is "a specific form of passivity that makes the man-person to be but the subject of what happens instead of being the actor or agent responsible for building his own attitudes and his own commitment to the community. Man then fails to accept

123 PDV, 69.

his share in constructing the community and allows himself to be carried with and by the anonymous majority."[124]

Closely connected with the attitude of conformism is that of non-involvement. The individual member may not want to get involved in the life of the seminary community because he thinks that the community nullifies him. The only case in which non-involvement in a community is justified is when one has to avoid cooperation with evil. Other than that, the attitude of non-involvement also springs from the individualistic mindset.

Authentic Participation

There are two particular attitudes that foster the virtue of justice within the context of acting in the seminary community: solidarity and opposition. Unlike the inauthentic attitudes for participation, these positive attitudes are founded upon a correct understanding of self-love. Consequently, they lead to an authentic fulfillment of the personalistic norm and of the human person in his acting together with others.

Solidarity and the Common Good

Wojtyła understands solidarity as the stable disposition whereby one accepts and fulfills his part in a given community and in view of the common good. For instance, a seminarian who is solidarious has the "constant readiness to accept and to realize one's share in the community because of one's membership within that particular community. In accepting the attitude of solidarity man does what he is supposed to do not only because of his membership in the group, but because he has the benefit of the whole in view: he does it for the 'common good'. The awareness of the common good

124 Wojtyła, *The Acting Person*, 289.

makes him look beyond his own share."[125]

Although the solidarious member of the seminary accepts his own part in the community, he does not try to perform the part of others, because he realizes that persons are complementary. Thanks to the attitude of solidarity, the individual members of the seminary community find their own fulfillment while working for the fulfillment of others. After all, each one of us contributes to the common good in a *unique* way, not only by our actions, but also with our own distinctive personality that always plays a role in instantiating, as it were, these general types of actions.

Healthy Spirit of Opposition

Opposition refers here to a healthy spirit that springs from the attitude of solidarity.[126] Through this healthy opposition, individual members participate proactively in the common good of the seminary community by expressing some disagreement with the way things are handled.[127] Within a seminary community, there must be a place for dialogue, a place where the voices of seminarians and other members of the seminary community are heard, and where all are capable of offering their opinions for the common good of the seminary.

For opposition to be constructive, it is not enough to create a "space" where these voices are heard. Additionally, the person in charge of the seminary community needs to "to allow the opposition that emerges from the soil of solidarity not only to *express* itself within the framework of the given community but also to *operate* for its benefit."[128]

So, we may need to rethink the way in which we have structured

125 Wojtyła, *The Acting Person*, 285.

126 See ibid., 287.

127 See ibid., 286.

128 Ibid., 287.

the seminary community. "The structure of a human community [like the seminary] is correct only if it admits not just the presence of a justified opposition but also that practical effectiveness of opposition required by the common good and the right of participation."[129] When the ruling of the seminary community is based on the truth and not on the imposition of the will, there is no fear to dialogue. Instead, as it happens in the dictatorship of relativism, where there is no objective truth, there is no meaningful dialogue but only the imposition of someone's will.

From Resentment to the Priestly "Munus Regendi"

I have already mentioned different ways of promoting distributive justice in the configuration of the seminary community. However, priestly formation in the virtue of justice also needs to form seminarians in their future exercise of power in the Church, in that peculiar form of *we–I* justice, which looks ahead at the future priestly exercise of authority and governance as a participation in Christ's *munus regendi*. The rationale behind this correlation is that "whoever speaks of distributive justice has to speak of exercise of power."[130]

The Experience of Authority and Power

Always granting room for freedom, the way in which we experience authority and the exercise of power greatly influence the way in which we exercise them in the future. *Resentment* may play a dangerous role in this process. Max Scheler has lucidly unveiled the phenomenon of resentment, describing it as a "self-poisoning

---

129 Wojtyła, *The Acting Person*, 287.

130 Pieper, *The Four Cardinal Virtues*, 81.

of the mind which has quite definite causes and consequences."[131]

The causes of resentment are "the systematic repression of certain emotions and affects which, as such, are normal components of human nature."[132] Such repression has as its consequence "the constant tendency to indulge in certain kinds of value delusions and corresponding value judgments. The emotions and affects primarily concerned are revenge, hatred, malice, envy, the impulse to detract, and spite."[133]

The individualistic or totalist configurations of the seminary community, as well as the attitudes of conformism and non-involvement, may foster such resentment against authority. Lack of solidarity and healthy opposition may lead to an experience of authority as the sheer tyrannical imposition of another's will.

The conformism and non-involvement of a seminarian, together with his position of vulnerability, could lead to a repression of his anger, frustration, detraction, spite, and even envy in this regard. Such repression leads to a false hope of reaching ordination in order to be able to be liberated from the authority of those responsible for priestly formation at the seminary.

Moreover, we could also foster the hope of finally being the one in authority, the one capable of exercising authority in like manner. That occasion could be seen, more or less consciously, as the time to effect the repressed revenge against the alleged injustices received during seminary.

In all of this, there can be a value delusion. The newly ordained priest, who has gotten out of seminary in this unfortunate condition, may actually think that his way of exercising authority is only a manifestation of love for and a promotion of obedience.

---

131 Max Scheler, *Ressentiment*, trans. Lewis Coser and William Holdheim (Milwaukee: Marquette University Press, 2010), 25.

132 Ibid.

133 Ibid.

Consider this other example that illustrates this same repression and delusion caused by resentment. A poor man working at a factory could be the object of verbal abuse by his boss. This injustice generates anger and hatred in his heart.

However, his vulnerable condition forces him to stay on the job. He has to repress his anger, hatred, frustration, his impulse to detract, and his spite toward his boss. He may envy his boss for his riches and for his way of exercising authority.

Now, imagine that this poor man has the opportunity to get out of this job. He gets money from an inheritance, studies, and becomes a social worker in defense of the poor. In this new scenario, he often speaks about the benefits of a life of simplicity.

Yet his co-workers notice that he is quite abusive toward them. He easily gets angry and blows up. These periodic episodes contrast with his sincere efforts in favor of the poor and in favor of a life of simplicity and equality among members of society.

Scheler would say that this man's talk and defense of simplicity may *seem* purely motivated by his love for this value. Nonetheless, in reality, his resentment against the rich and those in authority has caused that certain delusion Scheler is referring to. He does not really love simplicity.

Because of his traumatic experience at the factory, he hates not being the one in authority and control. He occasionally takes revenge by treating others the same way as he was treated at the factory. He envies those who are rich and secretly desires to be like them.

Deep down, in a habitual and subconscious way, those forces are moving him to act in the way that he does. These forces explain the contrast between his actual good intentions and his habitual dispositions to act against those who are working for him. Paradoxically, he imitates exactly that which he hated in his boss at the factory.

Something quite similar may happen to a seminarian who has a bad experience of authority at the seminary. When he becomes a priest, he may have very good actual intentions. However, some of his repressed habitual dispositions of anger, hatred, spite, etc., may lead him to act in a contrary way to those good intentions.

Pointing precisely at this phenomenon, Spanish popular wisdom says that, in general, "there is no worse ruler than the ruler who once was a slave." A bad experience with respect to authority and more concretely, with respect to priestly authority, may lead to resentment. And this resentment may lead to a *tyrannical* use of authority in which people are only the means to one's ends.

Virtuous Priestly Authority

As we know, priestly authority should be a virtuous fatherly authority. Even Aristotle understood that the relationship between a father and a son should be a very special kind of virtuous friendship.

The philosopher also noted that its worst corruption is its transformation into a form of *tyranny*. Commenting on the Aristotelian text, Thomas Aquinas explains:

> Friendship consists in sharing in common . . . Obviously then if nothing is shared between ruler and ruled—as when the ruler aims at his own good—no friendship can exist between them; nor can there be any justice between them inasmuch as the ruler usurps for himself all the good due to the subject. But this happens under tyranny because the tyrant does not strive for the common good but for his own. Thus he acts with his subjects like a workman with a tool, a soul with the body, or a master with a slave, for the tyrant uses his subjects as slaves . . . However, those who use things do not have friendships toward them. Even if they somehow benefit the things, they intend by this the good of the things only as it is related to their own good.[134]

134 *In VIII Ethic.*, lect. 11, nos. 1698–99.

Aquinas's words anticipate Wojtyła's personalistic norm. At the same time, they indirectly offer a way to overcome the resentment previously mentioned.

If a ruler has not learned how to overcome the obstacles of utilitarianism, as well as the inauthentic attitudes for participating in the community toward the common good, he will not rule by serving. The evil of utilitarianism can creep into the ruler, who is in this case, the priest. Instead of having a ruling relationship with his parishioners or seminarians in terms of service and the kind of friendship that is inherent to fatherhood, he will look out only for himself.

He will become a tyrant who does not strive for the common good but only for his own, a priest who will see other people as sheer tools, as sorts of slaves. In this bad scenario, things may get done. Perhaps those being ruled are somehow benefited in some measure. Being a tyrant, the priest-ruler may actually seek the good of those under his charge, never for their own sake, but only insofar as their good is a means to the priest's ends. He will never love them as persons. He will only use them. He will want their good only inasmuch as it impacts his.

One should recall the practical principle I stated before: *treat seminarians the way they are to treat others in the future; love them, and they will learn how to love others*. The education or formation of seminarians happens mostly by example.

Thomas explains that "when we are dealing with the conduct of people, example has more influence than words. A person chooses and does what seems good to him, and so what one chooses is a better indication of what is good than what one teaches should be chosen. This is why when someone says one thing and does another, what he does has more influence on others than what he has taught. Thus it is especially necessary to give example by one's actions."[135]

---

135 *Super Io.,* cap. 13, lect. 3, no. 1781.

In the school of love that the seminary is supposed to be, a priest should rule and govern as a servant. It is not in vain that the doorway into the sacrament of Orders is the permanent configuration with Christ, the Deacon. Christ is the model for human and infused distributive justice.

Configured to Christ the Head, a priest is to govern like Christ governs his Church: in a spirit of submission and *diaconia*. Christ has fulfilled the prophecies of the servant of Yahweh in his obedience unto death (see Is 52:13–53:12; Phil 2:8). Through suffering, he was made perfect in obedience (see Heb 5:8–9).

Christ has been submissive first of all to the will of his Father. Moreover, this very submissiveness constitutes the essence of his filial relation of love. The temptations of the devil for Jesus to exercise his sonship outside the Father's will, as well as the many messianic expectations of the people that went along the same lines, were rejected and overcome by the crucified King of the Universe, who manifests how to exercise a true filiation and kingship in service and obedience.

The entirety of the life of Christ is a giving of his self for the ransom of many, which unveils his diaconal-filial obedience (see Mk 10:45; Eph 5:25). Because of that obedience, God exalted and gave him all power and authority (see Mt 28:18). It is precisely from that obedience that Christ the Head of all rules over the universe, handing everything back to the Father (see Col 1:16; 2:10).

In this way, Christ washing the feet of his disciples, before his supreme act of freedom in obedience, is the paradigm that teaches in the seminary, as a school of love, how to govern and rule in love (see Jn 13:1–17). Through the exercise of the evangelical counsel of obedience, a priest shows the essence of love and its sacrificial dimension just as Christ obeyed unto death, death on a cross. The priest governs in love by being obedient, by emptying his own self. By this obedience, the priest expropriates himself from his own ego in an exodus of love toward the Church that makes him the head of the body.

Spiritual Exercises in Justice

After providing the essential knowledge to understand the virtue of justice, we will conclude our reflections, offering some spiritual exercises in this virtue. These spiritual exercises are to be done within the context of the Examen prayer. In addition, we should also bring them up in spiritual direction and *mutatis mutandis* in formation meetings. Keep in mind that, according to John Paul II, the Holy Spirit is the main agent of priestly formation. The seminarian's responsible freedom is irreplaceable. Everyone else involved in formation—spiritual directors, formation advisors, teachers, and so on—are mere instruments, all of them participating in attaining the common good of the seminary community.

	I acknowledge the value or importance of the virtue of justice, not only for my human formation but also for my spiritual life.
	I always have the impression that cultivating my virtues is a bit narcissistic.
	I have the practical conviction that my own good is not obtained in isolation, but in acting together with others.
	I acknowledge my responsibility to grow in all virtues not only for my own sake, but also for the sake of the seminary community and my future parish.
	I realize that my sins are not really private; they have a negative impact on the seminary community.
	I often notice a disordered self-love in my actions because I require glory from men.
	I often notice a disordered self-love in my actions because I boast in myself and not in the Lord.
	I often notice in my conduct an ordered self-love because I seek God's glory.
	I often notice in my conduct an ordered self-love because I esteem above all God's witness in my well-formed conscience.

	I often notice in my conduct an ordered self-love because I am willing to despise in myself everything that separates me from God.
	I often notice in my conduct an ordered self-love because I take pleasure in entering into my own heart in silence and recollection.
	I desire to become free from sin and a servant of justice in order to share in the freedom of God's children, loving God with all my strength.
	I envision the seminary as a place where I can grow in acquired responsible freedom.
	I have the practical conviction that I am a necessary and irreplaceable agent of my own priestly formation, that all priestly formation is in the end, self-formation.
	I freely welcome the human mediating forces of my priestly formation as instruments coming from God, the Holy Spirit.
	I experience some difficulties in acknowledging and affirming the dignity of others as another *I*, as my neighbors.
	I still need to grow in the conscious awareness of my own personal dignity.
	I have a difficulty moving beyond the level of friendships of utility.
	I experience loneliness in my life at the seminary.
	My being goal-oriented is an obstacle in respecting the natural right of others not to be used as a sheer tool.
	I view the common good of the seminary as my own good.
	In my relationship with other seminarians and seminary staff, I have a utilitarian mindset.
	I often fall into reviling.
	I often fall into backbiting.
	I often fall into talebearing.
	I often fall into derision.

	I am fighting reviling by working on speaking to others in accordance with their dignity, cultivating the virtues of meekness, clemency, and humility.
	I avoid conversations that involve backbiting.
	I realize the gravity of the sin of backbiting against those responsible for priestly formation.
	I have fallen into backbiting because of envy.
	I am fighting backbiting with being benevolent toward others, exercising in humility, and learning how to rejoice in their good.
	I have fallen into talebearing.
	I am fighting talebearing by fostering friendship and communion.
	I have fallen into derision.
	I am fighting derision by promoting a healthy humor that fosters a spirit of Christian cheerfulness.
	I adopt an attitude of individualism when it comes to the common good of the seminary.
	I adopt an attitude of conformism and non-involvement when it comes to the common good of the seminary.
	I feel resentment about the way authority is exercised on me at the seminary.
	I view seminary formation as an ally and not as an obstacle to my future ordination.
	I tend to assimilate in the seminary community in an exterior and superficial way, "flying under the radar."
	I have a humble and sincere dialogue with my formation advisor about the things at the seminary that in my judgment are neither right nor in favor of the common good.

CHAPTER 3

FRIENDSHIP AND AFFABILITY

THE VALUE OF FRIENDSHIP AND AFFABILITY

THE human person is social by nature. He is a being that experiences himself as destined for communion. For this reason, Aristotle already noted that we are political animals.[1] Justice regulates and orders this relational nature, bringing it to a greater perfection by establishing the foundations for affability.

In turn, affability contributes to the perfection of justice as one way of authentically participating in the community. Ultimately, our social nature finds its natural fulfillment in virtuous friendship, in that communion of persons (*communio personarum*) and gift of self inherent in it.[2] As Vatican II teaches, the human person, being "the only creature on earth which God willed for itself, cannot fully find himself except through a sincere gift of himself."[3]

COMMUNITY AND UNION IN LOVE AND NATURE

From a theological viewpoint, when charity enters into play, one can consider that the human person is created in the image of the

---

1 See Aristotle, *Politics*, I. 1. 1153a2–3.

2 Aristotle also considered friendship as the perfection of justice. See Aristotle, *Nichomachean Ethics*, VIII, 1. 1155a, 1-30. See also Gerald B. Phelan, "Justicia y Amistad," *Finisterre* 1 (1948) 221–45.

3 GS, 24.

Triune God. Consequently, our social nature is perfected at a higher and supernatural level. Thus, any interpersonal community in the Church, such as a seminary or a parish, is called to image the Trinity.

Indeed, "the Lord Jesus, when He prayed to the Father, 'that all may be one . . . as we are one' opened up vistas closed to human reason, for He implied a certain likeness between the union of the divine Persons, and *the unity of God's sons in truth and charity*."[4] Hence, members of the seminary community, "*in their common humanity*, are called to live in a *communion of love*, and in this way to mirror in the world the *communion of love that is in God*, through which the Three Persons love each other in the intimate mystery of the one divine life."[5] As John Paul II teaches in this text, the communion inherent to true friendship *imitates God's unity of nature and love*.[6]

In God, there is *unity of nature*. Accordingly, there is a certain similitude in the unity of human persons. We also share amongst ourselves in the same specific nature and natural dignity. The dissimilarity, of course, is even greater. While the Divine Persons, in the unity of their nature, are one simplest being without any composition whatsoever, human persons, in the unity of their specific nature, remain different beings united at the accidental level.

In God, there is also a spiritual *unity of love*. Accordingly, there is a certain similitude in the spiritual loving union of human persons. Once again, the dissimilarity is even greater. The unity

---

4 GS, 24. Emphasis added.

5 MD, 7.

6 Aquinas explains that "the perfection of each thing is nothing but sharing a *likeness* to God; for we are good to the extent that we resemble God [*Deo assimilatur*]. Accordingly, our unity contributes to our perfection to the extent that it shares in the unity of God" (*In Io.*, cap. 17, lect. 3, no. 2214).

of love in the Divine Persons is not given by another. God does not participate in another. Instead, the union or common union in charity between human persons that images God in the supernatural realm is a gift received from sanctifying grace. It is given by God. It is a participation in God.

What is more, it is a union with other human persons because of our communion with God. Priestly formation in friendship and affability, from the perspective of charity, must always keep in mind this broader theological context. Formation in friendship and affability approaches this same reality from the natural perspective, concentrating on how they perfect man's social nature.

True Friendship and Affability in the Seminary Community

Both friendship and affability find their root in the Latin word '*amicitia*.'[7] This word translates Aristotle's use of the Greek term '*philia*.' Commenting on Aristotle, Aquinas notes that we do not know the name of every virtue. He says that many virtues "are without special names, but, as we have done with the others, we shall try to invent names to clarify what is said for the sake of the good that will ensue."[8]

Aristotle did not find a proper and special name to describe the virtue that regulates this one particular aspect of our life in community: speaking and acting together with others in such a way that sometimes we approve of and please others, while other times

7 For a very good study on affability, see Carlo De Marchi, *L'affabilitas Nei Rapporti Sociali. Studio Comparativo Sulla Socievolezza El Il Buonumore in Tommaso d'Aquino, Thomas More e Francesco Di Sales* (Rome: EDUSC, 2010). For a concise treatment, see Baptista Mondin, "Affabilità/Cortesia," *Dizionario Enciclopedico Del Pensiero Di San Tommaso d'Aquino* (Bologna: ESD, 1991), 25–26.

8 *In II Ethic.*, lect. 9, no. 351.

we disapprove of and displease them. However, Aristotle did find proper names for the excess and the defect of this unnamed virtue. The excess consisted in being a people pleaser, in being obsequious, or a flatterer. The defect, in turn, had to do with quarreling.

Yet, since the Greek philosopher noticed some similarities between this unnamed virtue and friendship, he used the term *philia* to describe both of them. Thomas followed this same line of thought. Nevertheless, inspired by the Latin version of Sir 4: 7, he invented a proper and special name for this precise virtue: affability.[9]

The value of human friendship should not be underestimated. Aristotle said that "without friends no one would choose to live, though he had all other goods."[10] True or virtuous friendship is the greatest expression of human love. It is absolutely necessary for the human person.

As John Paul II explains, "Man cannot live without love. He remains a being that is incomprehensible for himself, his life is senseless, if love is not revealed to him, if he does not encounter love, if he does not experience it and make it his own, if he does not participate intimately in it."[11] In a certain sense, friendship is the natural substratum, as it were, that is assumed, purified, and elevated by the virtue of charity.

Describing charity, Jesus said to his disciples: "No longer do I call you servants, for the servant does not know what his master is doing; *but I have called you friends*, for all that I have heard from my Father I have made known to you" (Jn 15:15). From this same perspective of charity, friendship is the basis for some

---

9 The Vulgate renders Sir 4:7 as "make yourself affable in the congregation of the poor [*congregationi pauperum affabilem te facito*]."

10 Aristotle, *Nichomachean Ethics*, VIII. 1.

11 RH, 10.

key interpersonal relationships for every priest, such as paternity, filiation, and fraternity.[12]

Moreover, true human friendship on this earth is necessary, not only for our natural but also for our supernatural happiness. In this life, a priest needs human friends "for the purpose of a good operation, namely, that he may do good to them; that he may delight in seeing them do good; and again that he may be helped by them in his good work."[13]

And yet, true friendship is not common; this treasure is rarely found. "A faithful friend is a sturdy shelter / he that has found one has found a treasure" (Sir 6:14). Nowadays, we are in a severe need to rehabilitate friendship. In a culture that has forgotten this important value, the priest is to be "a man of communion."[14] As von Hildebrand explains, "The drama of the society in which we live lies in the fact that we put the greatest weight on social contacts, while living in a tragic isolation."[15]

Our technological progress is not always used for the good of the human person. Thus, it has often meant a sort of expansion in our social contacts, accompanied by a paradoxical effect: a depersonalization of our social relations and a sort of self-inflicted solitary confinement.

On the other hand, the importance of the virtue of affability for priestly formation is also beyond doubt. Sometimes this virtue goes unnoticed because it is falsified. It is confused with "being nice." However, as we will see, "being nice" can be a vice.

Yet, rightly understood, affability promotes the needed social skills to become a man of communion, both at the seminary and at the parish. This virtue is fundamental in order to live with others in

---

12 See *In VIII Ethic.*, lect. 12, nos. 1706, 1715; lect. 11, no. 1695.

13 *ST* I–II, q. 4, a. 8, c.

14 PDV, 18.

15 Von Hildebrand, *The Art of Living*, 59.

a community. In and of itself, the specific virtue of particular justice does not suffice for the attainment of the seminary's common good.[16] Other virtues like affability are needed as well. The latter insert us into a deeper layer of authentic participation.

Since such a life is not possible without joy, Thomas explains the need for the virtue of affability by pointing out that "no one could abide a day with the sad nor with the joyless. Therefore, a certain natural equity (*debito naturali honestatis*) obliges a man to live agreeably with his fellow-men; unless some reason should oblige him to sadden them for their good."[17]

Authentic Participation and Affability

Within this joyful context, affability orders, in accordance with right reason, when to approve and please others, and when to disapprove and displease them. As a result, affability is one way of authentic participation in the seminary community that avoids alienation. It promotes solidarity and healthy opposition, while directly attacking the inauthentic attitudes of conformism and non-involvement.

Consequently, the virtue of affability frees the future priest from assimilating in the seminary by a purely external and superficial way: "flying under the radar." The virtue of affability helps the seminarian not to go through seminary without seminary going through him. It takes the future priest out of the passivity of going through the motions in his priestly formation, a passivity that also ends up absorbing him into the bad attitudes inherent in some seminary subcultures. By promoting all these things, the virtue of affability collaborates to make the seminarian take effective ownership of his future priesthood, thereby knowing himself and acting as the "necessary and irreplaceable agent in his own formation."[18]

---

16 See Rodríguez Luño, *Ética General* (Pamplona: EUNSA, 2001), 249.

17 *ST* II–II, q. 114, a. 2, ad 1.

18 PDV, 69.

Affability overcomes the fear of conflict and trouble when one has to displease others and not succumb to peer pressure for the sake of virtue. It promotes the proper soil, as it were, for fraternal correction. Looking ahead, the virtue of affability promotes the future priest's correct participation in Christ's *munus regendi.*

Affability and the Munus Regendi

John Paul II especially underlines the importance of being affable and not quarrelsome for this ministry in priestly life. He says that "of special importance is the capacity to relate to others. This is truly fundamental for a person who is called to be responsible for a community and to be a 'man of communion.' This demands that the priest *not* be arrogant, or *quarrelsome*, but *affable*, hospitable, sincere in his words and heart, prudent and discreet, generous and ready to serve, capable of opening himself to clear and brotherly relationships and of encouraging the same in others, and quick to understand, forgive and console."[19]

Previously in the same document, the pope had explained that "the priest is called to express in his life the authority and service of Jesus Christ the head and priest of the Church by encouraging and leading the ecclesial community."[20] John Paul listed the following qualities needed for the correct exercise of this *munus regendi*: "faithfulness, integrity, consistency, wisdom, a welcoming spirit, *friendliness*, goodness of heart, decisive firmness in essentials, freedom from overly subjective viewpoints, personal disinterestedness, patience, an enthusiasm for daily tasks, confidence in the value of the hidden workings of grace as manifested in the simple and the poor."[21] Among these needed

19 PDV, 43. Emphasis added.

20 Ibid., 26.

21 Ibid.

qualities, the virtue of affability encompasses that welcoming spirit, friendliness, goodness of heart, decisive firmness in essentials, and freedom from overly subjective viewpoints.

The Scriptures offer us a fitting testimony of bad kingly ruling, a testimony of the lack of affability and of the danger of compromising virtue for the sake of pleasing people. King Saul was rejected for this exact reason. In his fight against the Amalekites, he disobeyed the Lord's command to destroy all the spoils of war (see 1 Sm 15:1–3). He was afraid to displease the people of his army. He allowed them to take "of the spoil, sheep and oxen, the best of the things devoted to destruction" (1 Sm 15:21). Saul plainly confessed to Samuel, the prophet: "I have transgressed the commandment of the Lord and your words, *because I feared the people and obeyed their voice*" (1 Sm 15:24; emphasis added).

Being afraid to displease them and disapprove of their actions, he disobeyed God. In light of this sin, Samuel told him: "Behold, to obey is better than sacrifice . . . Because you have rejected the word of the Lord, he has also rejected you from being king" (1 Sm 15:22–23).

Saul's temptation is also present in priestly life. Out of one's incapacity to practice the virtue of affability, a priest may condone sinful behaviors without finding the courage to disapprove of them and displease the people afflicted.

From the perspective of charity, the value of affability gleams as that kindness (*suavitas*) which springs from supernatural love, very different from the superficial and false kindness of the world.[22]

---

22 See AL, 99–100. For an interesting study on kindness, see Lawrence G. Lovasik, *The Hidden Power of Kindness. A Practical Handbook for Souls Who Dare to Transform the World, One Deed at a Time* (Manchester, NH: Sophia Institute Press, 1999). The author does not identify kindness with affability. His understanding is much broader, including many of the aspects treated under the virtue of justice. Nevertheless, this is a great resource with many appropriate Scriptural references and good practical advice.

Affability, as kindness that springs from charity, entails no fiction or pretense. It is truthful and authentic. Commenting on 2 Cor 6: 6–7, Thomas explains that charity has an exterior and an interior effect. He explains that affability is exactly that exterior effect.

Aquinas describes affability as a peculiar "kindness toward one's neighbor [*suavitatem ad proximum*]: for it is unseemly for a person not to be kind toward those he loves; therefore he says, in kindness, in our behavior toward others, and gentle . . . Not in the kindness of the world, but in that which is caused by the love of God, i.e., by the Holy Spirit . . . In the internal effect it has truth without deception [*veritatem absque fictione*], i.e., that a person not pretend outwardly the contrary of what he has within; hence he says, in genuine love: 'Let us not love in word or speech but in deed and in truth'."[23]

These brief remarks on the value of friendship or affability should initiate our reflection by motivating us to devote ourselves to its spiritual exercise. Now, let us briefly pause and reflect on the following questions:

(1) What does lack of friendship and affability do to my life?

(2) What does lack of friendship and affability do to the life of the seminary?

(3) What will lack of friendship and affability do in my future life as a priest?

(4) What will my incapacity to be an example of friendship and affability mean for the life of my spiritual children?

(5) How will my growth in the virtues of friendship and affability impact my life as a seminarian and as a future priest, as well as the life of those around me in the seminary and in my future parish?

---

23 *Super II Cor.*, cap. 6, lect. 2, no. 220. I have altered the translation. The English version has mistaken the interior and the exterior manifestations of charity.

A Community that Fosters Virtuous Friendship

Nominally, the English word *friendship* is a reflection or abstraction on the word *friend*, which in turn comes from the Old English *freond*. This is a word of Germanic origin related to the Dutch *vriend* and the German *freund*. These Germanic words find their origin in an Indo-European root, meaning "to love," a love that is characteristically free. As was already noted, friendship translates the Latin *amicitia*, the abstract concept derived from *amicus* (friend). Just as it happens in Greek and in English, one also notes a close connection between friendship and love: *amicus* comes from the verb *amare*, to love.[24]

Virtuous Friendship and Priestly Fatherhood

Friendship has many of the qualities of good operative habits. However, it entails a certain reciprocity foreign to the essence of virtues: "Friendship is a kind of equality precisely as it requires *mutual love*. This seems to be an addition to the mode of virtue, for

---

24 See Marcos Manzanedo, "La Amistad En La Filosofia Greco-Romana," *Angelicum* 70 (1993): 329–61. For other helpful studies on friendship, see Neera Badhwar, "Introduction: The Nature and Significance of Friendship," in *Friendship: A Philosophical Reader* (Ithaca: Cornell University Press, 1993), 1–38; Paul J. Wadell, *Friendship & the Moral Life* (Notre Dame, IN: University of Notre Dame Press, 1991); Suzanne Stern-Gillet, *Aristotle's Philosophy of Friendship* (Albany: State University of New York Press, 1995); Donald X. Burt, *Friendship and Society: An Introduction to Augustine's Practical Philosophy* (Grand Rapids, MI: William B. Eerdmans, 1999); Leonardo Polo, "La Amistad En Aristóteles." *Anuario Filosófico* 32 (1999): 477–85; Andrés Vázquez de Prada, *Estudio Sobre La Amistad* (Madrid: Ediciones Rialp, 1975).

in any virtue the act of the virtuous man is enough. But in friendship the act of one is not sufficient but the acts of two mutually loving one another must concur."[25] Thus, friendship is not a virtue but results from being virtuous.[26] It is a habitual, reciprocal, and mutually known benevolence founded upon a certain "*communicatio*."[27]

This sort of descriptive definition of friendship is valid for all of its kinds: for paternity, filiation, fraternity, etc. Therefore, all of the elements that I am going to discuss have to do with a seminarian preparing himself to become a good father to his spiritual children by being a good son to his spiritual fathers and by being a good brother to his fellow seminarians. Since friendship is not one particular virtue but the result of being virtuous, the whole of priestly formation in the human virtues should be viewed as formation in friendship as well. It is a formation in virtuous priestly fatherhood.

Elective Love

A future priest enjoys a real friendship when his act of love for another is not only an occasional thing that takes place once or twice. Friendship is a habit.[28] It is not a fixed routine, but a firm and stable inclination to love with a creative spontaneity, which also includes ease and delight.[29] The love in question is neither a sensible passion nor a spiritual affection of the rational appetite.[30]

---

25 *In VIII Ethic.*, lect. 5, no. 1605. Emphasis added.

26 See *De Virtutibus*, q. 1, a. 5, ad 5; q. 2, a. 2, ad 8.

27 See Ramírez, *De Caritate*, 38–39; Aquila, "The Priest as Man of Charity," 39–44.

28 See *In VIII Ethic.*, lect. 5, nos. 1596, 1603, 1604.

29 See *In III Sent.*, d. 27, q. 2, a. 1, c.

30 See *ST* I–II, q. 26, a. 3, c.; Abelardo Rivera, "El Amor de Amistad En Santo Tomás de Aquino" (Facultad de Teología de la Universidad de Navarra, 2008).

It is an *elective* love of the will, a freely chosen act, whose objects are both the good of the other as well as the good things willed for him.[31]

In this kind of elective love, we have two different objects or *termini ad quem* that specify two different kinds of love. The first is the person loved; the second is the "thing" that is loved for this person. We love the person for his own sake, while we love the "thing" *for the person*. Hence, there are two kinds of elective love inherent in friendship: love for the person and love for "things."[32] A future priest enjoys friendship for another when he has this habitual form of elective love toward the person of the other, for whom one wills good "things"—here understanding by "things" any sensible substance or any sensible or spiritual accident.[33]

The Three Degrees of Friendship

A seminarian may will another's good for different reasons.[34] Perhaps he wants it because the other is useful to him in some way, or because the other is the cause of some form of pleasure. In these two instances, the *degree* of friendship is unmistakably low.

Still, there is a third and more perfect degree of friendship, wherein the good of the other is willed for its own sake. In true friendship, "the good of a friend must be willed for his sake and not for the sake of the one loving."[35] As a result, we can rightly speak of an analogous sense of the word "friendship." It is found first and

31 See *ST* II–II, q. 27, a. 2, c.

32 See Jesús García López, *Tomás de Aquino: Maestro Del Orden* (Madrid: Ediciones Pedagógicas, 1996), 210–12.

33 See *ST* II–II, q. 25, a. 3, c.

34 See *In VIII Ethic.*, lect. 3, no. 1563.

35 Ibid., lect. 2, no. 1558.

foremost, not in the love of utility or pleasure, but in the love which aims at the good of the other for its own sake: "These [loves] do not differ in kind as three equal species of a genus but are *classified by priority and posteriority*."[36]

Consequently, we can speak of three degrees of friendship. Aquinas reasons their distinction by pointing out three different acts of love specified by their different objects: "Since acts are diversified according to the difference of objects, the types of love will differ in kind according to these three: thus there is one type of love by which a thing is loved for the good, another for the pleasurable, and a third for the useful."[37]

These three different acts of love find their habitual expression in three different degrees of friendship: "Because love is an act of friendship, there will be three kinds of friendship equal to the three objects of love. One is friendship for the honorable good or the good as such, another for the pleasurable, and a third for the useful."[38] The highest degree of friendship is often called "virtuous" friendship.[39] It integrates utility and pleasure without making of them its main motive.

Further, friendship is reciprocal love that is known to both persons. Two people "cannot be friends while they are unaware of one another's feelings."[40] And friendship is all about loving and being loved. Therefore, "we say friendship is benevolence with corresponding requital inasmuch as the one loving is loved in return."[41]

---

36 *In VIII Ethic.*, lect. 3, no. 1563. Emphasis added.

37 Ibid.

38 Ibid.

39 See *In VIII Ethic.*, lect. 3, no. 1575.

40 *In VIII Ethic.*, lect. 2, no. 1560.

41 *In VIII Ethic.*, lect. 2, no. 1559.

"COMMUNICATIO"

Moreover, virtuous or 'true' friendship is founded upon a certain *communicatio*.[42] I have purposefully left *communicatio* untranslated because the English cognate 'communication' does not render justice to the Latin. In addition to communication, it also conveys a sense of sharing, mutual belonging, and even communion. As Thomas explains, "Men are accustomed to call friends those *who share in any common undertaking*."[43] Indeed, "friendship seems to exist among people to the extent that they share with one another."[44]

Thus, true friendship is also founded upon the communication of secrets. Friends share in a certain intimacy: "This is the proper mark of friendship: that one reveals his secrets to his friend."[45] In true friendship, the affections of persons are united, as it were. There is a sort of communion of hearts (*communicatio cordis*). For this reason, by confiding a secret, "one seems not to have dismissed from his heart that which he reveals to a friend."[46] As a result, "this appears to be especially proper to friendship: really to converse with the friend."[47]

As I mentioned, friendship entails a communion of hearts, a *communicatio* of intellect and will in their reciprocal immanence, and mutual synergy. Thomas often uses the word "concord" to signify such a communion precisely because, nominally, concord means "with [the same] heart" (*con-cordia*). Thus, "concord, properly speaking, is between one man and another, in so far as

---

42 See Joseph Bobik, "Aquinas on Communicatio, The Foundation on Friendship and Caritas," *The Modern Schoolman* 64 (1986): 1–18.

43 *In VIII Ethic.*, lect. 9, no. 1659. Emphasis added.

44 Ibid.

45 *SCG* IV. 21.

46 Ibid.

47 *SCG* IV. 22. See Phil 3:20; 2 Cor 3:18.

the wills of various hearts agree together in consenting to the same thing."[48]

Although friends do not agree in everything, they do share a common worldview (*Weltanshauung*). Friends may have a common worldview and share in a common good, while disagreeing on the exact way in which this common good is instantiated.[49] Nevertheless, sharing the same worldview implies willing and nilling very similar things.[50]

The reciprocal love inherent in true friendship is also marked by the virtue of gratitude. The friend always aims to surpass the primordial gift of another's benevolent love. In the context of this virtuous circle of benevolence explained in chapter 2, we can speak of a gift of self-inherence in true friendship because, as Thomas explains, "We are related as to ourselves to those whom we love in that love, thereby *communicating ourselves to them in some way*."[51]

Celibacy and Friendship

To be educated in the kind of friendship just described is essential for priestly formation. John Paul explains that it is foundational for those who live in celibacy. As is known, "the charism of celibacy, even when it is genuine and has proved itself, leaves one's affections and instinctive impulses intact."[52] To be sure, celibacy implies an invitation to a peculiar solitude for God. But this solitude does *not*

48 *ST* II–II, q. 29, a. 1, c. Emphasis added.

49 See *In II Sent*., d. 11, q. 2, a. 5, c; *ST* II–II, q. 37, a. 1, c.; Daniel Schwartz, "Friendship and the Circumstances of Justice According to Aquinas," *The Review of Politics* 66, no. 1 (2004) 35–54. See also this broader study, Daniel Schwartz, *Aquinas on Friendship* (Oxford: Clarendon Press, 2007).

50 See *SCG* IV. 22.

51 *Super Io*., cap. 15, lect. 4, no. 2036.

52 PDV, 44.

imply a denial of the human person's social nature and of his need for human friendship.

In celibacy, the human person reaches self-fulfillment preserving "the integral truth of his humanity, without losing along the way any of the essential elements of the vocation of the person 'created in the image and likeness of God'."[53] As a result, this solitude does not entail a renunciation of *all* friendships or communions of persons. It only means renunciation of marriage as conjugal friendship and of physical paternity.

Even so, this initial renunciation is transformed by a certain abundance in other friendships, in other forms of the communion of persons, even in other forms of paternity. The celibate is able to discover in his solitude for God "a new and *even fuller form of intersubjective communion with others*."[54] He "has the awareness that in this way he can realize himself 'differently,' and in some sense *'more' than in marriage*, by becoming 'a sincere gift for others'."[55]

Solitude for God ends up meaning a *fuller* way of being in communion with other human persons, an even greater fulfillment of the human person's vocation to the gift of self for others, a greater capacity for friendship. For this reason, John Paul II makes the following recommendation for priestly formation: "A precious help can be given by a suitable education to true friendship, following the image of the bonds of fraternal affection which Christ himself lived on earth."[56]

The seminary must be a community where this education in true friendship takes place. True or virtuous friendship should be promoted not only among seminarians. Without a doubt, that kind of fraternal friendship is important, as it is the groundwork for

53 TOB, 77:1.

54 TOB, 77:2. Emphasis added.

55 Ibid. Emphasis added.

56 PDV, 44.

future priestly fraternity. However, seminarians need to learn not only priestly fraternity, but also how to exercise priestly paternal friendship toward their future parishioners, and filial friendship toward their bishop.[57] The best way to teach all of these dimensions of friendship is to experience them with formation advisors, spiritual directors, teachers, seminarians, and other members of the seminary community.

Besides, as Aristotle and Aquinas explained, friendship is greatly needed for young men to be educated: "Friendship is necessary for young men that the help of friends may restrain them from sin, for they themselves are inclined to desires for pleasures."[58] Obviously, not everyone can be friends with everyone at the virtuous level just described. Nonetheless, some meaningful friendships are absolutely necessary in priestly formation. The virtue of affability promotes the suitable environment in seminary, so that these deeper friendships flourish among the members of the community.[59]

Affability as Authentic Participation

The virtue of affability can be considered from the viewpoint of the rational ordering of the passion's objects.[60] These objects can be related to the sensible appetite or to the intellect. Their relationship to the sensible appetite specifies this or that passion in its kind. It determines if it is love, desire, pleasure, hate, aversion, pain, hope, fear, etc.

---

57 John Paul II conceives the relationship between priests and laity as friendship in PDV, 17. Likewise, the relationship between bishop and priests is also one of friendship. See PDV, 41.

58 *In VIII Ethic.*, lect. 1, no. 1540.

59 See De Marchi, *L'affabilitas*, 110.

60 This is the Aristotelian perspective explained in *ST* I–II, q. 60, a. 5, c.

The relation of the passion's objects to reason helps to specify the essence of different virtues. The same object—for instance, the pleasurable good—can have multiple relations to the intellect. Each of these relations corresponds to a distinct virtue.

For example, the pleasurable good can be related to reason considered simply as good, and as it concerns the individual under the aspect of a certain moderation. This is the characteristic relationship with the intellect that specifies virtues in the province of temperance. Further determinations to this relationship could be added, thereby resulting in different specific virtues within that province.

For instance, chastity falls under the province of temperance as the virtue that moderates one's rational relationship with the pleasurable good of human sexuality. On the other hand, the pleasurable good could be related to reason as it concerns the individual, but now under the aspect of its being difficult to obtain, under its arduousness. This is the characteristic relationship with the intellect that specifies virtues within the province of fortitude.

In our context, priestly affability establishes yet a different relationship between reason and the pleasurable good, a relationship distinct from the ones already mentioned. It relates the pleasurable good to the intellect under the aspect of acting together with others within the seminary community. It is also under the aspect of ordering one's behavior toward another "as being pleasant in his regard, by becoming speech and deeds."[61] Priestly affability relates the pleasurable good of acting together with others to reason by aiming at "living with others without offense or even with pleasure."[62]

Despite its relationship to the pleasurable good, the virtue of affability is part of justice and not of temperance. Unlike the virtues in the province of temperance, affability relates to reason

---

61 *ST* I–II, q. 60, a. 5, c.

62 *In IV Ethic.*, lect. 14, no. 824.

as it concerns another's good and under a certain aspect of debt. What really needs to be regulated within ourselves by right reason is not a potential excess of joy in living with others. Rather, right reason regulates in affability a debt toward others and toward the community by preventing two potential deviations: first, is by not paying the debt because we do not enjoy the spiritual pleasure of living with others, or second, by compromising the payment of the debt because of fear or other factors. As a result, priestly affability is a matter of justice and the rational appetite, a matter of the true order of reason in our will. Thus, sometimes, in order to live with others at the seminary without offense, the affable seminarian or priest "*refuses to give pleasure to another, in fact sometimes chooses to cause pain*."[63]

Against popular belief, to be affable does not always mean to be nice. There are many potential scenarios in which the affable priest or seminarian is obliged to rebuke or to disapprove of another's conduct. Herein lies the great importance of this virtue for priestly formation. It determines when a seminarian or priest should please others and when he should displease them in accordance with right reason.

A priest or a seminarian may be obliged to displease others "if a thing is not honorable to him, for instance, another uses indecent language; or if a thing is harmful to him, for instance, another injures him in word."[64] Obviously, there are many more potential scenarios that could be listed. Yet, given the context of this book, we could keep in mind at least all of the offenses against justice and its related virtues here treated, offenses which evidently harm the seminary's common good.

---

63 *In IV Ethic*., lect. 14, no. 825. Emphasis added.

64 Ibid.

Our reflections on the essence of affability unveil it as an annexed virtue to justice. Like justice, it is a virtue that inheres in the will, is characteristic of one's life in community, and is concerned with a certain debt toward others. Unlike justice, affability entails a *moral* and not a legal debt, and is even different from the moral debt of gratitude.

Affability's debt is natural and required by that which is *honestum*, that is to say, by the very intrinsic goodness of this virtue. In our case, it is a debt of honesty to live pleasantly together with other members of the seminary community.[65] Whence, affability "falls short of the notion of justice, because it lacks the full aspect of debt, whereby one man is bound to another, either by legal debt, which the law binds him to pay, or by some debt arising out of a favor received. For it regards merely a certain debt of equity [*debitum honestitatis*], namely, that we behave pleasantly to those among whom we dwell, unless at times, for some reason, it be necessary to displease them for some good purpose."[66]

Since we are social or political animals, we have an obligation toward other persons regarding the things without which society or interpersonal communities could not exist.[67] Without affability, the seminary community is compromised. Affability's debt concerns this exact obligation. It belongs to the natural law. Its binding character arises from ordering part of man's inclination "to good, according to the nature of his reason, which nature is proper to him: thus man has a natural inclination to know the truth about God, and *to live in society*: and in this respect, whatever pertains to this inclination belongs to the natural law; for instance, to shun

65 See *ST* II–II, q. 114, a. 2, c; *In III Sent.*, d. 33, q. 3, a. 4, qc. 1, c.

66 *ST* II–II, q. 114, a. 2, c.

67 See *ST* II–II, q. 109, a. 3, ad 1.

ignorance, *to avoid offending those among whom one has to live*, and other such things regarding the above inclination."[68]

This natural inclination is like the impression of the eternal law in our human or rational nature.[69] It needs to be subsequently ordered by right reason. The virtue of priestly affability is one of the ways in which we do so, one way in which we freely and rationally second the motion of this peculiar natural inclination within the context of the seminary community. Thereby, we instill an added rational order to our life in community and to our avoiding offending those among whom we live.

Affability borrows from friendship some of its qualities and extends them sincerely to many more people.[70] Remember, affability is not always being nice, no matter what. That is a false caricature of this vital virtue that majorly hinders its rehabilitation for priestly life. Rather, the virtue of affability is the "habit by which a man accepts what others say or do, or rightly rejects and contradicts it."[71]

Virtuous friends excel in carrying out these precise actions, thanks to their intimate *communicatio*. For instance, when two seminarians enjoy a true or honorable friendship, they approve and accept each other's good actions, as these actions contribute to their common good and communion. In turn, they disapprove, reject, and contradict each other's bad actions, as these actions directly harm the very foundation of their friendship and communion of persons, namely, their common *munus* of being virtuous in view of their future priesthood. Therefore, priests or seminarians who

---

68 *ST* I–II, q. 94, a. 2, c. Emphasis added.

69 See *ST* II–II, q. 152, a. 12, c; See Martin Rhonheimer, *Natural Law and Practical Reason: A Thomist View of Moral Autonomy*, trans. Gerald Malsbary (New York: Fordham University Press, 2000), 66–70, 104.

70 See De Marchi, *L'affabilitas*, 110.

71 *In IV Ethic.*, lect. 14, no. 818. See *ST* II–II, q. 114, a. 1, c.

are true friends live with one another in an amicable way, both by pleasing and approving each other, and also by "calling each other out" when their actions are in blatant contradiction with what is *honestum*. Affability resembles friendship in this exact trait.[72] For this reason, this virtue is often called "friendliness."[73]

Indeed, "that person, who is disposed according to the mean habit of affability, conducts himself in agreeable association with others in a manner becoming to a friend whose friendship is moderated by reason, a thing that pertains to honorable friendship."[74] The seminarian or priest, having the very opposite vice, would be described as contentious and perverse. He is a person "who falls short in this matter and does not fear to sadden those with whom he lives."[75]

Both Aristotle and Thomas would consider vicious the seminarian or priest who is always nice, no matter what. Anyone afflicted by this vice of excess, if he "overdoes this [being agreeable to others] merely for the purpose of pleasing, is called obsequious. If he acts for his own utility, for example, his profit, he is called a sycophant or a flatterer."[76]

Yet seminarians or priests need not be in a relationship of intimate and perfect friendship in order to be affable.[77] It suffices to strive for a life of virtue, and to have for the other that generic love owed to every human person: "Every man is naturally every man's friend by a certain general love . . . This love is signified by signs

72 See *In II Ethic.*, lect. 9, no. 354.

73 *ST* II–II, q. 114, a. 1, ad 1.

74 *In IV Ethic.*, lect. 14, no. 820.

75 *In II Ethic.*, lect. 9, no. 354.

76 Ibid.

77 See *In IV Ethic.*, lect. 14, no. 821; *In III Sent.*, d. 33, q. 3, a. 4, qc. 2, c.

of friendship, which we show outwardly by words or deeds, even to those who are strangers or unknown to us."[78]

The affable seminarian or priest is quite *objective* in his estimation of another's conduct. His evaluation has to do with his own virtuous character and his desire to be virtuous. He "does not take the particular things said or done by others as becoming, because he is influenced by hatred or love of them but because he is disposed in this way by habit. This is proved by the fact that he observes the same not only with friends but generally with all acquaintances and strangers, intimates and outsiders."[79]

The affable future priest distinguishes different ways of relating to people. It is not unjust to treat people differently. What is determinant is to treat different people as it is due to them. The kind of sharing or *communicatio* one should have with a superior or with a peer are not exactly the same. Likewise, the conversations with an intimate friend and with an acquaintance are also quite different: "A virtuous man speaks and converses in a different way with persons in high places and with private persons, with friends and with acquaintances, and so on according to other distinctions of persons, ascribing to each individual what is appropriate."[80]

Thus, affability is very important for priestly formation. It helps the future priest to relate appropriately with formation advisors, spiritual directors, teachers, and other seminarians, and to do so in different ways. For instance, a seminarian may have cultivated a filial virtuous friendship with his formation advisor.

---

78 See *ST* II–II, q. 114, a. 1, ad 2. In another place, Thomas identifies as one of the motives for loving others "our sharing in the same nature… Since all men are alike in nature, they should love one another. So to hate one's neighbor is not only against the divine law, but also against the law of nature" (*In Duo Praec.*, a. 2, tit. 1).

79 *In IV Ethic.*, lect. 14, no. 821.

80 *In IV Ethic.*, lect. 14, no. 826.

That relationship requires from the future priest an intimate level of sharing very different from the one appropriate with a newly arrived seminarian. Yet this *filial* friendship toward his formation advisor requires different attitudes from the ones appropriate in the *fraternal* virtuous friendship he may enjoy with one of his fellow seminarians.

Our spiritual exercises in priestly affability should also take into consideration that this virtue is closely related with other virtues from the province of temperance, especially meekness, modesty, and humility. It relates with meekness because inordinate anger is a common obstacle to being affable. In fact, sinful anger can often lead to quarrels and litigation. The virtue of meekness is a powerful ally of affability, inasmuch as it moderates anger according to right reason.

In addition, affability relates with modesty because the latter moderates our external actions directed toward others, such as our spoken words and visible deeds. These actions express our internal attitudes or emotions. Based on these same actions, others judge and interpret what is internal to us.[81] Thence, moderation is a powerful ally of affability inasmuch as these external acts need to be moderated in order to cause pleasure or pain in others, according to right reason.

In turn, affability is also closely connected with humility and indirectly with patience. Often, a proud seminarian or priest will have no patience with others. Such a proud person, "who thinks big about himself and despises another, cannot endure the latter's shortcomings."[82] Thus, a combination of spiritual exercises in these virtues may be in order, if a future priest needs special attention in matters of affability.

---

81 See *In Duo Praec.*, a. 2, tit. 1.

82 Ibid.

Quarrelling and Flattery as Inauthentic Participation

The vice directly opposed to affability by way of defect consists in wishing "to be contrary to everything said or done as if trying to make others sad and taking care to emphasize anything that will make life unpleasant for others."[83] Obviously, not every disagreement is a direct obstacle to affability. As we know, there is an authentic spirit of opposition that fosters authentic participation.

However, quarrelling promotes alienation. It is not simply the absence of that concord or *communicatio* of intellect and will, which characterizes true and honorable friendship. Quarreling contradicts the more generic love that is owed to every human person, especially as members of the same community. The quarreler acts in the community by manifesting opposition and contradiction in an inauthentic manner, trying to make life uncomfortable for others. He is not worried about the common good.

Instead, his contradiction "has the intention of displeasing."[84] Pursuing this intent, the quarreler is not afraid of displeasing others by being disagreeable with other members of the seminary community. Thereby, those who fall into quarreling "are opposed to everything with the intent of being disagreeable, and care for nobody."[85]

Moving to the opposite side of the spectrum, it is important to notice that, although it is important to please those with whom we live in the seminary community, we are not to do so at the expense of virtue, or at the expense of their own good. One is not to please others beyond the limits of honesty. Unlike King Saul, the affable priest or seminarian "does not fear to displease when it is a question

---

83 *In IV Ethic.*, lect. 14, no. 817.

84 *ST* II–II, q. 116, a. 1, ad 1.

85 *ST* II–II, q. 116, a. 1, c.

of obtaining a certain good, or of avoiding a certain evil."[86]

Being nice no matter what is not virtuous. "If a man were to wish always to speak pleasantly to others, he would exceed the mode of pleasing, and would therefore sin by excess."[87] A seminarian or priest may sin in this regard with the sheer intention to please others. He is complaisant or obsequious. He praises and approves anything that is said or done so as to avoid conflict, to not sadden anyone.

As it was mentioned, this vice leads to inauthentic ways of participating in the seminary community, especially to a lack of solidarity and healthy opposition, substituted by conformism and non-involvement. Thomas describes people afflicted by this vice, saying that "they praise everything that others say and do for the purpose of making themselves agreeable. They never contradict people for fear of giving offense, thinking they must live without causing pain to anyone."[88]

On the other hand, when the seminarian or priest is "nice no matter what," because he wants to get something out of the other by means of pleasing him, then he is properly and strictly speaking a flatterer. Aquinas admits a broader sense in which both scenarios described could be encompassed by a more generic meaning of flattery. Thus, in this generic sense, flattery is "wont to be applied to all who wish to exceed the mode of virtue in pleasing others by words or deeds in their ordinary behavior toward their fellows."[89]

Flattery could be also looked at from the viewpoint of the formation advisor and the seminarian and the expectations that the latter has from his formation meetings. To be sure, the formation advisor needs to acknowledge and affirm the seminarian's virtues,

86 *ST* II–II, q. 115, a. 1, c.

87 Ibid.

88 *In IV Ethic.*, lect. 14, no. 816.

89 *ST* II–II, q. 115, a. 1, c.

sometimes, even in public. Among seminarians, it is also needed to affirm one another and encourage one another by pointing out the progress we are making in following the Lord and his call to the priesthood.

But then, how are we to distinguish between this good and important way of affirming the virtues other people have from flattery? Indeed, "one may praise a person both well and ill, according as one observes or omits the due circumstances. For if while observing other due circumstances one were to wish to please a person by praising him, in order thereby to *console* him, or *that he may strive to make progress in good*, this will belong to the aforesaid virtue of friendship."[90]

At times, others have a need of consolation and/or encouragement. To truthfully affirm the goodness that another person has is a virtuous act, provided we respect these due circumstances and have the other's good as the goal of praising him, let that good be to console the other or to encourage him to strive for virtue. Following Ignatius's rules of discernment for the first week of the Spiritual Exercises, we may say that, by acting in this manner, we are imitating the good Spirit.

Nevertheless, one has to avoid naiveté, thinking that to praise others is always a good thing. The *Catechism* explains that "every word or attitude is forbidden which by flattery, adulation, or complaisance encourages and confirms another in malicious acts and perverse conduct. Adulation is a grave fault if it makes us an accomplice in another's vices or grave sins. Neither the desire to be of service nor friendship justifies duplicitous speech. Adulation is a venial sin when it only seeks to be agreeable, to avoid evil, to meet a need, or to obtain legitimate advantages."[91]

Hence, there is always a certain danger in praising others, even

---

90 *ST* II–II, q. 115, a. 1, ad 1. See De Marchi, *L'affabilitas*, 123.

91 CCC 2480.

with the good intention previously described. Still, we need to be careful to respect due circumstances.

It would be grave matter and against charity to praise another for that which he should not be praised, like his vices or sins. For instance, we should not be praised for always being nice to people, no matter what. Thomas explains that this kind of praise "is contrary to the love of God, against Whose justice he speaks, and contrary to the love of his neighbor, whom he encourages to sin."[92]

Moreover, we should not praise another for a good quality, whose real presence is uncertain. We should not praise another's meekness or humility if the real presence of these virtues in another is not evidently manifested by their proper acts. Furthermore, even if the quality being praised is truly good and is truly present in the other, we should not praise another if this becomes the occasion of sin in another, for instance, inciting him to vainglory.[93] This may happen, "by way of occasion, as when the praise of a flatterer, even without his intending it, becomes to another an occasion of sin."[94]

When Thomas explains the sin of scandal, he makes an important consideration regarding whether the occasion of sin is given or taken. He distinguishes between active and passive scandal.[95] For this reason, our praise of another may be given as an occasion of sin in an active manner, or it may be taken as an occasion of sin by the person being praised. In this last case of passive scandal, the agent may praise another without actually intending that the other may be led to sin and respecting the other circumstances previously described. Nevertheless, the person being praised may take it as an occasion of sin.

In turn, active scandal may be direct when we actually intend

---

92 *ST* II–II, q. 115, a. 2, c.

93 See *ST* II-II, q. 115, a. 1, ad 1.

94 *ST* II–II, q. 115, a. 2, c.

95 See *ST* II–II, q. 43, aa. 3–4.

it. However, it may also be accidental or indirect, that is, outside of the agent's intention: "Active scandal may be understood in two ways, directly and accidently. The scandal is accidental when it is beside the agent's intention, as when a man does not intend, by his inordinate deed or word, to occasion another's spiritual downfall, but merely to satisfy his own will."[96]

In this last scenario, the action in itself is inordinate, but the agent does not intend to lead others to sin. We may praise something objectively not truly good or not truly present in another. This is an inordinate deed or word. It may essentially contribute to and cause the occasion of another's spiritual downfall. Yet the intention of our praising may have been only to please him and not to induce him to sin.

Thomas Aquinas compares quarreling and flattery so as to determine their gravity. It really depends on two different viewpoints. On the one hand, these vices can be seen in relation to the virtue they oppose, namely, the virtue of affability. In this case, flattery is an excess that looks like the virtue in some instances although in reality, it is not. For this reason, being a vice by way of defect, quarreling looks less like affability; it is more opposed to the virtue, so to speak.

On the other hand, we may consider these vices in and of themselves and in their causes. In this second viewpoint, it really depends on the circumstances. It is difficult to say which of the two is graver. "We may consider them as regards certain external motives, and thus flattery is sometimes more grievous, for instance when one intends by deception to acquire undue honor or gain: while sometimes quarreling is more grievous; for instance, when one intends either to deny the truth, or to hold up the speaker to contempt."[97]

---

96 *ST* II–II, q. 43, a. 3, c.

97 *ST* II–II, q. 116, a. 2, c.

Spiritual Exercises in Friendship and Affability

After providing the essential knowledge to understand friendship and the virtue of affability, we will conclude our reflections, offering some spiritual exercises in them. As usual, these spiritual exercises are to be done within the context of the Examen prayer. Moreover, we should also bring them up in spiritual direction and *mutatis mutandis* in formation meetings.

	I have a distinct experience of myself as a being destined for communion.
	I strive to collaborate with supernatural grace so that the seminary community images the Trinity as a community where there is unity in common humanity and in love.
	I experience that I cannot live without love, that without it I am incomprehensible to myself.
	I nurture my friendship with Christ by means of prayer and by having a secret life hidden in him.
	I experience concord with Christ; I make my own his thoughts, feelings, and desires.
	I desire to love others in Christ because I want to do his will.
	I already have some virtuous friendships that are preparing me to exercise priestly paternity, filiation, and fraternity.
	I realize that I need virtuous friendships to be happy on this earth. I need others to do good to them, to delight in them doing good, and so that they may help me in my good work.
	I consider myself as a man of communion.
	Although I have a great deal of social contacts, I experience a certain depersonalization in my relationships. Sometimes, I live in a sort of self-inflicted solitary confinement.
	I strive to be nice to all no matter what.
	I value the virtue of affability as the virtue whereby I will learn to become a man of communion.

	I aim at promoting joy in the seminary community by growing in the virtue of affability.
	I practice affability in the seminary community as a way to be solidarious and to express, when needed, a healthy spirit of opposition against those things that undermine the seminary's common good.
	The virtue of affability is helping me not to go through seminary without seminary going through me.
	The virtue of affability is helping me to take ownership of my formation and not succumb to bad peer pressure.
	The exercise of affability is helping me to overcome fear of conflict and trouble for the sake of virtue.
	I exercise the virtue of affability with an eye open to my future priesthood and my future participation in Christ's *munus regendi*.
	I have prayed with 1 Sm 15:1–24, meditating on what lack of affability can do to my future priesthood.
	I have asked God to grant me the kindness toward others that is the result of charity.
	All of my friendships are either friendships of utility or friendships of pleasure.
	I want to learn how to become a good spiritual father by being a good spiritual son and brother within the seminary community.
	I realize the importance to foster authentic and virtuous friendships in order to lead a good and healthy life as a celibate.
	I tend to be obsequious by pleasing others at the expense of virtue and truth.
	I flatter others to get something out of them by pleasing them.
	I acknowledge and affirm others' virtues, in the right circumstances, to console them and to encourage them in their strides to make progress in the good.
	I praise others for their vices and sins.

	I praise others for goods whose real presence in them is uncertain.
	I am not afraid to displease others and cause pain in them, when necessary, for the sake of virtue and honesty.
	I manifest opposition in the seminary community, trying to make life uncomfortable for others, not worrying about the common good but intending to displease.
	I strive to live with others at the seminary community without offense and even with pleasure.
	I have called out other seminarians when their words or actions have been in blatant contradiction with what is *honestum*.
	I am able to relate to diverse people at the seminary community, by treating them differently in accordance with what is due to them.
	I have been exercising in affability by working also in meekness, modesty, humility, and patience.

CHAPTER 4

VERACITY AND SELF-KNOWLEDGE IN CHRIST

THE VALUE OF VERACITY

SINCE God is Truth, as part of God's people, the seminary community is called to live in the truth.[1] Yet nowadays, veracity (*veritas*, *veracitas*) is a virtue that has been severely damaged. As a result, we are in grave need of rehabilitating our interest to *know* and to *communicate* the truth.[2]

Properly speaking, the virtue of veracity is a good operative habit that inheres in the will. It is directly related to the truth of the intellect, especially to the truth about ourselves. Aquinas describes it as "that truth whereby a man, both in life and in speech, shows himself to be such as he is, and the things that concern him, not other, and neither greater nor less, than they are."[3] Thomas adds somewhere else that "'faithfulness whereby a man's acts agree with his words', is contained in 'truthfulness' as to the observance of one's promises: yet 'truthfulness' covers a wider ground, as we shall state further on."[4]

---

1 See CCC 2465.

2 See Romano Guardini, *Learning the Virtues That Lead You to God*, trans. Stella Lange (Manchester, NH: Sophia Institute Press, 1998), 13; Antonio Millán-Puelles, "La Dimensiones Morales Del Interés Por La Verdad," *Anuario Filosófico* 62, no. 3 (2009): 531–56.

3 *ST* II–II, q. 109, a. 3, ad 3.

4 *ST* II–II, q. 80, a. 1, ad 3.

Accordingly, a seminarian has an especial obligation to manifest himself as he really is. He is to do so by means of his words and actions.[5] This particular moral responsibility is founded upon our rational inclination to live in community.

Nonetheless, such a debt is only experienced insofar as this natural inclination is known and ordered by right reason.[6] "Since man is a social animal, one man naturally owes another whatever is necessary for the preservation of human society. Now, it would be *impossible* for men to live together, unless they believed one another, as declaring the truth one to another."[7]

Without the virtue of truth, the seminary community and its whole mission would simply collapse. Imagine that no one could be trusted to be sincere. What would it mean for everyone at the seminary to take as fact that, until proven otherwise, everybody is lying about themselves and about things related to them?

Lack of veracity eventually disintegrates any community. For this reason, Guardini explains that "associations that are to endure, to grow, and to become fruitful must become ever more pure in the truthfulness of each toward the other; *if not, they will disintegrate*. Every falsehood destroys the community."[8] Consequently, priestly formation and the seminary community presuppose sincerity. Its absence jeopardizes the common good, as well as the good of

---

5 See *In Io.*, cap. 8, lect. 6, no. 1245.

6 See Aristotle, *Politics*, I. 1, 1153a2–3; *ST* I–II, q. 94, a. 2, c. For how we come to know the obligations of the natural law, see Steven Jensen, *Knowing the Natural Law: From Precepts and Inclinations to Deriving Oughts* (Washington, DC: Catholic University of America Press, 2015).

7 *ST* II–II, q. 109, a. 3, ad 1. Emphasis added. See also *ST* I–II, q. 60, a. 5, c; II–II, q. 114, a. 2, ad 1; Kevin White, "The Virtues of the 'Animal Sociale': Affabilitas and Veritas in Aquinas," *The Thomist* 57, no. 4 (1993): 641–53.

8 Guardini, *Learning the Virtues*, 18. Emphasis added.

the individual members of the seminary. Even real virtues would always be doubted; they could appear as inauthentic.

As von Hildebrand says, a mendacious person "not only embodies a great moral disvalue (as does the avaricious or intemperate man), but he is crippled in his whole personality and in the whole of his moral life. *Everything in him which is morally positive is threatened by his untruthfulness and even becomes doubtful.*"[9]

As a result, the virtue of truth is one foundational way of authentically participating with others in view of the seminary's common good. By contrast, lying, hypocrisy, boasting, and irony are alienating and untruthful attitudes. Our spiritual exercises in veracity promote their eradication. Conversely, these same exercises also foster the future priest's sincere and realistic self-manifestation that makes the whole formation project viable.

The future priest's obligation to manifest himself as he really is entails the duty to overcome a certain ignorance about himself. For this reason, to foster our desire for communicating the truth is not enough. We also need to rehabilitate our interest or motivation to know it, especially to know the truth about ourselves. Veracity and self-knowledge are inseparable; they go hand in hand; they are like two sides of one coin. A seminarian cannot manifest himself as he truly is, *unless he knows himself.*[10]

The perfect exercise of veracity entails a conformity (*adequatio*) between our words/actions and our *real* identity. Hence, were a future priest willfully to renounce exercising in self-knowledge, he would be falling into a *negligent* form of vincible and culpable ignorance, which hinders both the exercise of veracity as well as his entire formation. This voluntary renunciation would amount to conformism and non-involvement in one's future priesthood.

---

9 Von Hildebrand, *The Art of Living*, 37. Emphasis added.

10 See Antonio Millán-Puelles, "Las dimensiones morales del interes por la verdad," *Anuario Filosófico* 62, no. 3 (2009), 532.

The need to foster *both* our desire for communicating and for knowing the truth about ourselves can be illustrated with a simple example. Consider, for instance, the customary self-evaluation that many seminaries require from seminarians. This evaluation often concentrates on the candidate's virtues and vices. Formation advisors take it into consideration in order to write their own yearly report about the future priest. They find it a great aid if the seminarian's self-evaluation is not only sincere but also realistic.

Now, what does it look like when the seminarian, who is evaluating his own virtues and vices, has also been negligent about his own self-knowledge? What happens when, as a result, he lacks basic discernment about his own self?

By their own nature, virtues and vices are habits. As such, they are difficult to be known. They are *subconscious*. Hence, it often takes some serious reflection to identify them accurately. Habits are part of our consciousness, only when they are in act, and when their proper actions flow from them.[11]

Yet even when they are in act and are part of our awareness, we may inadvertently experience their existence, without even being able to *name* them. To be able to recognize and name our virtues or vices, we need to reflect upon the conscious awareness we have of them. Moreover, we need to do so with a certain knowledge of their essence.[12] Without this reflection and that essential knowledge, a future priest will inadvertently experience some of his own virtues or vices. He may not even know that he has them at all.

Given this state of affairs, can the seminarian in question be truthful in his self-evaluation? Certainly, he can intend to be

---

11 For a summary on consciousness, see Ángel Pérez-López, "Karol Wojtyła's Thomistic Understanding of Consciousness," *The Thomist* 79, no. 3 (2015): 407–37.

12 This whole question is best explained in *In III Sent.*, d. 23, q. 1, a. 2 and in *De Veritate*, q. 10, a. 9.

sincere and not to deceive anyone. However, he may say things about himself that are *materially false*.

For instance, he may say that he is affable, when in fact, he has the vice of flattery. He may not notice that he is insensible, and consequently affirm that he is temperate. He may mistake his vice of servility for the virtue of humility. He may say that he is generous when, in reality, he has the vice of prodigality. Of course, to say something that is materially false without the formal intent to deceive others does not amount to lying.[13]

Nevertheless, it represents a certain falsehood and, consequently, a certain obstacle to the virtue of veracity. It surely entails a self-manifestation that is *not realistic*, that is to say, a manifestation that is not in conformity (*adequatio*) with whom the seminarian really is. What is more, this negligent ignorance and consequent lack of realism can also close the door to the Holy Spirit's action and to the other mediating forces in priestly formation. How then can this future priest be truthful in the fullest sense of the term, avoiding even that kind of material falsehood? Presupposing the willingness to be sincere, diligent self-knowledge and discernment are the answer.

Keeping these brief reflections in mind, let us pause and discuss the following questions:

(1) What does lack of truth or veracity do to my life?
(2) What does lack of truth or veracity do to the life of the seminary?
(3) What will lack of truth or veracity do in my future life as a priest?
(4) What will my incapacity to be an example of truthfulness mean for the life of my spiritual children?

---

13 See *ST* II–II, q. 110, a. 1, c.

(5) How will my growth in the virtue of truth or veracity impact my life as a seminarian and as a future priest, as well as the life of those around me in the seminary, and in my future parish?

Self-Knowledge in Christ

As John Paul II explains, "The more human beings know reality and the world, the more they know themselves in their uniqueness, with the question of the meaning of things and of their very existence becoming ever more pressing."[14] Two different answers could be given to this very question. According to Augustine, these answers were based on two different kinds of self-love: love of oneself to the point of despising God, or love for God to the point of despising in oneself everything that is opposed to him.[15]

Those who properly know and estimate themselves, love themselves aright.[16] They fully follow the admonition "know yourself," "carved on the temple portal at Delphi."[17] Augustine elaborates on this same admonition: "Why then is the mind commanded to know itself?"[18] The interior man, the human spirit or mind (*mens*), "should *think about itself and live according to its nature*."[19]

Every sin results from an improper self-love. Therein, one subordinates in a disordered fashion that which is inferior to that which is superior. In other words, one does not subordinate his intellect and will to the truth about the good and, ultimately, to God.

---

14 FR, 1.

15 See *De Civitate Dei*, XIV. 28.

16 See *ST* II–II, q. 25, a. 7, c.

17 FR, 1.

18 *De Trinitate*, X. 2. 7.

19 Ibid. Emphasis added.

In sin, one does exactly the opposite. As a result, the intellect and the will do not rule over, but are ruled instead, by sensible desires.[20]

Thus, Augustine concludes that in every sin, the human spirit or mind (*mens*) "has twisted its desires the wrong way round *as though it had forgotten itself.*"[21] In a sense, when we sin, we have forgotten who we are. To properly exercise the virtue of veracity, we need to rediscover our own identity through diligent self-knowledge in Christ and in his Cross.

To be Aware and to Understand

To effectively grow in this kind of self-knowledge, we need to recall an important distinction made by Augustine in his controversies against those who misunderstood the nature of the human soul. Therein, he singled out one form of self-knowledge totally free from error. One can never err in one's consciousness, in one's existential awareness (*se nosse*). Mistakes in self-knowledge always take place, when one reflects upon his own awareness, when one tries to get to his own essence by *thinking* about or *understanding* (*se cogitare*) one's conscious experiences.[22]

We are all aware of ourselves every time we act consciously. However, it is very possible to be aware of the existence of something *without* knowing exactly what it is. For instance, all of us have had an awareness of our will every single time we have acted freely in our lives.

Yet to know what the human will essentially is, takes effort and self-reflection. Along the way, one can make many mistakes. Nevertheless, the challenge is worth accepting.

---

20 See *De Malo*, q. 4, a. 8, c; *ST* II–II, q. 164, a. 1, c; I, q. 95, a. 1; q. 97, a. 1.

21 *De Trinitate*, X. 2.7. Emphasis added.

22 See Augustine, *Confessions*, X. 11. 18. For a greater treatment of this topic, see Salvino Biolo, *L'autoconscienza in S. Agostino* (Roma: Editrice Pontificia Università Gregoriana, 2000).

The simple awareness of the human will does not give us much information about its nature. Similarly, in one's spiritual life, it is not sufficient to be aware. We need to accept the challenge of self-knowledge; we need to understand, to think about ourselves. Being aware (*se nosse*) and understanding (*se cogitare*) are like the conditions for the possibility of right action. They are an essential step for human formation in the priestly virtues.

Action and Self-Knowledge

Action and self-knowledge bring our subconscious faculties and habits into the sphere of consciousness in order to unveil their essence. Our intellect, our will, our memory, our virtues, our vices, and other customs acquired in our upbringing, or through the imitation of our parents, are all subconscious, as long as they remain in potency, as long as they are not in act. Thanks to our capacity to reflect and to think about ourselves, when these habits are enacted, not only do they pass into the realm of consciousness, they can also be understood, judged, evaluated, affirmed, or corrected. As was noted, this kind of knowledge about ourselves is quite foundational for the virtue of veracity, for a realistic self-manifestation. It is also axial for any moral growth and education in the virtues.

Furthermore, the relationship between being aware and understanding our own habits leads us to a difficult topic that I need to mention very briefly: the nature of the subconscious. Karol Wojtyła has rightly noted that the reality of "subconsciousness brings out vividly the hierarchy of human potentialities. There is something highly significant in *the constant drive toward the light of consciousness*, in the constant urge emanating from the subconscious to attain the level of consciousness and to be consciously experienced."[23]

---

23 Wojtyła, *The Acting Person*, 95. Emphasis added.

This drive toward the light of consciousness should be fostered. Formation in the priestly virtues takes place only in that light. In fact, "both the existence of subconsciousness and the functions it performs indubitably indicate that *consciousness is the sphere where man most appropriately fulfills himself*."[24]

Accordingly, a realistic and Christian view of the human person should not mystify the subconscious. Inadequate and reductionistic anthropologies have identified the human person with consciousness. Thus, denying man's substantial unity and not comprehending the distinction between potency and act, they have misunderstood the nature of the subconscious.

These reductionistic views are *totally incompatible with priestly human formation in the virtues*. They mystify the subconscious as that which is in me but is not me, because I am my consciousness. Moreover, they claim that the subconscious determines who I am and what I consciously do, to a point of jeopardizing the very reality of human freedom.

An Integral View of the Human Person

Human formation in the priestly virtues needs to adopt, instead, an integral view of the human person. Such a view needs to understand the subconscious in light of man's substantial unity and of the distinction between potency and act. In such a view, both the subconscious and consciousness are *in* me, but neither of them are me. I am the substantial unity of my rational soul and the matter of my human organism.

In addition, it is consciousness that shapes the subconscious. That which has been consciously experienced becomes part of one's subconscious. As a result, the latter is not an enigmatic unknown and inaccessible realm that questions the reality of human

---

24 Wojtyła, *The Acting Person*, 95. Emphasis added.

freedom. Rather, it is simply like a bank of experiences, stored in a potential or habitual state within me. These potential accidental entities are waiting to become actual and to pass into the realm of consciousness and free action.

Consequently, Wojtyła explains that "the subconscious is to a high degree shaped by consciousness, but *otherwise it is only a repository* where what is contained in the man-subject is *stored and awaits to emerge in awareness. For it is then that it will also assume a fully human significance*."[25]

Of course, this whole topic is of the utmost importance for priestly formation as education in the virtues. Our faculties, as well as all kinds of intellectual and moral habits, belong to that repository subconscious realm, which moves into the light of one's consciousness. Such movement is accompanied by our understanding, judging, evaluating, and even correcting these habits. For this reason, Wojtyła says that "the transfer to the domain of consciousness of moments captured in subconsciousness, and especially those hindered from coming to a genuine objectivization, stand out as one of *the chief tasks of morality and education*."[26]

The seminary should not abandon this task to psychology and therapy. Without any detriment to the value of the latter, we need to keep in mind Wojtyła's words. He clearly identifies this task as one pertaining to *morality* and to *education*. Hence, it cannot be excluded from priestly human and spiritual formation.[27]

Discerning Virtues and Vices

Teresa of Avila speaks about the need to move beyond a simple awareness about oneself and one's own habits. She explains to her nuns that "it is no small misfortune and disgrace that, through

25 Wojtyła, *The Acting Person*, 95. Emphasis added.

26 Ibid. Emphasis added.

27 See PDV, 45.

our own fault, we neither understand our nature nor our origin."[28] Such ignorance about oneself is harmful for the spiritual life. She offers the following example: "Would it not be gross ignorance, my daughters, if, when a man was questioned about his name, or country, or parents, he could not answer? Stupid as this would be, it is unspeakably more foolish to care to learn nothing of our nature except that we possess bodies, and only to realize vaguely that we have souls, because people say so and it is a doctrine of faith."[29]

We know that we have bodies, just because we are aware of them. Likewise, we are aware about our soul every time we act. However, this awareness is not enough. We need to reflect, we need to think about ourselves (*se cogitare*), about the things we are aware of.

To reflect upon the nature of graces or virtues received leads to that correct self-knowledge inherent in proper self-love as friendship with one's interior man. For this reason, Teresa laments that "rarely do we reflect upon what gifts our souls may possess, Who dwells within them, or how extremely precious they are. Therefore, we do little to preserve their beauty; all our care is concentrated on our bodies, which are but the coarse setting of the diamond, or the outer walls of the castle."[30]

Essential and Existential Knowledge of Habits

The seminarian's philosophical and theological studies would certainly be of benefit to this kind of diligent self-knowledge that Teresa of Avila recommends. Nonetheless, some pre-scientific knowledge about the essence of virtues and vices, as well as of

---

28 Teresa of Avila, *The Interior Castle or the Mansions,* (Charlotte, NC: TAN Books and Publishers, 2011), I. 3.

29 Ibid.

30 Ibid.

their proper acts, is a sufficient minimum to be of help. Thomas Aquinas distinguishes two kinds of knowledge concerning habits. "One knowledge is that by which one knows whether he has a habit. The other is that by which one knows what a habit is."[31]

A seminarian cannot know that he has this or that habit unless he knows what this habit is all about. "For the knowledge by which one knows he has a habit *presupposes the knowledge by which he knows what that habit is*. For I cannot know that I have chastity unless I know what chastity is."[32]

Essential Knowledge of Virtues and Vices

The essential knowledge of the virtue of chastity has to do with its proper acts. In fact, "we perceive that habits exist in us only by perceiving acts of which habits are the principles. And by its essence a habit is the principle of a certain kind of act. Thus, if we know a habit as the principle of such an act, we know what it is. Accordingly, I know what chastity is if I know it is that through which one refrains from illicit thoughts in matters of sex."[33]

Thomas's example is fairly clear. Hardly anyone would have a difficulty in identifying the virtue of chastity in that scenario. Yet the knowledge of one's habits is not always an easy matter, as sometimes it can be quite tricky to discern.

Consider the example of the vice of envy. A seminarian may experience envy without being able to name it. He only knows that he is sad. Sadness is the act he is aware of.

However, the formal motive of that sadness—that is, what

---

31 *De Veritate*, q. 10, a. 9, c.

32 Ibid. Emphasis added.

33 Ibid. Thomas is comparing in this text the knowledge of habits with the knowledge of the soul. I have eliminated the references to the soul from the quote in order to make it clearer.

drives it—is not entirely conscious or clear to him. He can only observe that it seems to be a constant pattern under certain similar circumstances. In this situation, the seminarian can be assailed by questions such as the following: "What is this sadness all about?" "Why do I experience it in me?" "What is its cause?" "Is it just being physically tired?" "Is it sloth?" "Is it envy?" The exact answers to these questions can be complicated.

To *be aware* of one's sadness, without *understanding* it, is not sufficient. To put this whole situation aside, until it fades away, is not the solution either. When this particular situation passes by, the disorder of envy may remain in that repository of a habitual and subconscious potency. It lingers without going anywhere. It remains until the next time, when envy makes its appearance even more violently, with a more intense spiritual act of sadness.

Thus, a seminarian would not be able to respond meaningfully to his own sadness until he is *aware* of what is going on in himself, until he *understands* that he has the exact vice of envy. Only then, can he *take* the appropriate *action*. In priestly formation and in Christian life, one needs these three things: to be aware, to understand, and to take action.[34]

We already know that one cannot be fully truthful about his own virtues and vices, unless he has an adequate knowledge about himself, unless he is able to discern and distinguish them. Yet, there is another scenario that should also be mentioned. Guardini explains that the human person, in the dynamism of his interior self-knowledge, "separates into two beings and confronts himself. I consider myself, test and judge myself, and decide about myself. Then this duality again unites into the single self and thereafter bears within itself the results of this encounter."[35]

---

34 For a superb explanation of how these three things are key to the spiritual life, according to Ignatius of Loyola, see Gallagher, *The Discernment of Spirits*, 11–26.

35 Guardini, *Learning the Virtues*, 18.

Imagine now that a seminarian is unwilling or simply afraid to be fully sincere with himself. This unwillingness can be problematic. Our higher faculties—our intellect and will—are the *custodians* of the threshold in that passage from subconsciousness to consciousness that is so characteristic of mental and moral habits. Thus, the future priest may adopt an attitude whereby he "simply erases from his mind everything in his life which is difficult or disagreeable."[36]

He may even care not to know himself for fear of the habits he may find. Then, the future priest behaves like one "who not only hides his head like an ostrich, but who persuades himself that he is going to do something, when he knows full well that he cannot do it. He does not want to recognize his own faults; he immediately twists the meaning of every situation which is humiliating or disagreeable for him so that it loses its stings."[37]

Obstacles to Self-Knowledge

As a result, one may willfully place serious obstacles before one's truthful self-knowledge and to the discernment of one's virtues and vices. These obstacles need not be actual. They can also be habitual.

The vice of pride, for instance, can be blind to the truth, especially to the truth about oneself.[38] The vice of lust is also a serious obstacle for an adequate self-knowledge. It blinds, as it were, the mind: "Just as bodily blindness is the privation of the principle of bodily sight, so blindness of mind is the privation of the principle of mental or intellectual sight."[39]

---

36 Von Hildebrand, *The Art of Living*, 38–39.

37 Ibid.

38 See *ST* II–II, q. 162, a. 3, ad 1.

39 *ST* II–II, q. 15, a. 1, c.

This blindness is generated by the disorder in the faculties engendered by lust. The latter subordinates the intellect and the will to the sensible passions, fixing their entire attention on corporeal things. As a result, "man's operation in regard to intelligible things is weakened."[40] This kind of blindness is quite serious, for it "excludes almost entirely the knowledge of spiritual things."[41]

Another habitual obstacle to the discernment of our own virtues and vices is lack of docility. As is known, docility is part of the virtue of prudence.[42] It is a certain aptness for being taught, that can be hampered by pride's self-sufficiency.

Since the proud person does not submit his intellect to God, much less does he do so to his human teachers. He prefers to be right about himself rather than to learn what is, in reality, true. The virtue of docility removes this obstacle of self-sufficiency. As Aquinas explains, "Even the learned should be docile in some respects, since no man is altogether self-sufficient."[43]

The virtue of docility helps us to accept the opinions of others.[44] While the person who is self-sufficient tends to always follow one's own judgment to the point of precipitation, the docile person is ready to descend, in an orderly fashion and without precipitation or rash action, from his own understanding to the opinion of those who may be more competent than him in one given area. Of course, the formation advisor and the spiritual directors are some of those agents of formation, which the Holy Spirit has chosen to help and teach the docile future priest. They are to help the seminarian to grow in his self-knowledge in Christ.

---

40 *ST* II–II, q. 15, a. 3, c.

41 Ibid.

42 See *ST* I–II, q. 57, a. 6, ad 4.

43 *ST* II–II, q. 49, a. 3, ad 3.

44 See *ST* II–II, q. 53, a. 3, c.

The Chair Wherefrom Christ Teaches Virtue

Self-knowledge is not to be understood in a narcissistic manner. It is certainly knowledge about ourselves. But it is not knowledge we acquire by ourselves. We do so together with others and in light of God. Indeed, the truth about the human person is inseparable from the truth about God.

Christ is God's eternal Logos, in whose redemptive incarnation and gift of self for the Church, we find the fullest revelation of the truth about the human person (see Jn 14:6; Eph 5:25). For this reason, when dealing with the virtue of truth, especially when speaking of the truth about ourselves, we need to keep in mind that "only in the mystery of the incarnate Word does the mystery of man take on light."[45] Christ's redemptive and spousal love for the Church is the greatest manifestation of this mystery.

Thus, "by the revelation of the mystery of the Father and His love, [Christ] fully reveals man to man himself and makes his supreme calling clear."[46] Veracity must be exercised in self-knowledge in Christ. Such self-knowledge in Christ discloses not only who we are, but also who we ought to be.

This last conclusion is applicable to every human person. However, it takes on a special dimension within the context of priestly formation. As John Paul II explains, "The priest finds the full truth of his identity in being a derivation, a specific participation in and continuation of Christ himself, the one high priest of the new and eternal covenant. The priest is a living and transparent image of Christ the priest."[47]

---

45 GS, 22.

46 Ibid.

47 PDV, 12.

Every truth, in some manner, points to Christ as the Truth. Teresa of Avila again offers a valuable reflection with respect to self-knowledge, which every candidate to the priesthood should take to heart: "I believe *we shall never learn to know ourselves except by endeavoring to know God*, for, beholding His greatness we are struck by our own baseness, His purity shows our foulness, and by meditating on His humility we find how very far we are from being humble."[48]

The contemplation of the crucified Christ, as he gives his own life for the Church, should take precedence here. In accordance with GS 22, the whole truth about man is therein expressed.

As Thomas Aquinas explains, referencing Heb 12:2, Jesus is the pioneer and perfecter of our faith. He has loved us to the end. In so doing, he has healed human nature. "The remedy for every tribulation is found in the Cross."[49]

Most importantly for this book, Thomas argues that "an example of *every virtue* is found in the Cross," because "the Cross was not only the altar on which He suffered, but also the *chair from which He taught*."[50] Christ's cross fulfills the Law perfectly. The authority of the crucified Lord sharply contrasts with that of the scribes and the Pharisees.

For this reason, Jesus had said, "The scribes and the Pharisees sit on Moses' seat; so practice and observe whatever they tell you, but not what they do; for they preach, but do not practice" (Mt 23:2–3). Unlike them, Christ taught the whole truth about man's vocation and every virtue with authority (*ex-ousia*) from the chair of the cross. In the *Liturgy of the Hours* for Aquinas's feast day,

48 Teresa of Avila, *The Interior Castle*, I. 2. 10. Emphasis added.

49 *Super Heb.*, cap. 12, lect. 1, no. 667.

50 Ibid.

we read: "Whoever wishes to live perfectly should do nothing but disdain what Christ disdained on the cross and desire what he desired, for the Cross *exemplifies every virtue*."[51]

John Paul II also concentrates on this same idea. Taking Christ's spousal gift of self for the Church, as expressed in Eph 5:25, the pope speaks about the spousal meaning of the body as the vocation and supreme calling of the human person.[52] Such a vocation consists in loving in the way in which Christ loved on the cross. This is the chair wherefrom Christ taught the whole truth about man. The entire vocation to virtue is exemplified right there.

Thus, our self-knowledge should always be in Christ, in light of his cross, and in his spousal love. Therein, the future priest knows his own shortcomings under the light of God's mercy. There, he also witnesses an example of every virtue in which he is to grow.

Most importantly, in Christ's cross, we also find the source of grace and power wherefrom that growth in virtue should take place in seminary. Knowing ourselves aright, and by doing so in Christ and in his cross, discloses every virtue God has given us and every vice, which needs to be destroyed within our soul. This is the proper Christian context, wherein to exercise veracity as "that truth whereby a man, both in life and in speech, shows himself to be such as he is."[53]

---

51 Thomas Aquinas, "Collatio 6 Super Credo in Deum," in *The Liturgy of the Hours*, vol. 3 (New York: Catholic Book Publishing, 1975), 1335. See also *ST* III, q. 46, a. 3, c.

52 I have dealt with this topic in Angel Perez-Lopez, *Procreation and the Spousal Meaning of the Body: A Thomistic Argument Grounded in Vatican II* (Eugene, OR: Pickwick, 2017).

53 *ST* II–II, q. 109, a. 3, ad 3.

Veracity as Authentic Participation

The virtue of truth is an annexed virtue to justice. Veracity coincides with justice in being directed to another and in establishing a certain equality—that between signs and realities. However, it differs from justice in that the virtue of veracity does not entail a legal but a moral debt of honesty, that is to say, a debt arising from the very goodness of this virtue.[54]

As we already know, this moral debt makes life in common possible.[55] Its payment promotes authentic participation within the seminary community. It really fosters the idea that "the candidate himself is a necessary and irreplaceable agent in his own formation."[56] Within this context, John Paul II's ideas about priestly formation as self-formation, in collaboration with the Holy Spirit and the other agents of priestly formation, gains an unsuspected force.

Allow me to illustrate what veracity, as authentic participation, looks like in seminary life by means of an image. One could picture a set of concentric circles. At the center, the seminarian should place himself, his conscience, and God.

Around that first circle, imagine another one in which we can place the seminarian's confessor. Around this second circle, picture a third one in which we find the spiritual director. The fourth circle includes, perhaps, a psychologist who works at the seminary. (More and more seminaries in the country employ their services.) The fifth circle contains the formation advisor. In the sixth, we could place all the other agents of formation.[57]

---

54 See *ST* II–II, q. 109, a. 3, c.

55 See *ST* II–II, q. 109, a. 3, ad 1.

56 PDV, 69.

57 I am grateful to Fr. Scott Traynor for this image.

The virtue of veracity regulates the proper knowledge and manifestation of ourselves in all of these concentric circles. We do not always perform a good action by telling the truth. We must always tell the truth in *the right circumstances*.[58] We need to say what is true to the right person, in the correct way, and in the right time and place.[59]

To each of these concentric circles corresponds one prudent way of being truthful. Confession and a formation meeting are not the same thing. However, this does not mean that veracity or the forum of conscience are to be excluded from formation meetings. The Church requires the formation advisor to judge the seminarian on matters that belong to that precise forum. Therefore, the seminarian must be truthful about matters such as chastity, even if his veracity does not entail that he speaks to his formation advisor as if the latter were his confessor or spiritual director.

Most importantly, all of these "circles" presuppose veracity in order to contribute effectively to the formation of the seminarian. All of them represent the different agents of formation, which are instrumental in different ways to the action of the Holy Spirit. He is the one that will lead us to the whole truth about ourselves (see Jn 16:13).

All of these agents of formation should help the future priest to know himself better. They should aid him in manifesting himself in veracity. As a result, these different circles and agents of formation should help the future priest to be transformed deeply by the God who created us without our consent, but will not save us without that same consent.[60]

---

58 See *ST* II–II, q. 109, a. 1, ad 2.

59 See *ST* II–II, q. 109, a. 1, ad 3.

60 See *Sermon* 169, 13 in Augustine of Hippo, *Sermons 151–183 (III/5)*.

The seminarian or priest who has the virtue of veracity "is truthful inasmuch as the things he divulges about himself are true. He does this not only by word but also by his manner of living, according as his exterior conduct and his speech conform to his nature."[61]

Yet veracity sometimes inclines a seminarian or a priest to speak and represent himself as less than he really is. It would be against the very virtue of veracity to *deny* something good that is truly present in us. This would imply falsehood.

However, a priest or a seminarian could act in accordance with veracity while *affirming* true things about himself, without showing *all* of his goodness (see 2 Cor 12:6). This need not be a lack of humility or truthfulness. On the contrary, it can be a prudent and good thing to do at times. A seminarian or priest may affirm things about himself and not show the whole good that is in him in matters of science or holiness. In this case, Aquinas explains, "This is done without prejudice to truth, since the lesser is contained in the greater."[62]

Within seminary life, it is often convenient to adopt this attitude. We should avoid boasting as much as possible, as well as its semblance. Exaggerations about my virtue can be really vexing for other people and for life in community. Conversely, those who are truthful but also do not show the whole good that is in them are a source of pleasure for others. It is easier to live with them: "Those who represent themselves as being greater than they are, are a source of annoyance to others, since they seem to wish to surpass others: whereas those who make less account of themselves are a source of pleasure, since they seem to defer to others by their moderation."[63]

---

61 *In IV Ethic.*, lect. 15, no. 835.

62 *ST* II–II, q. 109, a. 4, c.

63 Ibid.

Alienating and Untruthful Attitudes

Rejecting the Father of Lies By Putting Away Falsehood

To grow in veracity, we need to eradicate some alienating and untruthful attitudes, which are sometimes present in the seminary community. As part of God's people, we are called to live in union with Christ. As a result, the seminary is called to avoid and reject association with the "father of lies."

Jesus clearly taught that the devil "was a murderer from the beginning, and has nothing to do with the truth, because there is no truth in him. When he lies, he speaks according to his own nature, for he is a liar and the father of lies" (Jn 8:44). As a fallen angel, the devil turned away from God in aversion. He recoiled entirely from the Truth.[64] Thus, in these spiritual exercises in veracity, future priests are faced with the renewal of an important choice: are we with Christ or against him? (see Mt 12:30).

If we are with Christ, we belong to the truth and we walk in the light, because "God is light and in him there is no darkness at all" (1 Jn 1:5. See also Jn 14:6; 1 Jn 1:7). Instead, if we are against him, we belong to the devil and we walk in darkness: "If we say we have fellowship with him [Christ], while we walk in darkness, we lie and do not live according to the truth" (1 Jn 1:6). Aquinas explains that "God alone, when speaking on his own, speaks the truth, for truth is an enlightenment of the intellect, and God is light itself and all are enlightened by him."[65]

The future priest should be united with God in the truth, walking in the light. When he is not united with God, but "speaks on his

---

64 See *In Io.*, cap. 8, lect. 6, nos. 1244, 1247.

65 *In Io.*, cap. 8, lect. 6, no. 1250.

own, [he] speaks a lie; but when he speaks from God, he speaks the truth."[66] To walk in darkness, abandoning the light of Truth, entails belonging to the devil, insofar as this conduct closely imitates the father of lies, as children imitate the conduct of their parents (see Jn 8:44). In this scenario, one associates with him "who did not stand in the truth and who first invented lying."[67]

Indeed, the devil did not learn to lie from anyone. He invented falsehood, when he told Eve that she would not die (see Gn 3: 4). We should not trust him. We should renounce him and all his works once again. We should reject every form of falsehood and embrace the truth. As God says, "No man who practices deceit / shall dwell in my house / no man who utters lies / shall continue in my presence" (Ps 101:7).

Do we really want to dwell in God's house and live in his presence forever? Ignatius of Loyola's principle and foundation, as well as his spiritual exercises on the two standards, could be very helpful in order to renew our answers to these crucial questions.

St. Paul also establishes an intrinsic connection between the Christian vocation and putting away falsehood. He urges us: "Put on the new nature, created after the likeness of God in true righteousness and holiness. Therefore, putting away falsehood, let every one speak the truth with his neighbor, for we are members one of another" (Eph 4:24–25). Falsehood belongs to the old man, which needs to be mortified by the Spirit (see Rom 8:13).

Instead, the future priest lives in Christ. He made us; we belong to him (see Ps 100:3). From the perspective of charity and of this new life, we are to be truthful, because we are members of one another. For members are to love and mutually assist one another in truth (see Zec 8:16; Rom 12:5).[68]

---

66 *In Io.*, cap. 8, lect. 6, no. 1250.

67 Ibid.

68 *In Eph.*, cap. 4, lect. 8.

Thus, we need to treat briefly some of the untruthful attitudes to be mortified in us. These attitudes all render being members of one another, as well as this love that assists others in the truth, utterly impossible. For this reason, following Wojtyła and the explanations in chapter 3, I characterize these untruthful attitudes as alienating.[69]

Five Alienating Untruthful Attitudes

In order to mortify and put away falsehood, we need to assail five main vices: lying, dissimulation, hypocrisy, boasting, and irony. These vices are morally evil for the individual, but they are also harmful to the common good of the seminary.

Lying

The moral act of *lying* is a *voluntary* or human act. We tend to think that one lies by simply saying or manifesting something false. Yet, this alone does not constitute the moral act of lying: "The essential notion of a lie is taken from *formal* falsehood, from the fact namely, that a person *intends* to say what is false; wherefore also the word *mendacium* [lie] is derived from its being in opposition to the 'mind'."[70]

There is another element, besides the intention of saying what is false, which adds a certain fullness to the lie: the intention to deceive, that is to say, to will that the other may have a false opinion. Thomas explains that such an additional intention "does not belong to the species of lying, but to perfection thereof."[71]

However, as I explained before, a seminarian may say something false, thinking that it is true and with no intent to

---

69 See Wojtyła, *Person and Community*, 206.

70 *ST* II–II, q. 110, a. 1, c.

71 Ibid.

deceive. In this case, there is no moral act of lying. Aquinas explains that "if one says what is false, thinking it to be true, it is false materially, but not formally, because the falseness is beside the intention of the speaker so that it is not a perfect lie, since what is beside the speaker's intention is accidental for which reason it cannot be a specific difference."[72]

The opposite is also true. If a seminarian says something factually true, but thinking that it was false and willing to be mendacious, he is lying. When "one utters falsehood formally, through *having the will to deceive*, even if what one says be true, yet inasmuch as this is a voluntary and moral act, it contains falseness essentially and truth accidentally, and attains the specific nature of a lie."[73]

Every philosophy student, sooner or later, has to deal with the difficult moral scenario about lying in order to do something good and avoid something severely evil. For instance, should one lie to the Nazis in order to save the Jews hidden in one's basement? Since this is not an academic book, I will not treat this difficult but fascinating topic here with all the rigor it deserves.[74] However, I would like to make some practical remarks, which will end up being useful for priestly formation in the virtue of veracity.

There are distinct ways of classifying the different *kinds of lies*. From the objective and essential viewpoint, there are two fundamental kinds of lies. The first one *goes beyond* truth. It is called *boasting*. The second one *falls short* of the truth and it is called *irony*.[75]

---

72 *ST* II–II, q. 110, a. 1, c.

73 Ibid.

74 For a brief but very good treatment, see Dewan, *Wisdom and Law*, 374–386.

75 See *ST* II–II, q. 110, a. 2, c.

From the viewpoint of what aggravates the sin of lying, there is another possible division. When one intends to injure the other by lying, we have a serious sin called *a mischievous lie*. The same lie may be diminished in its evil character when it is directed to some good.

Thomas Aquinas speaks of two different kinds of lies under this category: jocose and officious lies. *Jocose lies* are oriented to some pleasure, like a desire to please another. Instead, *officious lies* are intended to help another person or to save him from some injury. Consequently, the question about the Nazis and the Jews has to do with the moral nature of officious lies.

There is no doubt, lying is intrinsically evil. Holy Scripture affirms categorically: "Be not willing to make *any manner of lie*" (Sir 7:13; emphasis added). As Thomas says, "A lie is essentially evil and to be avoided, but truth is good and to be praised."[76]

To lie violates the very nature of signs. They "were instituted to represent things as they are. Therefore, if a person represents a thing otherwise than it is by lying, he acts in an inordinate and vicious manner. But if he speaks the truth, he acts in an orderly and virtuous manner."[77]

Thomas is clear about it. "A lie is sinful not only because it injures one's neighbor, but also on account of its inordinateness."[78] Wherefrom, we should not conclude that it is allowed "to make use of anything inordinate in order to ward off injury or defects from another: as neither is it lawful to steal in order to give an alms, except perhaps in a case of necessity when all things are common."[79]

---

76 *In IV Ethic.*, lect. 15, no. 836.

77 Ibid.

78 *ST* II–II, q. 110, a. 3, ad 4.

79 Ibid.

Aquinas concludes that, "it is not lawful to tell a lie in order to deliver another *from any danger whatever.*"[80] The correct thing to do in these difficult moral scenarios, such as the one previously mentioned, is not to lie but "to hide the truth prudently, by keeping it back."[81]

Then, what would Thomas say in confession to someone who has lied in order to save the Jews? Certainly, he would have explained to the penitent that it would have been better to hide the truth prudently than lying. Perhaps fear or other factors hindered this prudent reasoning. For this reason, Aquinas might have reminded the penitent that "the greater the good intended, the more is the sin of lying diminished in gravity."[82]

Thomas would perhaps have said that although every lie is sinful, not every lie is equally so. Probably, the Angelic Doctor would have reminded the penitent about the midwives in Egypt, who lied to save the life of innocent children (see Ex 1:21). The midwives' lying was not meritorious, but their goodwill and fear of God was. Indeed, because of that goodwill and their fear of God, they were rewarded.[83]

However, at the seminary, formation advisors are not like Nazis persecuting seminarians, as if the latter were the innocent Jews of the story hidden in the basement. I cannot think of a scenario at the seminary in which lying to a formation advisor could classify as an officious lie comparable to the midwives'. Seminarians should remember that lying is always sinful, *semper et pro semper*.

---

80 *ST* II–II, q. 110, a. 3, ad 4. Emphasis added.

81 Ibid.

82 *ST* II–II, q. 110, a. 2, c.

83 "The midwives were rewarded, not for their lie, but for their fear of God, and for their good-will, which latter led them to tell a lie. Hence it is expressly stated: 'And because the midwives feared God, He built them houses'. But the subsequent lie was not meritorious" (*ST* II–II, q. 110, a. 3, ad 2).

In addition, lying in order to cover up the mistakes of another seminarian, or lying so as not to "rat out" another's sins, for instance, do not seem to be officious lies. Unlike the lies of the midwives, these do not intend another's true good. Added to the intrinsic disorder of lying, one has to factor in here the intending of a *merely apparent* good. It is merely "apparent" because, in *truth*, it entails at least two serious moral evils.

First, it involves a clear harm done to the individuals not exposed to the light of truth (see 1 Jn 1:6). Second, it also involves inauthentic and alienating ways of participation, which directly harm both the individuals involved as well as the seminary's common good. Members of the seminary community are to love and assist one another mutually, but always in the truth.

Dissimulation and Hypocrisy

Let us move on to our next set of alienating and untruthful attitudes. The *Catechism* teaches that veracity guards against the duplicity inherent in *dissimulation and hypocrisy*.[84] A future priest falls into dissimulation when he willfully manifests through his deeds something contrary to who he really is.[85] In this way, a hypocritical seminarian pretends to have a virtue that, in reality, is absent in his life.[86]

But remember, Jesus had very harsh words against *hypocrisy*. He usually addressed these words to religious people, to the Pharisees and the scribes. "Woe to you, scribes and Pharisees, hypocrites! for you are like whitewashed tombs, which outwardly appear beautiful, but within they are full of dead men's bones and all uncleanness" (Mt 23:27).

---

84 See CCC 2468.

85 See *ST* II–II, q. 111, a. 1, c.

86 See *ST* II–II, q. 111, a. 2, c.

The practice of hypocrisy leads to a vain and false worship. It promotes honoring God only with one's lips, while one's heart is far from him (see Mt 15:7–9). But no one can deceive God. Thus, Jesus said to the Pharisees, "You are those who justify yourselves before men, but God knows your hearts; for what is exalted among men is an abomination in the sight of God" (Lk 16:15). The Lord warns us: "Beware of practicing your piety before men *in order to be seen by them*; for then you will have no reward from your Father who is in heaven" (Mt 6:1; emphasis added).

To give the semblance of holiness for the sake of being honored, while being unjust in a less obvious way, is very dangerous for one's salvation. Jesus said to his disciples about this very danger: "Beware of the scribes, who like to go about in long robes, and love salutations in the market places and the best seats in the synagogues and the places of honor at feasts, who devour widows' houses and for a pretense make long prayers. They will receive the greater condemnation" (Lk 20:46-47).

Aquinas explains that "hypocrisy is a kind of dissimulation, whereby a man simulates a character which is not his."[87] The hypocrite does not oppose the virtue he is faking, but veracity.

For instance, a future priest may choose to appear grateful when in fact he is not. He does not intend the existence of the virtue of gratitude, but only its semblance. Thus, "*his hypocrisy is not opposed to that virtue, but to truth,* inasmuch as he wishes to deceive men with regard to that virtue."[88] He may even express appreciation and thankfulness for favors received. However, he does not intend this act for its own sake, but only as means to the end by faking gratitude in order to cut a good figure.

In this manner, hypocrisy implies a certain *duplicity*. The future priest who falls into this sin "shows one thing outwardly

---

87 *ST* II–II, q. 111, a. 3, c.

88 *ST* II–II, q. 111, a. 3, ad 1.

while having another in his heart."[89] One of the best remedies against hypocrisy is the practice of the virtue of simplicity. The latter rectifies one's intention so that it does not tend to two things at once, one inwardly and another outwardly.[90]

Dissimulation and hypocrisy are alienating and untruthful attitudes in the seminary community. They directly hinder the attainment of its common good. They render priestly formation inefficacious and superficial. They promote a subculture of walking, not in the light, but in darkness.

At the end, these attitudes are most harmful for the candidate to the priesthood himself. He will go through seminary without seminary going through him. If the candidate persists in these attitudes while in formation, he may manage to deceive others, but he cannot deceive God.

Moreover, he will have to experience the pain of being ordained without the sufficient preparation in order to joyfully exercise his own ministry. His entire priesthood could be permeated by an aura of inauthenticity, which ultimately leads to a double life.

Boasting and Irony

There are two other alienating false attitudes against veracity and the seminary's common good, which have to do with a clear excess and defect with respect to the mean of the virtue of truth. I already mentioned them as different kinds of lies. On the one hand, boasting (*jactantia*) consists in the lifting up of myself by words above who I really am.[91] Boasting finds its roots in pride and vainglory.[92] It is clearly opposed to truth by way of excess.

---

89 *ST* II–II, q. 109, a. 2, ad 4.

90 See *ST* II–II, q. 111, a. 3, ad 2.

91 See *ST* II–II, q. 112, a. 1, c.

92 See *ST* II–II, q. 112, a. 1, ad 2.

Commenting on Aristotle, Aquinas tells us that "the boaster who sins by excess pretends certain praiseworthy qualities, and this in two ways. In one way, he pretends to have some distinctions that he does not possess. In the other way, he claims distinctions greater than they really are."[93]

On the other hand, what Aquinas calls "irony" is opposed to truth by way of defect. Irony is used here in a special way. It does not signify a humorous and emphatic way of speaking, whereby one uses the very opposite adjective that would describe the real situation. For instance, to a person leaving no tip at the restaurant, I could say with irony: "Do not be that generous."

This is not the way Thomas uses irony here. He refers to one peculiar way of *belittling oneself against truth*. As we already know, not every belittling of oneself is irony, and most importantly, not every belittling of oneself is sinful.

For example, a priest or a seminarian may belittle oneself "*so as to safeguard truth*, as when a man *conceals the greater things in himself, but discovers and asserts* lesser things of himself the presence of which in himself he perceives."[94] This is not in itself sinful, nor does it amount to irony. Instead, a seminarian or priest could belittle himself "*by forsaking the truth*, for instance by *ascribing to himself something mean the existence of which in himself he does not perceive*, or by *denying something great of himself, which nevertheless he perceives himself to possess*: this pertains to irony, and is *always* a sin."[95]

Both boasting and irony are lies about one's person. However, they have a very different source. While boasting finds its roots in pride and vainglory, irony is usually rooted in a desire to

---

93 *In IV Ethic.*, lect. 15, no. 835.

94 *ST* II–II, q. 113, a. 1, c. Emphasis added.

95 Ibid. Emphasis added.

please others and not to come across as the person who boasts about himself.[96]

In the Gospels, we find the warning not to pretend to be lacking in external things by outward signs, in order to make a show of our spiritual excellence. Thus Jesus said: "When you fast, do not look dismal, like the hypocrites, for they disfigure their faces that their fasting may be seen by men. Truly, I say to you, they have received their reward. But when you fast, anoint your head and wash your face, that your fasting may not be seen by men but by your Father who is in secret; and your Father who sees *in secret* will reward you" (Mt 6:16–18).

The person who falls into this error, Aquinas teaches, is guilty of both irony and boasting under different aspects. But the main goal here is boasting. Belittling his outward appearance is only the means by which one attempts to show off one's spiritual excellence.

Spiritual Exercises in Veracity

After providing the essential knowledge to understand the virtue of veracity, we will conclude our reflections, offering some spiritual exercises in this virtue. Remember that for these exercises to be fruitful, we are not to examine ourselves, looking at what we are supposed to say or to do, as if looking for the correct answer. Instead, we are to honestly, realistically, and humbly find out the acts and areas in which we have the opportunity to exercise spiritually.

---

96 See *ST* II–II, q. 113, a. 2, c.

	I am interested in knowing and in communicating the truth.
	I understand the depth of my responsibility to be truthful for both my own good and for that of the seminary community.
	My lack of veracity has created a certain aura of suspicion around me, even around my own real moral virtues.
	I am diligent in my exercise of self-knowledge.
	Without any formal intent to deceive, out of ignorance, I have often said materially false things about myself in evaluations and formation meetings.
	I strive to grow in a more realistic manifestation of my own self before those responsible for my priestly formation.
	I have experienced the values of awareness and understanding as conditions for the possibility of right action in the spiritual and moral life.
	I desire to know myself more truly in order to act in better accordance with my own nature and dignity.
	I want to explore some of my habitual dispositions acquired by imitation of my parents that separate me from God and the Church.
	I have begun to reflect upon what gifts my soul possesses, how God dwells within them, or how extremely precious they are. Such meditation has motivated me to preserve their beauty.
	I am looking forward to applying my studies in philosophy and theology to my spiritual life, to understand better which virtues I already have and which vices I need to eradicate.
	I am afraid of seriously laboring to know myself better in order to be more truthful in seminary.
	I have often hidden my head like an ostrich in the sand during formation meetings, trying to convince myself that I am okay, and that my faults or vices are only a private matter between myself and my confessor.
	I have experienced the vice of pride hampering my authentic self-knowledge.

	I have experienced the vice of lust, blinding me to the truth about myself.
	I lack docility toward those responsible for my priestly formation.
	I have experienced the joy of self-knowledge as knowledge about myself not acquired only by myself but also together with others and in the light of God.
	I have prayed before Christ's cross for the virtue of veracity.
	I have experienced how the virtue of veracity promotes my being the irreplaceable agent of my own priestly formation.
	The virtue of veracity is helping me to manifest myself prudently and realistically to my confessor, spiritual director, formation advisor, etc. I trust that all of them are for my good and benefit.
	I have prayed to the Holy Spirit to lead me to the whole truth about myself.
	Sometimes I affirm true things about myself without showing all of my goodness in matters of science and holiness, so as not to annoy other seminarians.
	I have gone back to Ignatius of Loyola's principle and foundation, as well as his spiritual exercises on the two standards, in order to renew my renunciation to Satan as the father of lies and my desire to follow Christ, the Truth.
	I want to walk in God's light and not in darkness.
	I have prayed for at least one hour with Eph 4:22–25.
	I seek to show the excellence of my own opinion without giving credit to others.
	I delight more in my own excellence than in the excellence of the truth.
	I am self-sufficient in matters of self-knowledge and truth.
	I lie out of fear and in order to get out of trouble.
	Through my deeds, I try to come across as someone I am not.
	I have a duplicity of heart.

	What I intend inwardly and what I intend outwardly is one and the same thing.
	I talk about myself above myself.
	I belittle myself against truth, ascribing to myself an evil that I do not really have or denying the existence of a good that I really have.
	I practice my penances openly, trying to let others know about my own spiritual excellence.

CHAPTER 5

OBSERVANCE AND OBEDIENCE

THE VALUE OF OBSERVANCE AND OBEDIENCE

THE value of observance and obedience is explicitly underlined in the Scriptures. Jesus gave us a supreme example of obedience: "Being found in human form he humbled himself and became obedient unto death, even death on a cross" (Phil 2:8–9). The fruit of Christ's obedience is our justification: "By one man's disobedience many were made sinners, so by one man's obedience many will be made righteous" (Rom 5:19).

The learning experience of Christ's obedience gave us access to salvation. "Although he was a Son, he learned obedience through what he suffered; and being made perfect he became the source of eternal salvation to all who obey him" (Heb 5:8–9). The Holy Spirit has been poured into our hearts (Rom 5:5). Through him, we have a supernatural friendship with Christ, which manifests itself in an internal and loving obedience to the Son of God: "You are my friends if you do what I command you" (Jn 15:14). This renewed obedience to God's commandments leads to eternal life (see Mt 19:17).[1]

Moreover, we are not only to obey Christ, but also those in legitimate authority: "Obey your leaders and submit to them; for they are keeping watch over your souls, as men who will have to give account. Let them do this joyfully, and not sadly, for that would

---

1 VS, 12.

be of no advantage to you" (Heb 13:17). As Paul says, we should "outdo one another in showing honor" (Rom 12:10). Peter gives us encouragement to purify one's soul "by obedience to the truth" (1 Pt 1:22). We all should "be subject to the governing authorities. For there is no authority except from God, and those that exist have been instituted by God" (Rom 13:1). Rulers and authority are not necessarily bad news. They "are not a terror to good conduct, but to bad" (Rom 13:3).

Every priest, on the day of his ordination, hears his bishop say: "Do you promise *reverence* and *obedience* to me and my successors?" Following the Scriptures and anticipating that very moment, we want to prepare the candidate to the priesthood to be truthful or faithful to this future promise.

Today, reverence and respect have become the usual terms to signify the reality of observance (*observantia*). This virtue involves being attentive, respectful of, and reverent to another's dignity and authority. Consequently, out of that respect and reverence, one is willing to serve his superiors. Aquinas views observance as the virtue "whereby worship and honor are paid to persons in positions of dignity."[2] As a result, obedience is closely related to observance as one of its due acts, since "both reverential honor and obedience are due to persons who excel."[3]

The virtues of observance and obedience are in great need of rehabilitation. Their value or importance has been severely obscured by our culture's egalitarian emphasis and difficulty with accepting hierarchies.[4] Nonetheless, as I like to tell my students,

---

2 *ST* II–II, q. 102, a. 1, c. For a good study on this virtue in Aquinas, see Joseph Benedict, *The Virtue of Observance According to St. Thomas Aquinas* (Washington, DC: Thomist Press, 1954).

3 *ST* II–II, q. 80, a. 1, ad 3.

4 See Walter Farrell, *The Fullness of Life: A Companion to the Summa,* vol. 3 (New York: Sheed and Ward, 1940), 247–51.

God is neither a communist nor an anarchist. In his eternal ordering of the cosmos, he did *not* intend a "classless universe," in which all beings are equally good and equally gifted. In fact, we are not.

Every species has its own level of perfection. And even amongst those who belong to the same species, not everyone is equally good and equally gifted. As Thomas says, "One man may be superior to another, and there is the same possibility among angels."[5]

To be sure, all human persons have the same natural dignity. Yet not all of them are equally worthy of respect and honor. Some have a greater "acquired" dignity than others. This acquired dignity may spring from their virtues, their office, or hopefully both.

This hierarchical worldview is further obscured by our overemphasis on moral autonomy.[6] Despite the fact that we call our culture post-modern, it is deeply affected by the modern philosophy of Immanuel Kant. In truth, most people have never read his writings.

Nevertheless, most people currently share many of Kant's views. Postmodernity critiques and rejects many aspects from modernity. Yet it also retains some of the major axioms of the latter.[7]

Based on the nominalistic crisis in the Middle Ages and in the Renaissance, modernity underlines an anthropocentrism wherein the human person is irreducible to the world.[8] Modernity looks at this anthropocentrism from the viewpoint of the emancipation of the *sola ratio*.[9] Within this emancipation, truth is known absolutely

---

5 *SCG* III. 120.

6 See VS, 35–37.

7 See Luis Romera Oñate, *El Hombre Ante El Misterio de Dios: Curso de Teología Natural* (Madrid: Ediciones Palabra, 2007).

8 I have partially dealt with this question in my *De la experiencia*, 135–200.

9 See Romano Guardini, *The End of the Modern World: A Search for Orientation*, trans. J. Theman and H. Burke (London: Sheed and Ward, 1957).

under a mathematical and deductive model, whose point of departure is human reason in relation to itself.

Certainly, postmodernity critiques and rejects modernity's absolutistic and prideful pretensions to reach an absolute knowledge in an absolute manner. Indeed, no postmodern philosopher would develop a philosophical system like Hegel's. Instead, postmodernity overemphasizes man's finitude, his being conditioned by his cultural and linguistic context, as well as truth's *relative* character. Yet, postmodernity's rebellion is not so beyond modernity, or so meta-modern, as it may seem. It still retains intact the core modern principle of autonomy and emancipation from any external authority.

In this sense, postmodernity would still adhere to the Kantian motto "*sapere aude*"—"dare to know." As Kant says, "Enlightenment is man's emergence from his self-incurred tutelage."[10] The German philosopher understands this tutelage as "man's inability to make use of his understanding *without direction from another*."[11]

Kant invited people to be autonomous. He wanted them to be courageous enough to move beyond heteronomy, beyond this being directed by others. He argued that "self-incurred is this tutelage when its cause lies not in lack of reason but *in lack of resolution and courage* to use it without direction from another."[12]

Thus, he admonished, "*Sapere aude*. 'Have the courage to use your own reason!'—that is the motto of enlightenment."[13] Consequently, within this modern worldview, observance and

---

10 Immanuel Kant, "What is Enlightenment," in *On History*, ed. L. White Beck (New York: Bobbs-Merrill, 1963), 3.

11 Ibid.

12 Ibid.

13 Ibid.

obedience are perceived as heteronomy, that is to say, as violations of one's autonomy and personal dignity.

Postmodernity retains this exact core element from modernity. It fosters a crisis of truth, in which we have lost metaphysics, the knowledge of God, and consequently, man's true identity. Even today's unique revival of religion also seems to leave intact that modern claim for autonomy.

For this reason, many people today claim to be "spiritual," but not "religious." With this alleged contrast, they mean to exclude organized religion as one way of being guided by others. In turn, their profession to be "spiritual" entails not only a rejection of observance and obedience, but also a claim for autonomy detached from objective truth. As a result, such an avowal carries with it the complete absence of an objective ethical dimension to their "spirituality."

This assertion also entails that postmodern spirituality is a matter of sheer individual opinion, with no say whatsoever in the public square. Hence, we continue to promote a social order without God—*etsi Deus non daretur*. Make no mistake, all of us have been afflicted by these cultural phenomena in one way or another. Priests and seminarians are not exempt from this Western cultural influence.

Thus, we cannot ignore it. Instead, we need to acknowledge and identify it, in order to further evaluate its suitability for priestly formation. A priestly formation, which really prepares the seminarian to make the promise of respect and obedience, should take this fact into consideration.

Perhaps we should begin by pointing out how the value of observance and obedience shines particularly in their capacity to defend every other virtue. "All acts of virtue, in so far as they come under a precept, belong to obedience. Wherefore according as acts of virtue act causally or dispositively toward their generation and preservation, obedience is said to ingraft and protect all virtues."[14]

The entirety of priestly formation is based on the assumption that candidates to the priesthood, when beginning seminary, are not yet fully formed. They certainly need another's guidance and some precepts in order to develop virtues. Even if priestly formation is self-formation, it is certainly not autonomous. It essentially involves a participated theonomy, "since man's free obedience to God's law effectively implies that human reason and human will participate in God's wisdom and providence."[15]

Above all, priestly formation entails an authentic collaboration with the Holy Spirit as the *main* agent of priestly formation. Moreover, it also involves a collaboration with other mediating forces, such as formation advisors and spiritual directors.[16] As a result, without observance and obedience to them, seminary formation is not viable. In turn, when the seminarian rejects autonomy and embraces participated theonomy, when he accepts the value of observance and obedience to all these other agents of formation, the growth in every virtue fostered by their precepts is safeguarded or protected.

The value of observance and obedience is also evidenced by their connection to the common good of the seminary community. The obedience, which is part of priestly observance, takes place not only within the context of charity as friendship with God, but also within the context of justice and acting together with others. Under this last perspective, obedience is an authentic way of participating in the community and in view of the common good. Formation in priestly obedience should always remember this other dimension pertaining to the virtue of justice and authentic participation.

---

14 *ST* II–II, q. 104, a. 3, ad 2.

15 See VS, 41.

16 See PDV, 69.

In fact, Vatican II stresses the importance of understanding obedience in light of the priest's collaboration with the bishop. *Presbyterorum Ordinis* explains that priests should never lose "sight of the fullness of the priesthood which the bishops enjoy."[17] In light of this fullness, priests "must respect in them the authority of Christ, the Supreme Shepherd. They must therefore stand by their bishops in sincere charity and obedience. This priestly obedience, *imbued with a spirit of cooperation* is based on the very sharing in the episcopal ministry which is conferred on priests both through the Sacrament of Orders and the canonical mission."[18]

John Paul II has beautifully expanded on this same teaching. Implicitly echoing Aquinas, for whom the cross is the model of every virtue, the pope explains the model and source for priestly obedience. "Jesus Christ, who brought his pastoral charity to perfection on the cross with a complete exterior and interior emptying of self, is both the model and source of the virtues of obedience, chastity and poverty which the priest is called to live out as an expression of his pastoral charity for his brothers and sisters."[19]

John Paul has also underlined that priestly obedience has *apostolic*, *communitarian*, and *pastoral* dimensions. Obedience is *apostolic* because of its connection with observance; that is, because "it recognizes, loves and serves the Church in her hierarchical structure."[20] As the pope continues, "There can be no genuine priestly ministry except in communion with the supreme pontiff and the episcopal college, especially with one's own diocesan bishop, who deserves that 'filial respect and obedience' promised during the rite of ordination."[21]

---

17 PO, 7.

18 Ibid. Emphasis added.

19 PDV, 30. See PO, 15.

20 PDV, 28.

21 Ibid.

Priestly obedience has a *communitarian* dimension because it is one way of authentic participation in view of the common good. "It is not the obedience of an individual who alone relates to authority, but rather an obedience which is deeply a part of the unity of the presbyterate, which as such is called to cooperate harmoniously with the bishop and, through him, with Peter's successor."[22] For this reason, the pope explains that, as authentic participation, "priestly obedience should be *one of solidarity*, based *on belonging to a single presbyterate*."[23]

Lastly, priestly obedience has a *pastoral* dimension of self-giving to others, because it entails a "constant readiness to allow oneself to be taken up, as it were 'consumed', by the needs and demands of the flock."[24]

Keeping these brief reflections in mind, let us pause and discuss the following questions:

(1) What does lack of observance and obedience do to my life?
(2) What does lack of observance and obedience do to the life of the seminary?
(3) What will lack of observance and obedience do in my future life as a priest?
(4) What will my incapacity to be an example of observance and obedience mean for the life of my spiritual children?
(5) How will my growth in the virtues of observance and obedience impact my life as a seminarian and as a future priest, as well as the life of those around me in the seminary, and in my future parish?

---

22 PDV, 28.

23 Ibid.

24 Ibid.

Excellence, Honor, and Worship

As a general virtue, observance introduces us into a peculiar realm within the province of justice. It leads us into the area of honoring and worshiping another's excellence and dignity. This peculiar realm includes three specifically distinct virtues: religion, piety, and observance.

As was said, the virtue of obedience is closely linked to them. It finds its own characteristic expression in each of these three virtues.[25] Thus, "in so far as it proceeds from reverence for a superior, it is contained, in a way, under observance; while in so far as it proceeds from reverence for one's parents, it is contained under piety; and in so far as it proceeds from reverence for God, it comes under religion, and pertains to devotion, which is the principal act of religion."[26]

We will deal with piety and religion in our next chapter, indicating their peculiar connection to obedience. Yet our considerations now have more of a foundational character. We need to answer the following question: what do we mean by honoring and worshiping another's excellence and dignity?

Excellence, Dignity, and Goodness

Excellence and dignity are interrelated notions. They imply a certain a degree of goodness. The greater the goodness possessed, the greater the excellence or dignity. To explain the excellence and dignity honored and worshiped in the general realm of observance, we need to appeal to three interrelated metaphysical and theological topics: the convertibility between being (*ens*) and good (*bonum*),

---

25 Nevertheless, as Benedict explains, there are not three specifically distinct virtues of obedience corresponding to religion, piety, and observance. See Benedict, *The Virtue of Observance*, 70–73.

26 *ST* II–II, q. 104, a. 3, ad 1.

our participation in God as *the* Good and Exemplar, and the image of God in the human person.[27]

Allow me to clarify these highly philosophical assertions in simpler terms. In the case of the human person, a man is good, firstly, by virtue of his rational soul created directly by God. Since every agent produces something like itself (*omnes agens agit sibi simile*), this soul has a certain likeness to God as Supreme Good.

Man's substantial immanent form—that is to say, his rational soul—is the basis for this metaphysical participation. And since man has an intellectual nature similar to that of God, he is the being in the *visible* world who resembles him the most. Thus, the human being is made in God's image. The innate indelible dignity and excellence of every human person, a dignity and excellence that derive from the simple fact of being human, find their source right here, in this kind of metaphysical participation in God as *the* Good.[28]

Man's substantial form or spiritual soul inclines the human person naturally. It does so in accordance with his rational and social mode of being. As we know, in the human person there are natural inclinations to the acquisition of the virtues.[29] Hence, we find another sense in which the human person is good, another sense in which we can speak about excellence and dignity.

The human person is good in second act (*actus secundus*) because of the *conformity* to God as extrinsic form or supreme good. In other words, the human person is morally good because of his *conformity* to God as the final end and exemplar, because "an image is related to that of which it is the image as what is

---

27 See Wojtyła, *Person and Community*, 73–94.

28 See Wojtyła, *Sources of Renewal: The Implementation of the Second Vatican Council*, trans. P. S. Falla (San Francisco: Harper & Row, 1980), 284, 312; Wojtyła, *Person and Community*, 265.

29 See *ST* I, q. 76, a. 6, ad 1; I–II, q. 94, a. 3, c; *In IV Sent.*, d. 26, q. 1, a. 1, c.

measurable is related to its measure."[30] The human person is substantially permanent but perfectible in the accidental order.

Hence, when he lives a virtuous life conforming to the Divine Exemplar, he resembles God even more. A virtuous person looks more like God than a morally deprived one. Mother Teresa looks more like God than Hitler does. This is the sense in which *likeness*—in the expression "in God's image and *likeness*"—means the perfection of the *imago Dei*.[31] In this way, a person may grow in this excellence and dignity.

Honoring and Worship

The acts that have another's excellence or dignity as their objects are *honoring* and *worship*. In this way, the honor we are interested in unveiling now is not the object of hope but the act performed by the one honoring.[32] It is all about due excellence in another.[33]

Although such excellence includes power, nobility, or wealth, it does so only in reference to virtue.[34] Thomas explains that "honor is a kind of reverence due to a very excellent good."[35] It "denotes a witnessing to a person's excellence."[36] A seminarian, for instance, honors his spiritual director because he has reverence for him, and because he wants others to reverence him as well.[37] The reverence in question is a kind of good fear arising not from a

---

30 *In V Meta.*, lect. 17, no. 1003.

31 See Wojtyła, *Person and Community*, 45–56, 48, 74; *ST* I, q. 5, a. 1; q. 93, a. 9, c; I–II, q. 18, a. 1.

32 See *ST* I–II, q. 2, a. 2, c; *In I Ethic.*, lect. 5, no. 64.

33 See *ST* II–II, q. 81, a. 4, c.

34 See *ST* II–II, q. 25, a. 1, ad 2; II–II, q. 145, a. 1, c; *In I Ethic.*, lect. 5, no. 65.

35 *In IV Ethic.*, lect. 9, no. 756.

36 *ST* II–II, q. 103, a. 1, c.

37 See *ST* II–II, q. 103, a. 1, ad 1.

defect of punishment or guilt but rather from a certain inequality in being and goodness.

Consider, for instance, the reverence of the blessed in heaven. It springs from the contemplation of God's perfection in the face of their inequality as a natural imperfection. Thus, "the fear we will have in our heavenly homeland concerns this [natural] defect, a fear that will show reverence for our creator as we dart from the contemplation of his majesty to our own meagerness."[38] Likewise, we experience a similar inequality in being and goodness in the presence of a virtuous person or a person in authority, wherefrom, arises our reverence and honor for him.

Honoring someone entails not only the intellectual acknowledgement of their excellence, but also a certain *witness* to it. When one honors God, this witness can be internal to one's heart. Instead, when one honors human persons, "one cannot bear witness, save by means of signs, either by words, as when one proclaims another's excellence by word of mouth, or by deeds, for instance by bowing, saluting, and so forth, or by external things, as by offering gifts, erecting statues, and the like. Accordingly honor consists of signs, external and corporal."[39]

Moreover, another's dignity and excellence can be recognized apart from their relationship to the excellence of the one honoring him or her. The seminarian does not need to be constantly comparing himself with his superiors in order to determine whether or not they deserved to be honored. The excellence of his superiors can also be considered in itself, or in relation to other seminarians, or other persons. Thus, "in this way, honor is always due to a person, on account of some excellence or superiority."[40]

---

38 *De Spe*, q. 1, a. 4, ad 2.

39 *ST* II–II, q. 103, a. 1, c.

40 *ST* II–II, q. 103, a. 2, c.

Indeed, it is theoretically possible for a seminarian to be more virtuous than his spiritual director, formation advisor, or rector. Likewise, a priest could be more virtuous than his bishop. Yet in both scenarios, the seminarian should honor his superiors, just as the priest should honor his bishop. "For the person honored has no need to be more excellent than those who honor him; it may suffice for him to be more excellent than some others, or again he may be more excellent than those who honor him in some respect and not simply."[41]

Let us consider now the second act that has another's excellence or dignity as its object: the act of worship. The use of this word has a strange ring to our contemporary ears. Thomas does not mean that a seminarian should worship his spiritual director or his rector as he worships God. He clearly does not mean the worship that is due only to God, *latria*. Evidently, he does not mean either the worship that is due to saints (*dulia*) and to the Virgin Mary in a most excellent way (*hyperdulia*).[42]

The worship that is an act of observance, as a general virtue, is an act given to persons and to things only insofar as they are related to persons. It adds to one's honoring a certain *subjection* or *subordination* caused by the other's excellence and dignity. For this reason, we can certainly say that God honors the saints. However,

---

41 *ST* II–II, q. 103, a. 2, c.

42 We often hear the word *dulia* as applied to the kind of reverence that we give to saints and angels. Within this context, we hear that there is a distinction between *dulia* and *latria*. The first corresponds to the reverence that we give to saints and angels, while the second corresponds to the worship given to God alone. This distinction was especially highlighted after the Protestant Reformation. Thus, the Second Vatican Council distinguishes between devotion and adoration. See LG, 66; CCC 971. Although this distinction is extremely important and totally accurate, in order to understand the precise and fruitful connection between the virtue of observance and that of *dulia*, we need to go back to a more primitive or radical meaning of *dulia*.

although the saints worship God, they are not worshiped by him, because he is neither subject nor subordinated to anyone. Worship is formally characterized by the will to manifest this peculiar subordination, ordinarily through corporeal acts.[43] This is the act that is present in the specifically distinct virtues of religion, piety, and observance.

Observance and Participated Parenthood

Observance is a special virtue with a particular formal object, which distinguishes its own honoring and worshiping another's excellence from the one present in religion and piety. The special virtue of observance inheres in the human will. It belongs to the province of justice as an annexed virtue. As such, it has similarities and dissimilarities with justice. Like justice, observance is ordered to another, and it deals with a legal debt. Unlike justice, in observance, one cannot exactly repay what is received.[44] Observance's debt is one of *inequality*, just like the debts inherent in the virtues of piety and religion.

A person becomes another's debtor in different ways. It really depends on the other's excellence and on the diverse benefits received from him.[45] Religion is directly concerned with God. It deals with God's excellence and with the favors he bestows on us in his providence and government, as our supreme and most radical principle of being and conduct. No one has God's excellence and no one bestows gifts on us like God does. Hence, our distinct debt toward him specifies a whole particular virtue called religion.

Piety, instead, is directly concerned with our parents. It deals

43 See *ST* II–II, q. 82, a. 2, c.

44 See *In III Sent.*, d. 33, q. 3, a. 4.

45 See *ST* II–II, q. 101, a. 1, c.

with their excellence and with the benefits given to us by them, insofar as they participate in God's governance, thanks to their procreative *munus*. Piety's distinct debt results from the excellence and the benefits received from our parents' collaboration with the Creator in the transmission and education of human life.[46] Such collaboration goes beyond physical generation; it also implies the education of offspring unto heaven.[47] Consequently, piety's debt results from having received our own life and our education from our parents.

In turn, the debt pertaining to observance is distinct from the one of piety. Nevertheless, both are related. The virtue of observance considers the excellence of one's superiors, as well as the benefits received from them, insofar as our superiors participate in and extend, as it were, our parents' mission. One could almost say that observance deals with our superiors in their participated parenthood.

Hence, observance is a virtue whereby one honors and worships the excellence and dignity of our superiors as spiritual fathers and mothers. Of course, this is very pertinent for priestly formation and for the context of the seminary community. It also places priestly obedience to one's bishop within the right context.

Thomas explains that "a carnal father partakes of the character of principle in a particular way, which character is found in God in a universal way, so too a person who, in some way, exercises providence in one respect, partakes of the character of father in a particular way, since *a father is the principle of generation, of education, of learning and of whatever pertains to the perfection of human life*."[48] Thomas's words do not contradict Jesus's: "Call

---

46 See Wojtyła, *Love and Responsibility*, 226.

47 See *SCG* IV. 78; *Super I Cor.*, cap. 7, lect. 1; Pius XI, *Casti Connubi*, 12.

48 *ST* II–II, q. 102, a. 1, c. Emphasis added.

no man your father on earth, for you have one Father, who is in heaven" (Mt 23:9). Although no one is Father like God, there are plenty of persons who are not *the* Father, but *a* father to us. Think about priests, for instance. They are rightly called "fathers."

St. Paul says: "For this reason I bow my knees before the Father, from whom every *patría* in heaven and on earth is named" (Eph 3:14–15).[49] I have left untranslated the Greek word *patria* (see also Lk 2:14; Acts 3:25). It could mean paternity, family, homeland, or clan. All of these meanings are acceptable, as long as we acknowledge in them a certain priority and posteriority.

First and foremost, *patría* signifies a subject that is a principle of being. God, parents, families, homelands, clans, priests, educators, are all principles of being. But they are not so in the same way.

There is one principle of being from whom all of the rest receive their name. God, *the Father*, is the *principium sine principio*. He is Fatherhood in person.[50] Absolutely no one is a father like he is. No one else is a principle without a principle.[51] In this sense, we should call no one father except him (see Mt 23:9).

Nevertheless, any creature who participates in being a principle of life and education shares in God's *patría*. Priests are fathers for this very reason. Thus, Paul considers himself as a father in 1 Cor 4:15. Formation advisors, spiritual directors, and teachers at the seminary each exercise a peculiar spiritual parenthood toward seminarians, which deserves their observance.

Thomas said that being a parent includes being "*the principle of generation, of education, of learning and of whatever pertains to the perfection of human life*."[52] Of course, Aquinas is thinking in this text of education, understood as "the conducting and promoting

---

49 See MD, 8.

50 *ST* I, q. 33, a. 2, c.

51 See *ST* I, q. 33, a. 4, c.

52 *ST* II–II, q. 102, a. 1, c.

[of the human person] to the perfect state of man inasmuch as he is man, that is to say, to the state of virtue."[53]

Everything that pertains to the state of virtue and leads us into heaven is part of our education. Hence, the virtue of observance is a virtue directed to those who, not being God or our physical parents, partake in our education as the latter finds its fulfillment in love.[54] Our debt toward them not only is impossible to repay but also is closely linked to gratitude.

Education and governance are very closely related in this context. The latter is understood here as moving others to their due end, as leading them toward their perfection. As a result, Aquinas identifies a twofold consideration of the person in a position of dignity and authority.

First, one can consider this person's excellence of position and power. The virtue of observance responds to this excellence with the act of honoring. Second, one can consider this person's exercise of government. The virtue of observance responds to this exercise with the act of worship "consisting in rendering him service, by obeying his commands, and by repaying him, according to one's faculty, for the benefits we received from him."[55]

Benedict unifies all of these acts under a certain devotion. It consists in the "prompt will to give oneself to the things concerning the service of those constituted in dignity or authority and by extension to all those who excel in some virtue or knowledge."[56] This same author offers some hints on how to grow in these particular acts.

Benedict argues that the devotion characteristic in observance is closely related to meditation. Thus, it is important to consider

53 *In IV Sent.*, d. 26, q. 1, a. 1, c.

54 See *ST* I–II, q. 65, a. 2, c.

55 *ST* II–II, q. 102, a. 2, c.

56 Benedict, *The Virtue of Observance*, 49.

our superiors as such, to meditate how much they do for us, and to ponder on their excellence and on the sacrifices that their mission entails. Such a meditation awakens and motivates the will with love in order to serve them. Moreover, in order to grow in the virtue of observance, one should also meditate on our own shortcomings, and on our need for paternal guidance.[57]

Again, this same twofold consideration could help us distinguish the particular virtue of observance from the virtue of religion. Although both imply a sort of observance in a general sense, the service or servitude inherent in them is different. As Thomas says, "Servitude is due to God and to man under different aspects: even as lordship is competent to God and to man under different aspects."[58]

The virtue of religion is directed to God, who "has absolute and paramount lordship over the creature wholly and singly, which is entirely subject to His power."[59] In turn, the virtue of observance is directed to those who, not being our physical parents, exercise some government over us. Their government "partakes of a certain likeness to the divine lordship, forasmuch as he exercises a particular power over some man or creature."[60]

But what if my formation advisor, my rector, my bishop, or any other superior of mine is not as virtuous as he should be? Thomas teaches with a great deal of realism that, even in this case, honor is to be given to one's superior: "A wicked superior is honored for the excellence, not of his virtue but of his dignity, as being God's minister, and because the honor paid to him is paid to the whole community over which he presides."[61]

---

57 See Benedict, *The Virtue of Observance*, 49–50.

58 *ST* II–II, q. 102, a. 3, c.

59 Ibid.

60 Ibid.

61 *ST* II–II, q. 102, a. 2, ad 2.

Furthermore, if we are humble, it will not be too difficult to find something in another person for which we can honor him or her: “In every man is to be found something that makes it possible to deem him better than ourselves, according to Phil 2:3; ‘In humility, let each esteem others better than themselves,’ and thus, too, we should all be on the alert to do honor to one another.”[62]

Obedience and One’s Counsel

The virtue of observance places obedience within the right context. Obedience is seen as a loving and grateful response to the excellence of one’s superiors. Additionally, it is also a response to the benefits received from them as participants of God’s governance.

This right context promotes the exercise of obedience in accordance with the natural dignity of every human person. God left man to the hand of his own counsel.[63] The human person “is not compelled by natural necessity to do what he ought to do, but is left the free choice proceeding from his own counsel. And *just as he has to proceed on his own counsel in doing other things, so too has he in the point of obeying his superiors*.”[64]

God himself rules us as free agents. He governs us as beings capable of *understanding* his law, as beings who can willingly be the cause of their own obedience. Any exercise of authority and demand for obedience must imitate God’s.

In truth, in the seminary, or as a priest, we may not always be able to understand fully *all* the reasons behind a superior’s command.

---

62 *ST* II–II, q. 102, a. 2, ad 3.

63 See Sir 15:14. The act of counsel is an act of the intellect essential for the free choice of the will. See Daniel Westberg, *Right Practical Reason: Aristotle, Action, and Prudence in Aquinas* (Oxford: Clarendon Press, 1994); Federica Bergamino, *La Razionalità Della Libertà Della Scelta in Tommaso d’Aquino* (Roma: EDUSC, 2002).

64 *ST* II–II, q. 104, a. 1, ad 1. Emphasis added.

However, at the very least, in order to obey in accordance with the dignity that corresponds to personal beings, we need to be certain that the one commanding wants our good. We need to trust in the superior and in his capacity for his moral insight.

We want to stay away from two extremes. On the one hand, we want to avoid falling into the Kantian error of conceiving ourselves as the sole source of law. As Wojtyła explicitly says, "There is no question of assigning to the conscience, as Kant argued, the power to make its own laws—followed by an identification of this power with the notion of autonomy and thus in a way with an unrestricted freedom of the person. The *conscience is no lawmaker; it does not itself create norms; rather it discovers them, as it were, in the objective order of morality or law*."[65]

On the other hand, we do not want to fall into the other extreme. This end sees no role whatsoever in our understanding the commands we obey or the authority from whence they come. Aquinas has just said that, as the human person follows his own counsel for other things, he must do the same in obeying his superiors.

Accordingly, obedience can never mean "a denial of man's self-determination or the imposition of norms unrelated to his good."[66] Such a heteronomous obedience "would be in contradiction to the Revelation of the Covenant and of the redemptive Incarnation. Such a heteronomy would be nothing but a form of alienation, contrary to divine wisdom and to the dignity of the human person."[67]

Opposing Kant, Scheler also explains that moral insight should not be simply replaced by another's authority either, in a sort of blind obedience based solely on the affirmation "because I say

---

65 Wojtyła, *The Acting Person*, 165. Emphasis added. See also VS, 54.

66 VS, 41.

67 Ibid.

so." Moral insight—or what Thomas called counsel—should always be present in one's obedience. Even when a seminarian or a priest does not fully understand what he is being commanded to do, provided there is no contradiction to God's authority, he can at least understand and trust in the authority and moral insight of the one ruling. In this case "of pure obedience to authority it is *presupposed that the moral value of the commanding authority, or, more precisely, the truly authoritative nature of the commanding institution, is itself evident to the one who obeys*."[68]

Such moral insight closely connects obedience and observance. For instance, this connection is present when the seminarian acknowledges the excellence and dignity of the formation advisor or rector. The same connection is present when the priest acknowledges the excellence and dignity of his bishop. Then, one can trust in the moral insight of his legitimate superior, knowing full well and trusting in the authoritative nature of the commanding institution.

Based on that same experience, Scheler distinguishes (moral) authority from force: "Authority differs from mere power or force in that a person can possess authority only over *one who knows by evidence that this person possesses a deeper and wider moral insight than he does*. Moral 'trust' in an authority is based on this insight, and authority is based on this trust. If this trust is removed, authority becomes non-moral power and force."[69]

Consequently, personal obedience is always based on some rational understanding of the norm in itself, of the authoritative

68 Max Scheler, *Formalism in Ethics and Non-Formal Ethics of Values: A New Attempt toward the Foundation of an Ethical Personalism*, trans. M. Frings (Evanston: Northwestern University Press, 1973), 328. Emphasis added.

69 Ibid., 328.

nature of the commanding institution, of the capacity for moral insight of the commanding authority, and of the certainty that this authority wants what is good for me. This same obedience can be re-dimensioned by the virtue of religion. So, in addition to what has been said, one also can obey his superiors at the seminary or his bishop out of obedience for God.

Obedience as Gift of Self

In a broad sense, we can speak of obedience as "the performance of any action that may be a matter of precept."[70] In general, disobedience conversely consists in the omission of that due action, whatever the intention of the agent might be.[71] However, when dealing with the specific and special virtue of obedience, we are concentrating our attention upon the agent's intentional and formal consideration of the aspect of precept inherent to the good deed he is about to perform.

Then, the obedient agent performs an action of chastity, for example, with the intention to fulfill a precept. In turn, the specific sin of *disobedience* has to do with the intention of doing something evil with *actual contempt for the precept* that forbids it. Christian obedience is always related to following Christ and to our interpersonal relationship with him. It is not only "disposing oneself to hear a teaching and obediently accepting a commandment. More radically, it involves holding fast to the very person of Jesus, partaking of his life and his destiny, sharing in his free and loving obedience to the will of the Father."[72]

Aquinas also sees this inherent *interpersonal* dimension in obedience. The splendor of obedience's interpersonal dimension radiates with particular eloquence from the perspective of charity.

---

70 *ST* II–II, q. 104, a. 2, ad 1.

71 See *ST* II–II, q. 104, a. 2, ad 1.

72 VS, 19.

Therein, obedience leads to the spiritual sacrifice of one's will, to the offering of oneself to God.

As is known, sin consists in our contemning God, turning away from him and toward mutable goods. Conversely, a meritorious and virtuous act consists in contemning finite goods while adhering to God. The greater the finite good contemned in order to adhere to God, the greater offering and gift inherent in this good act.

But the greatest finite good we can contemn in order to follow God is our own will. There is nothing that we love more, because through our free will, we make use of all other finite goods. Consequently, Thomas explains that "the virtue of obedience, whereby we contemn our own will for God's sake, is more praiseworthy than the other moral virtues, which contemn other goods for the sake of God."[73] This is exactly what is meant by the gift of self.

From the *metaphysical* perspective, the human person possesses and governs himself. He does so in such an intimate way that no one else can take his place in making a free choice. Even God respects this very dignity. The human person is *alteri incomunicabilis*. Thus, from this viewpoint, Wojtyła explains that "it makes no sense to speak of a person giving himself or herself to another."[74]

However, from the *moral* perspective, the human person is able to decide freely to surrender his own free will to another. Moreover, one can do that out of charity, that is, out of love for God and others. Wojtyła explains that, in this moral sense, "one person can give himself or herself, can surrender entirely to another, whether to a human person or to God."[75] As Thomas says, in the virtue of obedience, we give ourselves because "we slay our own will."[76]

73 *ST* II–II, q. 104, a. 3, c.

74 Wojtyła, *Love and Responsibility*, 96.

75 Ibid., 97.

76 *ST* II-II, q. 104, a. 3, c.

Indeed, "obedience is one of the greatest of the virtues: for to offer something from one's external things is great; to offer something from the body is greater; but the greatest is to offer something from your soul and will: and this is done by obedience."[77] For this reason, any act of virtue acquires this dimension of priestly sacrificial self-offering or self-gift, when inserted in the orbit of obedience: "Any other acts of virtue are meritorious before God through being performed out of obedience to God's will."[78] By spiritually exercising from this perspective, the seminarian will build a basis for the implementation of the pastoral dimension of priestly obedience, that is, for that "constant readiness to allow oneself to be taken up, as it were 'consumed', by the needs and demands of the flock."[79]

Christ's Obedience as Exemplar and Example

As John Paul II explained, Christ crucified is the model and source for our obedience.[80] Priestly formation in the virtue of obedience should take place within the context of charity: "In the general context of charity—which consists in the loving gift of oneself—is to be found, in the program of spiritual formation of the future priest, *education in obedience*, celibacy and poverty."[81] When properly understood, priestly human formation leads to priestly spiritual formation. Such a formation in priestly obedience aims in "living in conformity with the crucified Christ."[82]

---

77 *Super Phil.*, cap. 2, lect. 3.

78 *ST* II–II, q. 104, a. 3, c.

79 PDV, 28.

80 See ibid., 30.

81 Ibid., 49. Emphasis added.

82 Ibid. See PO, 15. For a good article on Christ's obedience, see Mark Armitage, "Obedient unto Death, Even Death on a Cross: Christ's Obedience in the Soteriology of St. Thomas Aquinas," *Nova et Vetera, English Edition* 8, no. 3 (2010): 505–26.

Christ's obedience is the exemplar and example for priestly obedience. His obedience is a lesson or a vivid example in humility, in justice, in the value of experientially learning through suffering, and in charity. In addition, Christ's obedience is the source of grace and the model for our humble obedience, our justification, our own experiential learning of obedience through suffering, and for our own charity.

Humble Obedience and Justification

Jesus gave us a supreme example of obedience: "Being found in human form he humbled himself and became obedient unto death, even death on a cross" (Phil 2:8–9). Christ was obedient because he subordinated his human will to the Divine Will. Obedience gleams brightest when one follows another's command, even if it is contrary to one's will. Christ did this exact thing by reordering the natural inclination of his human will to live and to his own honor. He freely accepted in obedience his own death and the ignominy of the cross.[83]

Although they are two distinct virtues, Paul presents herein obedience as humility: "The manner and the sign of His humility is obedience, whereas it is characteristic of the proud to follow their own will, for a proud person seeks greatness. But it pertains to a great thing that it not be ruled by something else, but that it rule other things; therefore, obedience is contrary to pride."[84] However, Christ did not only show the way; he also gave us the power to walk it. He is not only an example: he is also the exemplar, the cause that effects our imitation of him. Thus, Christ's humble obedience reverses Adam's prideful disobedience.[85]

---

83 See *ST* III, q. 21, aa. 3–4.

84 *Super Phil.*, cap. 2, lect. 2.

85 See *ST* II–II, q. 163, a. 1, ad 2.

Christ's cross is the chair wherefrom he teaches humility and obedience.[86] Empowered by Christ, in our obedience to God and to our superiors, we will be able to give ourselves completely, knowing that we will find our lives. We will be exalted just as Christ was exalted for his humble obedience.[87]

The fruit of Christ's obedience is our justification: "By one man's disobedience many were made sinners, so by one man's obedience many will be made righteous" (Rom 5:19). On the cross, Christ gives a lesson on legal justice as adjusting to God's will and fulfilling his precepts.[88] Moreover, he also gives us a lesson on justice as justification. He provides satisfaction for our sins out of charity.[89] Jesus's death can be considered "as it proceeds from the will of Christ suffering, which was a will formed to the endurance of death, in obedience to the Father . . . and out of love for men."[90]

This satisfaction for our sins does *not* consist in the mere legality of taking our place as the condemned, making God look the other way from our misery. Justification is the other name of mercy. And true mercy dispels the cause of our misery.

Christ's satisfaction embraces us in the depths of his own mission as redeemer of man. His satisfaction does not change God as such. Rather, it changes and transforms *us* from within by allowing us to share in the Divine Life: "We have been changed from enemies to friends."[91] It rectifies our primeval disobedience and that of Adam.

---

86 See *Super Heb.*, cap. 12, lect. 1, no. 667.

87 See *ST* III, q. 48, a. 1; q. 49, a. 6, c.

88 See *Super Rom.*, cap. 5, lect. 5.

89 See *ST* III, q. 48, a. 2, c.

90 *Super Rom.*, cap. 5, lect. 2, no. 403.

91 *Super Rom.*, cap. 5, lect. 2, no. 404.

Learning in Suffering

Christ's obedience is a lesson and a dramatic example in the value of experientially learning the virtue of obedience through suffering. "Although he was a Son, he learned obedience through what he suffered; and being made perfect he became the source of eternal salvation to all who obey him" (Heb 5:8–9). The author of Hebrews places this obedience within a sublime description of Christ's priesthood. His obedience is inserted within his priestly compassion and mercy.[92] As was said, God's mercy is the shape that his divine love adopts when confronted by our misery.

God is merciful because, out of love, he wills good things for us that destroy or alleviate what makes us most miserable, what hinders our eternal salvation.[93] Christ, the High Priest, is the Son of God who became man in order to be able to suffer and to feel with us, that is, in order to have compassion (*cum-passio*) (see Heb 4: 15). He makes our misery his own. And through his obedience and sacrifice on the cross, Christ fills us with his mercy by destroying the very cause of our misery; namely, sin and death. Therefore, the learnt obedience of Christ becomes the source of salvation for all those who obey him.

How did God's Son *learn* obedience from what he suffered? This learning would seem impossible. Only the ignorant can learn. However, in Scripture one reads the following words addressed to Jesus: "Now we know that you know all things" (Jn 16:30). Thomas Aquinas explains that even though the Son of God eternally knows the essence of obedience, he learnt in his human experience ("what it means") to be obedient.

Since one only learns voluntarily, Christ freely chooses to take the condition of a servant and to be obedient unto death on a

---

92 See *Super Heb.*, c. 5, no. 258.

93 See *ST*, I, q. 21, a. 3.

cross. This experience is fitting for the King of kings. According to our human experience, he who does not learn to submit himself to another does not know how to rule others well. For this reason, by their participation in the ministerial priesthood of Jesus Christ, those who are called to rule in the Church (*munus regendi*) need to learn to rule in the school of obedience.

Aquinas explains how fitting is Christ's lesson in obedience through what he suffered. He says that "this shows how difficult the good of obedience is, because those who have not experienced obedience and have not learned it in difficult matters, believe that obedience is very easy."[94]

Christ's obedience is *the* lesson and the example in *the* value of experientially learning through suffering, especially for future priests who are called to rule others: "In order to know what obedience is, one must learn to obey in difficult matters, and *one who has not learned to subject himself by obeying does not know how to rule others well.* Therefore, although Christ knew by simple recognition what obedience is, He nevertheless learned obedience from the things He suffered, i.e., from difficult things, by suffering and dying: 'By the obedience of one many shall be made just'."[95]

The second part of the text from Hebrews that we are commenting on announces the salvific effect of Christ's obedience: "and being made perfect He became the source of eternal salvation to all who obey him" (Heb 5:9).[96] Christ is made perfect through his obedience because he obtains a glorious body incapable of suffering again. Other than that, Christ was already perfect. His growing in grace—of which Luke speaks about—consists in doing ever greater works that manifest his perfection.[97] Being perfect, Christ *communicates* to us a similitude of his goodness.

---

94 *Super Heb.*, c. 5, no. 259. See Rom 5:19.

95 Ibid.

96 See also Armitage, "Obedient unto Death."

97 See *ST* III, q. 7, a. 12, ad 3.

Through his mercy, Christ not only destroys our misery by his obedience to the Father, but also becomes the source of salvation for those who obey him. All of us are called to salvation and, consequently, to obey Christ. However, those ordained to the ministerial priesthood are called to such obedience in a special way. They are to rule in the Church as servants, who obey unto death and who communicate the mercy of Christ, the High Priest. For this very reason, they are called to this obedience in a more intense way.

Example and Exemplar of Loving Obedience

Christ's obedience is a lesson and a graphic example in charity. Moreover, it is the source and the model for our own friendship with God, and with others in God, and because of God. The Holy Spirit has been poured into our hearts (Rom 5:5), and through him we have a supernatural friendship with Christ.

Thus, Jesus said: "Abide in me, and I in you. As the branch cannot bear fruit by itself, unless it abides in the vine, neither can you, unless you abide in me. I am the vine, you are the branches. He who abides in me, and I in him, he it is that bears much fruit, for apart from me you can do nothing" (Jn 15:4–5). These words are the foundation for everything the ordained priest *does*.

The entirety of priestly ministry is founded upon a *relationship* with Christ. To abide in Christ means to enter into a relationship of friendship with him. Such a relationship is analogous to the one between God the Father and the Son.

Christ's Love and Obedience

Christ's love for his Father is *manifested* in his obedience unto death. Analogously, our friendship with Christ is *manifested in our obedience to him*. For this reason, the Lord says: "If you keep my commandments, you will abide in my love, just as I have kept my Father's commandments and abide in His love" (Jn 15:10).[98]

The friendship referred to here is clearly supernatural.[99] It assumes all of the elements explained in chapter 4. Thus, it is a mutual and known benevolence between Christ and the future priest, a benevolence founded upon a certain "*communicatio*."

The Lord freely loves our person and wills for us good "things" for our own sake. The highest degree of friendship, often called "virtuous" friendship, is the one elevated to the supernatural level in our relationship of charity with God. This is the kind of friendship that God has for us. He wills our good for our own sake. He does not subordinate his love for us to some sort of usefulness or pleasure.

Before God's infinite goodness and perfection, we will always be useless (*achreioi*) servants (see Lk 17:10). Whatever good we can give God, was given to us by him beforehand: "Who has given a gift to him that he might be repaid?" (see Rom 11:35). As Paul teaches elsewhere, "What have you that you did not receive?" (1 Cor 4:7).

The concrete way by which God loves our good for its own sake is by willing our sanctification or salvation and the things needed to that end (see 1 Thes 4:3). God loved the world and sent his only Son not to judge the world but to save it (see Jn 3:16–17). Christ came so that we may have life and have it in abundance (see Jn 10:10). In this relationship, it was God who loved us first. *His is the initiative; ours is the responsibility.*[100]

God teaches how to love by loving us, especially when we were sinners (see Rom 5:8–9). Jesus, *the* teacher, gave his own life

---

98 See also Aquila, "The Priest as a Man of Charity," 39–44.

99 See Matthew Kauth, *Charity as Divine and Human Friendship: A Metaphysical and Scriptural Explanation According to the Thought of St. Thomas Aquinas* (Charlotte, NC: Saint Benedict Press, 2012).

100 See MD, 29.

for us, for his friends (see 1 Jn 3:16). Each and every one of us can say with Paul that Christ "loved me and gave himself up for me" (Gal 2:20). As a result, we are called to respond: to love *as* Christ has loved us (see Jn 13:34).

My Own Know Me

Further, our friendship with Christ is mutually known and reciprocal, a reciprocal love known to both parties: "I am the good shepherd; I know my own and my own know me" (Jn 10:14).[101] Although we cannot add any good to God's infinite perfection, we can certainly will to manifest and communicate it. We can seek God's greater glory.[102] Utility and pleasure also have their own place in charity. Just as the highest degree of human friendship integrates utility and pleasure without making of them its main motive, so our friendship with God makes us useful to him under a certain aspect (*secundum quid*).

Without usefulness being the main motive for love, in charity, we are useful to the Lord under a certain aspect, just as God is useful to us (see 2 Tm 2:21; Ti 3:7–8; Ws 8:16). Similarly, we can make a case for pleasure. God's friends delight and rejoice in him (see Ps 33:9; Phil 4:4). In turn, God is also well-pleased in those who love him (see Prv 8:31).[103]

Our friendship with Christ is founded upon a certain *communicatio*. The Father, who gave us his only Son, will also give us every sort of good that grants us access to God's intimate life (see Rom 8:32).[104] Thomas explains that "we are made lovers

---

101 See *ST* I–II, q. 65, a. 5, c.

102 See *ST* I, q. 19, a. 2, c; II–II, q. 132, a. 1, c.

103 *SCG* IV. 22.

104 *In II Sent.*, d. 26, q. 1, a. 1, ad 2.

of God by the Holy Spirit."[105] The Spirit conforms us to Christ, making our friendship with him possible.

Friendship with Christ is also founded upon the communication of secrets. Aquinas explains: "This is the proper mark of friendship: that one reveals his secrets to his friend. For, since charity unites affections and makes, as it were, one heart of two, one seems not to have dismissed from his heart that which he reveals to a friend."[106] For this reason, while for some Christ's message appears in parables, the secrets of the Kingdom have been revealed to us (see Mk 4:11). No human eye has seen and no human ear has heard what God has prepared for his children; yet, these are the things "God has revealed to us through the Spirit. For the Spirit searches everything, even the depths of God" (1 Cor 2:9–10).

Our Hidden Life in Christ

In turn, we are also to have a hidden life in Christ, so as to taste of the intimacy that friends enjoy (see Col 3:3). The Holy Spirit conforms us to Christ, making us capable of the contemplation of God and conversation with him. Accordingly, Aquinas also explains that "this appears to be especially proper to friendship: really to converse with the friend. Now, the conversation of man with God is by contemplation of Him . . . Since, therefore, the Holy Spirit makes us lovers of God, we are in consequence established by the Holy Spirit as contemplators of God" (see Phil 3:20; 2 Cor 3:18).[107]

Moreover, friendship with Christ consists in a love whereby there is a communication or communion of intellect and will. As we know, Thomas often uses the word "concord" to signify just

---

105 *SCG* IV. 21.

106 Ibid.

107 *SCG* IV. 22.

such a communion.[108] In this hidden and intimate life in Jesus, in this supernatural friendship with him, the Christian is called to think with the mind of Christ, to have the same feelings as Jesus, to will freely what Christ wills and to educate accordingly one's thoughts and feelings (see 1 Cor 2:16).

As Thomas explains, "It is proper to friendship to consent to a friend in what he wills. Of course, the will of God is set forth for us by His precepts. Therefore, it belongs to the love by which we love God that we fulfill His commandments . . . Hence, since we are established as God's lovers by the Holy Spirit, by Him, too, we are in a way driven to fulfill the precepts of God" (see Jn 14:15; Rom 8:14).[109]

Jesus expresses it simply but profoundly: "You are my friends if you do what I command you" (Jn 15:14). The Lord is asking us to make a gift of our own will to him. Once again, the gratuitous initiative belongs to God; ours is the responsibility. He is the example and the exemplar for this loving obedience.

Spiritual Exercises in Observance and Obedience

After providing the essential knowledge to understand the virtues of observance and obedience, we will conclude our reflections, offering some spiritual exercises in these virtues.

	I desire to prepare myself for my future promise of observance and obedience to my bishop.
	I find a certain obstacle or resistance within me to observance and obedience due to my egalitarian upbringing.

108 See *ST* II–II, q. 29, a. 1, c.

109 *SCG* IV. 22.

	I find a certain resistance to observance and obedience because of my desires for autonomy.
	Sometimes I wish priestly formation could take place without another's direction.
	I experience my priestly formation not as a heteronomous but as a participated theonomy.
	In the past, I used to identify myself as "spiritual" but not "religious."
	I value observance and obedience as the defenders of every other virtue.
	I experience observance and obedience as authentic ways of participating in the seminary community in view of its common good.
	Christ crucified is my model for priestly observance and obedience at the seminary.
	I have experienced the apostolic dimension of priestly obedience in its connection with observance by acknowledging and loving the Church's hierarchical structure.
	I have experienced the communitarian dimension of priestly obedience as authentic and solidarious participation.
	I have experienced the pastoral dimension of obedience as gift of self.
	I have a certain ease in acknowledging the excellence and dignity of my superiors at the seminary.
	I honor those responsible for my priestly formation, witnessing my reverence toward them by external signs.
	I honor my superiors, intending to promote that other members of the seminary community may reverence them as well.
	I dishonor those responsible for my priestly formation by backbiting them.
	I have a difficulty in honoring my superiors because I always compare myself to them and I think that I am more virtuous.

	The acknowledgement of my superiors' excellence and dignity moves me to desire to be subject and subordinated to them.
	I acknowledge that I have a debt toward those responsible for my priestly formation, which I will never be able to repay to them.
	I acknowledge that those responsible for my priestly formation collaborate with God and extend, as it were, my parents' mission. I envision those responsible for my priestly formation as spiritual fathers and mothers.
	I am grateful to those responsible for my priestly formation.
	I have the prompt will to give myself to the things concerning the service of those responsible for my priestly formation.
	I have meditated on how much my superiors do for me, and how much they have sacrificed in order to accomplish their mission.
	I have meditated on my own shortcomings and my need for "parental" guidance in my seminary formation.
	Even when I think that my superior is wicked, I am still able to honor him for his dignity of being God's instrument and because of the dignity and excellence of the entire seminary community.
	I have prayed with Phil 2:3, asking God to give me the grace to esteem others as better than myself.
	Even when I do not understand all the reasons behind my superior's commands, at least I trust them and I understand that in their moral insight, they want my good and that they belong to the authoritative commanding institution God's providence has put me in.
	I obey my legitimate superiors because through them, I want to obey God.
	My pride is an obstacle for my growth in observance and obedience.

	I have experienced the joy of the gift of self, inherent in the sacrifice and oblation of my own will to God, and to those responsible for my priestly formation.
	I have prayed and meditated on Christ as the exemplar and example of humble obedience in Phil 2:8–9.
	I have prayed and meditated on Christ as the exemplar and example of justice and justification in Rom 5:19.
	I have prayed and meditated on Christ as the exemplar and example of learning obedience in Heb 5:8–9. I have contemplated how fitting this experience is for me and for my future exercise of priestly authority in the Church.
	I have prayed and meditated on Christ as the exemplar and example of loving obedience in Jn 15:4–14.
	I understand the responsibility and burden inherent in positions of authority and leadership.
	I have a hidden life in Christ.
	My obedience is rooted in my friendship with Christ.
	I experience my obedience as a self-gift to God and the Church.

CHAPTER 6

RELIGION AND PIETY

THE VALUE OF RELIGION AND PIETY

IN this chapter, we will continue to exercise spiritually within this particular realm of justice, unveiled by the general virtue of observance. We will look at piety and religion from the perspective of charity, that is, as perfected by supernatural grace, by the infused virtues, and by the gifts of the Holy Spirit.

As is known, the English word "piety" comes from the Latin "*pietas*" and from the Greek "*eusebia.*" At the same time, "piety" also signifies what is meant by "*religio,*" "*latria,*" and "*theosebia.*" Aquinas explains this multiplicity of words by pointing out that "some special and supreme mode [of obedience] is owed to God, because in Him is the supreme reason of majesty and lordship."[1]

Some people use the term piety "inasmuch as it is ordered toward the bringing about of devotion."[2] Others call it *theosebia* (divine worship) or *eusebia* (good worship), as "it is ordered toward an attentive intention."[3] Still others call it *latria* or service, because "it is ordered toward works in recognition of God's lordship, works that are suitable to Him from the law of creation."[4] This same virtue "is also called religion insofar as it is ordered toward

---

1 *In III Sent.*, d. 9, q. 1, a. 2, qc. 1, c. See also *De Civitate Dei*, X.

2 Ibid.

3 Ibid. See *ST* II–II, q. 80, a. 1, ad 4.

4 *In III Sent.*, d. 9, q. 1, a. 2, qc. 1, c.

the determination of works to which man determines himself by binding himself in God's worship."[5]

Lastly, the English term "piety" is also used to signify both the kind of honor and respect that is due to one's parents, and one of the gifts of the Holy Spirit whereby we honor God as his adoptive children in Christ. Following Thomas's mature theology, I will use the term "religion" to refer to the specific virtue whereby one honors and worships God's supreme excellence.[6] Also, I will restrict my use of the term "piety" to signify either the virtue by which we honor our parents, or the Holy Spirit's gift just mentioned.

The virtues of piety and religion are important for our everyday lives as Christians and future priests. They help us to place ourselves exactly where we belong within the hierarchy of the universe.[7] They also aid us to grow in the awareness of our *filial* and *created* condition. In the natural order, one is first a son, then a spouse, and then a father. The supernatural order must find a certain correspondence with this natural sequence. As Fr. Dewan likes to say, "Grace not only completes but also *imitates* nature."[8]

Hence, the virtues of religion and piety place us at the beginning of this process. Within seminary formation, they teach us how to

---

5 *In III Sent.*, d. 9, q. 1, a. 2, qc. 1, c.

6 For a more scientific study of St. Thomas Aquinas's sources and main texts concerning piety, see José Antonio Senovilla García, "La Virtud de La Piedad En Santo Tomás de Aquino: Fuentes y Análisis Textual" (Universidad de Navarra, 2004); Robert Jared Staudt, "Religion as a Virtue: Thomas Aquinas on Worship Through Justice, Law, and Charity," (Ave Maria University, 2008); Dewan, *Wisdom and Law*, 349–373; Reinhard Hütter, "Happiness and Religion: Why the Virtue of Religion Is Indispensable for Attaining the Final End: A Re-Lecture of Thomas Aquinas with an Eye to His Contemporary Relevance," *Nova et Vetera, English Edition* 14, no. 1 (2016): 15–60.

7 See Farrell, *The Fullness of Life*, 254.

8 Dewan, *Wisdom and Law*, 358.

be better sons in order to be better priests, that is, better spiritual spouses and fathers. They help us to realize how much we have *received* from God and from our parents.

These two virtues transport the human person into a deeper awareness of our being dependent rational animals. They make us embrace our dependency from the viewpoint of the logic of the gift: "The main reason for rendering worship to God is to signify that *whatever a man has, he received from God and that he depends on Him for his entire perfection.*"[9] Indeed, "since all things in us are from God, we must exhibit *latria* to God according to all things."[10] For this reason, the Lord must always be present in our actions: "Out of all things we call Him to mind, thus also out of all things we honor Him."[11]

Religion is the greatest of the moral virtues.[12] It draws the future priest close to God. It enables the seminarian to offer up any good deed of any virtue to God as a spiritual sacrifice of worship.[13] Since Christ's spousal and priestly self-offering for the Church on the Cross reveals the full truth about the human vocation, the virtue of religion re-dimensions our entire life in light of this full truth, in light of the spousal meaning of our body and vocation to the gift of self.[14]

Within the context of the seminary community, the virtue of piety has a very important value. It places the whole of priestly formation as a continuation or extension, as it were, of the family's mission. Since grace not only elevates but also imitates nature, the rediscovery of the father figure inherent to the virtue of piety aids the future priest in relating to God as Father. Likewise, such

---

9 *Super Heb.*, cap. 7, lect. 1, no. 330. Emphasis added.

10 *In III Sent.*, d. 9, q. 1, a. 3, qc. 3, c.

11 Ibid.

12 See *ST* II–II, q. 80, a. 6, c.

13 See *ST* II–II, q. 82, a. 1, ad 1.

14 See GS, 22, 24.

a rediscovery also helps the seminarian to relate to other spiritual fathers at the seminary community in his exercises in the virtue of observance.

Within this same context, it is quite difficult to overestimate the importance of the virtue of religion. Its cultivation is an essential primary stage for any promotion of vocations to the priesthood.[15] Furthermore, this virtue should lead the future priest to participate in Jesus's filial dialogue with the Father. Establishing the model for any seminary, Christ called his disciples to be with him and to be sent out (see Mk 3:13–15). During this formational time, Jesus wanted his disciples "to be witnesses of his silent prayer to the Father."[16]

Following that same model, as Pope St. John Paul II explains, future priests should have an "experience of the genuine meaning of Christian prayer, as a living and personal meeting with the Father through the only begotten Son under the action of the Spirit, a dialogue that becomes a sharing in the filial conversation between Jesus and the Father."[17] Moreover, the priestly life of prayer also translates into pastoral activity. As we read in the Scriptures, "Religion that is pure and undefiled before God and the Father is this: to visit orphans and widows in their affliction, and to keep oneself unstained from the world" (Jas 1:27).

In fact, formation in the virtue of religion is essential for the priest's future mission as teacher: "One aspect of the priest's mission, and certainly *by no means a secondary aspect*, is that he is to be a 'teacher of prayer'. However, the priest *will only be able to train others in this school of Jesus at prayer if he himself has been trained in it and continues to receive its formation*."[18]

---

15 See PDV, 38.

16 Ibid., 42.

17 Ibid., 47.

18 Ibid. Emphasis added.

Therefore, every seminary should foster human formation in the acquired virtue of religion as the human and natural substratum for the future priest's life of devotion and prayer. The virtue of religion regulates the entire liturgical life of a seminary or a parish.

Perhaps there is no other acquired virtue in which the objective and intimate connection between human and spiritual formation is made more evident than here. At the same time, the virtue of religion connects human and intellectual formation, thanks to the integrating role of the spiritual life. For this reason, John Paul II explains that "intellectual formation in theology and formation in the spiritual life, in particular the life of prayer, meet and strengthen each other, without detracting in any way from the soundness of research or from the spiritual tenor of prayer."[19]

The pope then quotes a beautiful passage from Bonaventure in order to illustrate this point: "Let no one think that it is enough for him to read if he lacks devotion, or to engage in speculation without spiritual joy, or to be active if he has no piety, or to have knowledge without charity, or intelligence without humility, or study without God's grace, or to expect to know himself if he is lacking the infused wisdom of God."[20]

Yet the value of religion is in great need of rehabilitation in our Western culture, wherefrom emerge many of our candidates to the priesthood. More and more in these days, people consider religion as superstition, as something contrary to progress. The word "religion" is often used to signify an arbitrary set of private beliefs without rational grounds, which is imposed on others by way of psychological manipulation or other forms of violence.[21] This usage greatly contributes to religion being outlawed from

19 PDV, 53.

20 Ibid.

21 See Hütter, "Happiness and Religion," 18.

the public square. It also hampers an authentic view of religious freedom. The latter is not based on the alleged right to privacy.[22]

Rather, religious freedom is grounded on one's *rights and obligations concerning the truth*: "All men should be at once impelled by nature and also bound by a moral obligation to seek the truth, especially religious truth. They are also bound to adhere to the truth, once it is known, and to order their whole lives in accord with the demands of truth."[23] Other times, religion is rejected in favor of being "spiritual." In this way, religion is conceived as an institutionalized and intolerant set of organized beliefs and ethical values, which are not up for grabs according to one's whims.

All of these uses are defective. We need to rediscover that religion is absolutely necessary for our happiness here on earth and for the attainment of our final end in heaven. We need to reclaim the true meaning of this virtue. It should be rehabilitated as the good operative habit whereby one truthfully honors and worships God's excellence and supreme dignity, by means of the internal acts of devotion and prayer, and by means of the external acts of adoration, sacrifice, oblation, tithes, and vows.

After these introductory reflections, let us pause and reflect on the following questions:

(1) What does lack of piety and religion do to my life?
(2) What does lack of piety and religion do to the life of the seminary?
(3) What will lack of piety and religion do in my future life as a priest?
(4) What will my incapacity to be an example of piety and religion mean for the life of my spiritual children?
(5) How will my growth in the virtue of piety and religion impact

---

22 See Janet E. Smith, *The Right of Privacy* (San Francisco: Ignatius Press, 2008).

23 DH, 2.

my life as a seminarian and as a future priest, as well as the life of those around me in the seminary, and in my future parish?

UNIQUE SERVICE AND WORSHIP TO GOD'S LORDSHIP

The origin of the word "religion" is uncertain. It could find its root in the verb *relegit*, to read again. So, religion would be all about reading again the things that pertain to God's worship, because we ought to frequently ponder this in our hearts.[24] However, religion could come from *religare*, to bind together or to bind again.[25] In this manner, religion would be all about binding ourselves to God, clinging to him as our last end.

Whatever etymology of "religion" is the most accurate, what is clear is that it speaks about our relationship with God. It directs the human person to him. It binds man to God as his most radical principle and final end. Lordship belongs to God in this supreme way.[26]

The virtue of religion makes us grow in the awareness of the psalmist's words: "Know that the Lord is God! / It is he that made us, and we are his; / we are his people, and the sheep of his pasture" (Ps 100:3). Only in the sincere gift of self to him does our life find its true meaning.[27] Such a gift is another way of expressing the service and worship that is due to him.

Those who belong to religious orders manifest in a visible and special way the religious character that belongs to the life of every Christian.[28] Although not all religious men and women are holy,

---

24 *ST* II–II, q. 81, a. 1, c.

25 See *SCG* III. 119.

26 *ST* II–II, q. 81, a. 1, ad 3.

27 See GS, 24.

28 See *ST* II–II, q. 81, a. 1, ad 5.

every holy man or woman is religious, whether he or she belongs to an order or not. In short, we should all give ourselves in sacrifice for God, thereby imitating Christ's sacrificial self-offering for the Church (see Eph 5:25).

We should all make of our lives a spiritual host (see Rom 12:1). Such offering commands acts of other virtues as well. For instance, when a seminarian studies, by having a religious attitude, he can thus perform an elicited act of the virtue of studiousness, but also a commanded sacrificial act of religion. Similarly, when he visits those who are sick, he is performing an elicited act of the virtue of mercy, but also a commanded act of the virtue of religion.[29]

Religion is an annexed virtue to justice. Like justice, religion is ordered to another, and it deals with a legal debt. Unlike justice, in religion, one cannot exactly repay what is received.[30] As the psalmist says, "What shall I render to the Lord / for all his bounty to me?" (Ps 116:12).

Religion's debt is one of *inequality*.[31] "Whatever man renders to God is due, yet it cannot be equal, as though man rendered to God as much as he owes Him."[32] As I explained, a person becomes another's debtor in different ways, depending on the other's excellence and on the diverse benefits received from him.[33]

Religion is directly concerned with God. It deals with God's excellence and with the favors he bestows on us in his providence and government, as our supreme and most radical principle of being and conduct, and as our final end and ultimate happiness. No one has God's excellence and no one bestows gifts on us like God.

---

29 See *ST* II–II, q. 81, a. 1, ad 1.

30 See *In III Sent.*, d. 33, q. 3, a. 4.

31 See *ST* II–II, q. 80, a. 4, ad 3.

32 *ST* II–II, q. 80, a. 1, c.

33 See *ST* II–II, q. 101, a. 1, c.

Lordship belongs to God in a unique way. He is the Creator. He governs all things and has dominion over them. He is "the Alpha and the Omega, the first and the last, the beginning and the end" (Rev 22:13).

Religion is a tribute to these truths. "Consequently, a special kind of service is due to him, which is known as *latria* in Greek; and therefore it belongs to religion."[34] There is a unique service and worship that is owed to God's lordship. Such service and worship is closely linked not only with the Holy Spirit's gift of piety, but also with that of fear of the Lord. In the latter, we reverence God in the contemplation of his perfection and our imperfection.[35]

Yet God is not the object but the end of religion. The latter is not a theological virtue. Religion is about the debt owed to God and the actions by which we serve and worship him.[36]

Worship of God

God is to be worshipped with both internal acts of the heart and external actions that have to do with corporeal things. We do not pay worship to God because he needs it or because it adds anything to him. We worship him for our own sake "because by the very fact that we revere and honor God, *our mind is subjected to Him*; wherein its perfection consists, since a thing is perfected by being subjected to its superior."[37] We worship God so that our heart, mind, or spirit (*mens*) may be subjected to him. In this sense, we are to worship God in spirit and truth.

True worship is a movement in which our heart is in harmony with God. As Thomas explains, religion "consists in the act

34 *ST* II–II, q. 81, a. 1, ad 3. See Farrell, *The Fullness of Life*, 252.

35 See *De Spe*, q. 1, a. 4, ad 2; *ST* II–II, q. 80, a. 2, ad 1.

36 See *ST* II–II, q. 80, a. 4, c., ad 2.

37 *ST* II–II, q. 81, a. 7, c.

whereby we worship God by subjecting ourselves to Him. This act ought to be in harmony with the one who is worshipped and with the one who does the worshipping. Now He who is worshipped, being a spirit, cannot be contacted by the body but only by the spirit [*mens*]. Consequently, his adoration consists chiefly in the act of the heart [*mens*], by which the mind [*mens*] is oriented to God." (see Jn 4:24).[38]

The External Signs of Religion

To be sure, considered in themselves and according to their own importance or value, the internal acts of religion take precedence over the external ones. However, we are rational animals whose knowledge and love begins with sensible things. We need visible signs of invisible realities.

As Thomas explains, "It is connatural for man to receive knowledge through his senses, and since it is very difficult to transcend sensible objects, divine provision has been made for man so that a reminder of divine things might be made for him, even in the order of sensible things."[39] God has offered this help so that "the intention of man might be better recalled to divine matters, even in the case of the man whose mind is not strong enough to contemplate divine things in themselves. And it was for this reason that sensible sacrifices were instituted."[40]

Thus, in the pedagogical order of generation, the external acts of religion come first.[41] For this reason, Aquinas explains that "the human mind, in order to be united to God, needs to be guided by the sensible world."[42] Good and beautiful liturgy, for instance, is

38 *Super De Trinitate*, q. 3, a. 2, c. *ST* II–II, q. 81, a. 7, ad 1.

39 *SCG* III. 119.

40 Ibid.

41 See *De Civitate Dei*, X. 5.

42 *ST* II–II, q. 81, a. 7, c.

foundational. The use of corporeal things at the liturgy is meant to elicit all the interior acts of religion. It is meant to help us grow in devotion and prayer.

For this reason, it is part of the virtue of religion to take good care of the liturgy in the seminary community. Liturgy, without the internal acts of religion, is empty and hypocritical. However, liturgy is also the pedagogue that elicits devotion, prayer, and ultimately, union with God. Indeed, "in the Divine worship it is necessary to make use of corporeal things, that man's mind may be aroused thereby, as by signs, to the spiritual acts by means of which he is united to God. Therefore, the internal acts of religion take precedence of the others and belong to religion essentially, while its external acts are secondary, and subordinate to the internal acts."[43]

Moreover, to understand the full value of spiritually exercising in the virtue of religion, we should remember that we do not render cult to God because he needs it. We do not bow to God because he needs it as children need breakfast to be prepared for them.[44] Instead, we bow, kneel, or prostrate ourselves with great devotion, "so that a true opinion concerning God may be strengthened in us, even by means of sensible things."[45] We are in desperate need to fight against idolatry. In a certain sense, "from the sin of idolatry all other sins arise."[46]

Whence, our minds or hearts greatly need to be stimulated. They need to grow accustomed to love God above all things and all persons. They need to form the good operative habit of worshiping God alone. They need to spiritually exercise in the virtue of religion by means of external actions: "This kind of exterior worship is

---

43 *ST* II–II, q. 81, a. 7, c. See also *Super De Trinitate*, q. 3, a. 2, c.

44 See Farrell, *The Fullness of Life*, 256–57.

45 *SCG* III. 120. See also *Super Rom.*, cap. 1, lect. 7.

46 *Super I Cor.*, cap. 12, lect. 1, no. 713. See Wis 14:27.

necessary to man so that man's mind may be aroused to a spiritual reverence for God. Now, for the mind of man to be moved toward something custom plays a great part, since we are easily moved toward objectives that have become customary."[47]

Devotion and Spiritual Worship

The main act of the virtue of religion whereby we repay God for all the good things he gives, as Alpha and Omega, is devotion. This act is often confused with a sentimental array of fuzzy, warm, and overdone feelings. In reality, however, true devotion has to do with a sacrificial spiritual worship.

Devotion is a claim of love. It brings out "the best in man, lifting him out of himself, putting even superior things in his power."[48] St. Paul describes devotion when he urges the community in Rome with the following words: "I appeal to you therefore, brethren, by the mercies of God, to present your bodies as a living sacrifice, holy and acceptable to God, which is your spiritual worship" (Rom 12:1).

The term "devotion" comes from the Latin verb *devovere*, to sacrifice or to consecrate. A devout seminarian consecrates or dedicates himself to God, sacrificially subjecting himself totally to him. As a result, devotion is "the will to give oneself readily to things concerning the service of God."[49]

Devotion is both a special act and a mode of acting. One can be devout. But one can also do things devoutly. Every other moral virtue is about something that can be ordered to God. Thus, "religion approaches nearer to God than the other moral virtues,

---

47 *SCG* III. 120.

48 Farrell, *The Fullness of Life*, 253.

49 *ST* II–II, q. 82, a. 1, c.

in so far as its actions are directly and immediately ordered to the honor of God."[50]

The act of devotion is capable of referring all other virtues to God's service. Indeed, "since devotion is an act of the will whereby a man offers himself for the service of God Who is the last end, it follows that devotion prescribes the mode to human acts, whether they be acts of the will itself about things directed to the end, or acts of the other powers that are moved by the will."[51] Every act of moral virtue can be performed with devotion. It can be offered up to God: "Every virtuous deed is said to be a sacrifice, insofar as it is done out of reverence of God."[52]

As Aquinas also says: "Every deed, insofar as it is done in God's honor, belongs to religion, not as eliciting but as commanding."[53] Or again: "The very fact that we wish to cling to God in a spiritual fellowship pertains to reverence for God: and consequently the act of any virtue assumes the character of a sacrifice through being done in order that we may cling to God in holy fellowship."[54]

For this reason, Francis de Sales considers devotion in a very broad sense and from the perspective of charity as "a virtue extremely pleasing to the Divine Majesty."[55] In his proposal, devotion encompasses all of the other virtues as referred to God. Consequently, the devout life becomes synonymous with a holy life.[56]

---

50 *ST* II–II, q. 81, a. 6, c.

51 *ST* II–II, q. 82, a. 1, ad 1.

52 Ibid.

53 *ST* II–II, q. 81, a. 4, ad 2. See also *Super De Trinitate*, q. 3, a. 2, c; *ST* II–II, q. 85, a. 3, c.

54 *ST* II–II, q. 85, a. 3, ad 1.

55 Francis de Sales, *An Introduction to the Devout Life* (Dublin: M. H. Gill and Son, 1885), 1.

56 Aquinas also explains that there is only a distinction of reason between sanctity and the virtue of religion. See *ST* II–II, q. 81, a. 8, c.

As a mode of acting, devotion permeates other acts with a priestly attitude of sacrifice, described as such by Paul in Rom 12:1. For instance, a seminarian can devoutly study or do dishes. The act of devotion "presides over all our action in this domain of religion."[57] It permeates everything we do with a *rationabile obsequium*, that is, with a giving of one's whole self to God in the awareness that we are creatures and that without God, we are nothing.

The Devout Seminarian

How can a seminarian grow in devotion? Of course, devotion is something that can be asked of God in prayer. Moreover, a future priest can grow in devotion out of his charity for God. There is a reciprocal relationship of enrichment between devotion and charity.

A devout seminarian is such because of his love for God. At the same time, his devotion nourishes his friendship with Christ: "charity both causes devotion (inasmuch as love makes one ready to serve one's friend) and feeds on devotion. Even so all friendship is safeguarded and increased by the practice and consideration of friendly deeds."[58]

Another way of growing in one's devotion is cultivating the virtue of humility. The latter suppresses our presumptuous hopes based on reverence for God and on proper self-knowledge. Thus, in humility, "the chief reason for suppressing presumptuous hope is based on *divine reverence*, which shows that man ought not to ascribe to himself more than is competent to him according to the position in which God has placed him."[59]

---

57 Dewan, *Wisdom and Law*, 361.

58 *ST* II–II, q. 82, a. 2, ad 2.

59 *ST* II–II, q. 161, a. 2, ad 3. Emphasis added. Thomas again mentions reverence for God as the motive for humility in II–II, q. 161, a. 4, ad 1.

Still another practical way to grow in one's devotion consists in exercising in a particular meditation. Since devotion is an act of the will, it has a motive in a consideration of the intellect, for there is nothing willed that is not first known (*nihil volitum nisi praecognitum*). We will a good that we understand as such. To be sure, many intellectuals are not devout, while many devout people are not very intellectually cultivated. However, the problem with the former is not in the knowledge about God, but in the pride with which one puffs himself up in knowing philosophy or theology.[60]

Granted a humble attitude, a way to elicit one's devotion consists in meditating on God's goodness. A priest or a seminarian should never be too busy to think about God.

The future priest should consider God's goodness throughout his own life. The seminarian should be very attentive to dispel the lies of the devil concerning God's loving presence in particularly difficult situations. The candidate to the priesthood should appeal to his own faith in order to realize that God is at work in all things, as well as in those sufferings that he allowed, for the good of those who love him (see Rom 8:28). Thomas explains that such meditation "wakens love which is the proximate cause of devotion."[61]

Meditation for Devotion

A seminarian should meditate on his own sins and shortcomings in light of God's loving goodness. If he has never done a general confession, this exercise could also be quite helpful. The consideration of one's sins elicits gratitude and love toward God. Moreover, it also awakens our consciousness of needing to lean on God. As a result, such meditation combats the presumption and

60 See *ST* II–II, q. 82, a. 3, ad 3.

61 *ST* II–II, q. 82, a. 3, c.

pride "whereby man is hindered from submitting to God, because he leans on his own strength."[62]

Such spiritual exercises entail a certain spiritual joy (*spiritualem laetitiam mentis*).[63] Devout priests are happy priests. In fact, the consideration of God's goodness moves the will to a gift of self, to a total surrender to God that makes one deeply joyful. Even the consideration of one's sins engenders joy insofar as it elicits hope in the Divine Assistance.

Another way to get to this devout attitude consists in meditating on one's conscience as a tabernacle where God's voice can be heard.[64] In Christian morality, something is obligatory or commanded because it is truly good and not vice-versa.[65] Moral conscience is the subjective measure of the morality of one's actions that ought to be well formed.

Consequently, moral conscience is not the supreme or highest norm of human conduct, but only the closest understanding the subject has concerning the morality of one's actions. Within one's conscience, one experiences moral obligation as resulting from a good to be done or an evil to be avoided.[66] Such obligation is in reality an interpersonal experience wherein one is called to a *rationabile obsequium* to God-the-Creator.

Moral obligation implies a certain sacrificial devout offering of oneself out of love. Wojtyła explains it as follows: "The tension arising between the objective order of norms and the inner freedom

---

62 See *ST* II–II, q. 82, a. 3, ad 3.

63 See *ST* II–II, q. 82, a. 4.

64 See GS, 16. For a good and broad study on conscience, see Graziano Borgonovo, *Soggetto Morale E Chiesa: Lutero, Erasmo, Newman, e Guardini a Confronto* (Casale: Edizioni Piemme, 2000).

65 See Karol Wojtyła, *Max Scheler y La Ética Cristiana* (Madrid: BAC, 1980), 135; *De Veritate*, q. 17, a. 3, c and ad 3.

66 See Wojtyła, *The Acting Person*, 156–158; *In II Sent.*, d. 24, q. 2, a. 4, ad 2; *De Veritate*, q. 17, a. 1, ad 4.

of the subject-person is relieved by truth, by the conviction of the truthfulness of good. But it is, on the contrary, intensified and not relieved by external pressures, by the power of injunction or compulsion. This is best formulated in St. Paul, in his demand of *rationabile obsequium*, which is the personalistic synonym of obligation."[67]

In accordance with Wojtyła's interpretation of Vatican II, devotion is one of the ways in which we can participate in Christ's priesthood. According to him, Vatican II is, above all, a pastoral and an ecclesiological council. It poses one foundational question: "Church, what do you say about yourself?"[68]

The answer to this question should inform *both* the *mind* and the *will* of her members. We should regain consciousness of what the Church is all about, according to God's revelation. But for this knowledge to be a true enrichment in the faith, it should also have an impact in our daily lives.

Meditation on the Incarnation

In order to grow in our devotion, we should meditate on Christ's redemptive incarnation as it mediates the mission of the Holy Spirit, and as it confers power to the human person so that he may attain his supernatural vocation of being a son in the Son.[69] Thus, the human person finds meaning in his own existence in the sincere gift of himself, in that gift that is modeled by Christ himself in his spousal love for the Church (see Eph 5:25).[70] Such a gift of self is a participation in Christ's *tria munera*, especially in

67 Wojtyła, *The Acting Person*, 166. For an explanation of this thesis in light of its sources, see my *De la experiencia*, 160–63.

68 Wojtyła, *Sources of Renewal*, 38.

69 See ibid., 78–79.

70 GS, 24.

Christ's priesthood as the summit of his mission as redeemer, of his mediation in the mission of the Spirit, and of his being founder of the Church.[71]

Such a meditation should have a moral impact in our attitudes. It should increase our devotion. As members of the Church, we are called to participate in Christ's *priestly munus* "through the sacraments and the exercise of virtues."[72] We actualize our *priestly munus* when, by our good actions, we cooperate with the grace of the sacraments and devoutly offer our lives to God as a living host.

Hence, participation in Christ's priesthood is the attitude whereby one exercises devotion, the attitude by which the human person gives himself and offers the world to God in the manner of a sacrifice that is true spiritual worship (*rationabile obsequium*) (see Rom 12:1).[73] Wojtyła argues that this attitude "denotes the simplest and most complete attitude."[74] He goes on to clarify that this same attitude refers to GS 24, and it "expresses the *vocation* of the person in its existential nucleus—a vocation referred to by *Gaudium et Spes* in the words to which we must *constantly* return."[75]

Thus, the fulfillment of the attitude of participation, as it is condensed in the participation in Christ's priesthood, entails the exercise of what Thomas Aquinas calls devotion. Wojtyła sees in this devotion the very heart of the moral renewal proposed by the Second Vatican Council. He audaciously claims that, "the attitude which derives from sharing in the priesthood of Christ is seen as

71 See LG, 5; Wojtyła, *Sources of Renewal*, 84.

72 LG, 11; see also Wojtyła, *Sources of Renewal*, 97.

73 PO, 2; Wojtyła, *Sources of Renewal*, 223.

74 Wojtyła, *Sources of Renewal*, 224.

75 Ibid. Emphasis added.

one which contains in a special way *all the richness of faith*, both as regards *content* and as regards subjective *commitment*."[76]

This moral attitude "is at the very center of the teaching of Vatican II and contains in a certain manner *all that the Council wished to say about the Church, mankind and the world*."[77] Participation in Christ's priesthood "is expressed through *participation in the sacraments*."[78] As the future pope explains, "The priesthood of Christ has realized itself through the work of redemption, so that all those who truly participate in it enjoy the fruit of that work, which is holiness. This is the purpose and effect of sharing in Christ's priesthood through the sacraments of the Church."[79]

Anthropology and Metaphysics of Prayer

Prayer is the second internal act of religion. Ultimately, it also arises from love and it should be permeated by devotion; that is, by that prompt and priestly will to the gift of self for God. Just as love elicits devotion, so the latter moves us to prayer.[80]

Any seminarian or priest should be in awe at the fact that we can pray to God, since this action reveals our profound dignity. "Think what happiness is granted thee, what honor bestowed on thee, when thou conversest with God in prayer, when thou talkest with Christ, when thou askest what thou wilt, whatever thou desirest."[81]

Prayer effects spiritual consolation.[82] It is an expression of

---

76 Wojtyła, *Sources of Renewal*, 225. Emphasis added.

77 Ibid. Emphasis added.

78 Ibid., 237.

79 Ibid.

80 See Dewan, *Wisdom and Law*, 361.

81 *ST* II–II, q. 83, a. 2, ad 3.

82 See *ST* II–II, q. 83, a. 15, c.

charity, and it is strongly aided by humility and faith. We ought to pray, asking what is needed for our salvation and that same for others. We are to do so piously and perseveringly.

There are many aspects of prayer that I will have to omit in this brief treatment. I will concentrate only on some essential points, which result from looking at the act of religion we call "prayer" from the anthropological and metaphysical viewpoint. Adopting this peculiar perspective focalizes some fundamental aspects of prayer, which helps us to grow in the virtue of religion, to educate others on how to grow in this same virtue, and to instruct those who will teach about it.

Prayer has often been reduced to an emotional experience. It certainly impacts and involves our emotional life. It has to do with our feelings and desires. Yet, prayer is much more. It is an act of one's heart (*mens*). It involves the highest and most intimate part of our soul: our intellect and our will in their reciprocal synergy.

To be sure, prayer involves the whole person. But it does so in a special manner. Consider the following example. It is the whole man that eats breakfast. However, he does not eat it with his ears, but with his mouth. Similarly, Thomas Aquinas knows well that it is the whole person that prays. Yet the human person does not pray with his feelings or with his will, but rather with his intellect.[83] Equally, it is the whole person who is devout. Yet we are not devout with our intellect but with our will.

No one should be afraid of falling into a certain intellectualism here. The human intellect does not exist in the void. The fact that prayer is an intellectual operation does not mean, for Aquinas, that it has nothing to do with one's will, with one's internal senses, or with one's passions. In fact, although it is an act of the intellect, prayer arises from the devotion, that is, from an act of the will.

83 See *ST* II–II, q. 83, a. 1, c.

Moreover, in order to pray, we use our internal senses. Additionally, prayer clearly elicits feelings and expresses desires. Hence, the fact that prayer is an act of the intellect entails no intellectualism. It is far from excluding other faculties. It only means that every other reality within the human person, every other faculty, contributes to the act of prayer or is affected by such an act from an intellectual perspective.

As Thomas says, prayer (*oratio*) is like spoken reason. In it, the human person speaks his mind to God. It consists in the rising of the spirit or heart (*mens*) to the Lord, to bless and thank him, and to ask of him what is convenient for our eternal salvation or that of others.[84] In so doing, the human person subjects or subordinates his intellect and will to the Lord. This is most evident in petitionary prayer, wherein we manifest our needs to God as the source of every good.

In prayer, we also acknowledge and relate to the Lord what we *know* about ourselves and others. We can even *express* how we feel, or how we respond to the reception of what God has given us. For instance, we can express our gratitude toward him or our fear before a difficult situation.

To Dialogue with God

Yet every act of acknowledging, relating, responding, or expressing something to God is always a communication carried out by the intellect. It is a raising of the human spirit to God in dialogue (*dia-logos*) with him. Consequently, it happens through one's logos or intellect. For this reason, only intelligent beings can pray, because there is no conversation, no dialogue, and no prayer possible without *logos*.[85]

---

84 See *ST* II–II, q. 83, a. 17, c. Antonio Royo Marín, *Teología Moral Para Seglares: Moral Fundamental*, vol. 1 (Madrid: BAC, 1986), 337.

85 See *ST* II–II, q. 83, a. 10, c.

Our dialogue with God in prayer should always be an act of worship in spirit and in truth (see Jn 4:24). It should always be carried out with the fervor of love or devotion, always praying in accordance with the truth of faith. We should always pray with a correct intention and with a certain constancy.

Aquinas explains that prayer is spiritual because it is done "with *fervor of spirit*."[86] It should always avoid pretense and hypocrisy by being truthful, "because no fervent spiritual desire is meritorious unless united to the truth of faith."[87] Indeed, "for a man to merit receiving what he asks, he should ask for things which are not in opposition to the will of the giver, and also ask for them in a way which is acceptable to the giver. And so when we pray to God, we ought to be such as God seeks. But God seeks those who will worship him in spirit and in truth, in the fervor of love and in the truth of faith."[88]

In addition, our dialogue with God should be constant, because the desire which causes prayer, namely, charity, should be constant and without ceasing in our lives. The times of actual prayer during our day are to be long enough to refresh us and continue to enkindle in us this desire. But they should not be so long as to tire our soul and extinguish our charity (see 1 Thes 5:17).[89]

In the case of petitionary prayer, this dialogue involves our intellect in its most practical dimension, that is, in its orientation toward action. When we ask things of God in prayer, we truly act as (secondary) causes of what we are praying for.[90] Aquinas explains this very important and metaphysical topic for a simple

---

86 *Super Io.*, cap. 4, lect. 2, no. 611.

87 Ibid.

88 *Super Io.*, cap. 4, lect. 2, no. 614.

89 *ST* II–II, q. 83, a. 14.

90 See *ST* II–II, q. 83, a. 2, c.; Stephen Brock, "On the Causality of Petitionary Prayer: C. S. Lewis, Peter Geach, and Thomas Aquinas," *Living Faith* 12, no. 2 (2012): 11–22; Dewan, *Wisdom and Law*, 370.

and practical reason. If there were no true causality on our part, there would be no point in asking anything from God in prayer.

THREE ERRORS

This metaphysical and practical topic opens the door to three errors, which need to be avoided in order to make full sense of our life of prayer. The first error consists in concluding that Divine Providence does not regulate human affairs. If such were the case, there would not be a point in praying at all. God simply would not care.

The second error is to postulate that everything happens of necessity. Again, this would render petitionary prayer meaningless. My asking for humility, for instance, would not be a real cause in any way of God giving it to me.

The third error would be to affirm that Divine Providence can change. This other option would certainly make room for petitionary prayer. Yet, it would do so at the high cost of God's perfection. Within this view, I could really be the cause of the healing of my friend's cancer, for example, because I would have changed God's mind about it with my long hours of persistent prayer.

However, can a God who changes his mind be perfect? Can he be God? If God could actually change his mind, did he do it for better or for worse?

Thomas avoids these three potential errors, making full sense of our life of prayer, by explaining our true causality as secondary causes. He focuses on our personal dignity as beings, who can freely collaborate with the Creator, by being the cause of their own obedience to him. Thus, he argues:

> Divine providence disposes not only what effects shall take place, but *also from what causes and in what order these effects shall proceed.* Now among other causes human acts are the causes of certain effects. Wherefore it must be that men do certain actions, not that thereby they may change the Divine disposition, but that

> by those actions they may achieve certain effects according to the order of the Divine disposition: and the same is to be said of natural causes. And so is it with regard to prayer. For we pray not that we may change the Divine disposition, but that we may impetrate that which God has disposed to be fulfilled by our prayers in other words.[91]

In this manner, Aquinas maintains God's immutability of providence. However, this immutability "does not impose necessity on things that are foreseen."[92] At the same time, prayer is not seen as an attempt to change God's mind.

We need to be careful. As I like to tell my students, we will never surprise God. If God heals my friend from cancer, it is because he had already planned to do so. My asking him to heal my friend is truly a cause of this healing. Actually, in his eternal and perfect knowledge, God had already foreseen that I would pray in this way.

Nevertheless, his foreknowledge of my praying did not impose necessity on me praying for my friend's healing. I freely chose to pray in that manner. And God counted on my prayers to bring about his eternal design.

Remember, prayer does not change God but men. Prayer does not change providence but rather fulfills it. As we can see, this brief metaphysics of prayer leads us back to the key religious acknowledgment of our radical dependence on and subordination to God as Alpha and Omega.

Nevertheless, such dependence and subordination belongs, within the perspective of charity, to a relationship of friendship with God. Therein, prayer corresponds to that intimate conversation and *communicatio* of spirits between God and each one of us. In charity, our intellect and will conforms to God's in a secret life hidden in

---

91 *ST* II–II, q. 83, a. 2, c. Emphasis added.

92 *SCG* III. 95.

Christ. As a result, there is a union of hearts, as it were, a certain *concordia*. God's friends are of one mind and will with him.

Consequently, when they pray, they ask fitting things of the Lord. For this reason, it is also appropriate that Divine Providence fulfills their desires presented in prayer.[93] As we read in the psalms: "Take delight in the Lord, / and he will give you the desires of your heart" (Ps 37:4). Indeed, God "fulfills the desire of all who fear him; / he also hears their cry, and saves them" (Ps 145:19). In that sense, Jesus taught that "every one who asks receives, and he who seeks finds, and to him who knocks it will be opened" (Mt 7:8).

Moreover, prayer also belongs within the context of charity and the communion of saints. It is quite important for a seminarian to develop good and lasting friendships with the saints in heaven. Think about your guardian angel and other saintly persons that inspire your devotion. Prayer to them is an important way of doing so.

To be sure, when we pray to the saints, we do not pray to them as we pray to God. He alone gives us grace and glory. Yet our guardian angel or another human person in heaven can help us. They can intercede, advocate, and pray for us.[94] Thus, they can bring our prayers before God (see Rev 8:4).[95]

Furthermore, the perspective of charity reminds us that we should also pray for others, especially for our families, friends, and all the members of the seminary community. Certainly, out of charity, we can also pray for our enemies (see Mt 5:44).[96]

It is of the utmost importance to develop a solid habit of prayer during seminary. A special care should be devoted to the *Liturgy*

---

93 See *SCG* III. 95.

94 See *ST* II–II, q. 83, a. 11.

95 *ST* II–II, q. 83, a. 4, c.

96 *ST* II–II, q. 83, a. 8, c.

of the Hours. The seminarian should not restrict his prayer to communal prayer. That prayer should be done with great devotion and not just going through the motions.

Still, it is also very important to develop the habit of praying privately and in secret. All things being equal, one or two hours a day of silent prayer, preferably before the Blessed Sacrament, would be most appropriate. One would hope to continue this same rhythm prudently as an ordained priest. Pastoral activity is not an obstacle, provided one exercises authentic prudence. For instance, this kind of private prayer could always take place early in the morning or later at night, before or after parishioners need assistance.

For the seminarian, vacation is a sort of laboratory where to test the intensity of his prayer habits. Vacation is not only a time for rest; it also shows the real impact that the life of the seminary has had on the candidate to the priesthood. It manifests if the good habits promoted by the seminary community are sinking in or not. The future priest can examine, while on vacation, if there is in him a prompt inclination to pray with ease and pleasure, or if there is still internal resistance to such a discipline.

The seminarian should leave seminary to rest and be rejuvenated during his vacations but, in a certain sense, the seminary should never leave the seminarian. Within the context of seminary formation, the process of acquiring a solid habit of prayer could be approached gradually. Nevertheless, it should be firmly established by the time of being ordained a deacon.

There are many more things one could say about prayer. However, we need to bring our reflections to a conclusion. Thus, let us make a brief mention to the most perfect of prayers: the "Our Father."[97]

---

97 See *ST* II–II, q. 83, a. 9.

We begin by calling to God as Father, thereby evoking his love for us and our confidence in Him. The way this prayer continues has the great effect of ordering our desires. We pray for our final end: God's glory and his kingdom. We also ask for the necessary means to attain this end, namely, to do God's will and to receive from him our daily bread.

Moreover, in the Our Father, we also ask God to remove any obstacle that may hinder us from the attainment of this end: to forgive our sins, to help us not to fall into temptation, and to deliver us from the Evil One.

Informed by Devotion and Prayer

In reality, the exterior acts of religion are very present in the everyday life of the seminary. They correspond to our entire public liturgical life and to our private religious practices. Among the many things that could be said about this rich topic, I would like to focus on devotion and prayer's key role as the soul, as it were, of our true and spiritual worship. As Thomas says, "It is not enough merely to serve God, which can be done by outward action; we must also please Him by a right intention and by love." [98]

To run through the external acts of religion without the internal ones amounts to hypocrisy. It would entail a sort of lie. There will be no conformity (*adequatio*) between the external and the internal acts. The external acts of religion would be performed without sincerity. They would be counterfeits.

For instance, in the external act of adoration, a seminarian uses his body to reverence God. His external actions are meant to manifest the honor and reverence that is due to the Lord as well as the submission of his will to him.[99] To be sure, true adoration involves

---

98 *Super Heb.*, cap. 12, lect. 5, no. 724.

99 See *ST* II–II, q. 84, a. 3, c.; Royo Marín, *Teología Moral Para Seglares*, 345.

both body and soul. It is a bodily act of worship done in spirit and truth (see Jn 4:23).[100] In adopting humble bodily dispositions like kneeling or prostration, we incite interior reverence.

At the same time, these exterior acts of reverence are to express our interior disposition of devotion: "Exterior adoration is offered on account of interior adoration."[101] We are to show "signs of humility in our bodies in order to incite our affections to submit to God, since it is connatural to proceed from the sensible to the intelligible."[102] For instance, when a seminarian genuflects in the chapel, he is to express an interior attitude of acknowledgment of his weakness before God. When the future priest prostrates himself in prayer, he signifies that he belongs totally to God, that he is not his own anymore, that he has given his life to the Lord in its entirety.[103]

The Interior Disposition

But if our interior disposition is missing, these acts of adoration are not truly such. They have an external semblance of adoration but, in reality, they are a cheap forgery. As Jesus said, "This people honors me with their lips, but their heart is far from me" (Mt 15:8).

We have already spoken about devotion as an inward and spiritual sacrifice. Just as it happens with the bodily acts of adoration, outward sacrifices or oblations should also be animated by that same interior attitude. The outward signs in sacrifices are meant to signify that spiritual inward disposition by which one offers his own soul to God as Alpha and Omega: "The sacrifice that is offered outwardly represents the inward spiritual sacrifice."[104]

---

100 *ST* II–II, q. 84, a. 2, ad 1.

101 *ST* II–II, q. 84, a. 2, c.

102 Ibid.

103 See *ST* II–II, q. 84, a. 2, ad 2.

104 *ST* II–II, q. 85, a. 2, c.

The human person is naturally religious. He has always perceived that he is imperfect and in need of help and guidance from a supreme being, from God.[105] Thus, natural law is the foundation of the acquired virtue of religion, not the other way around.

Revelation assumes and elevates this same natural religiosity. Hence, just as it belongs to the natural law to offer sacrifices to God, it also belongs to the revealed law. Of course, we are not bound to offer animal sacrifices as they were prescribed in the Old Law. They were only a pedagogical tool. However, we are to offer other kinds of sacrifices or oblations.

Thomas Aquinas offers some examples. Other than the spiritual sacrifice of devotion and prayer, one can also offer bodily sacrifices in "martyrdom, and abstinence or continence."[106] Likewise, one can also offer a sacrifice to God by means of one's own material possessions: "We offer a sacrifice to God, directly when we offer our possession to God immediately, and indirectly when we share them with our neighbor for God's sake."[107]

In many countries, the offertory collection during Mass has provided a beautiful opportunity to exercise this kind of sacrificial action.[108] However, in our industrial societies, one does not have the chance to offer the first fruits of one's land nowadays.[109] Nonetheless, one can always give to God the first salary of a new job, or volunteer to do something for the Church in one's new business.

---

105 See *ST* II–II, q. 85, a. 1, c.

106 *ST* II–II, q. 85, a. 2, ad 2.

107 Ibid.

108 See Farrell, *The Fullness of Life*, 272.

109 Thomas treats of first fruits in *ST* II–II, q. 86.

Vows and Promises to God

Making vows or promises to God is another external act of the virtue of religion. Vows are promises to God. By taking these vows, the human person is bound to do or not do certain acts.[110]

The *Catechism* explains that "in many circumstances, the Christian is called to make *promises* to God. Baptism and Confirmation, Matrimony and Holy Orders always entail promises. Out of personal devotion, the Christian may also promise to God this action, that prayer, this alms-giving, that pilgrimage, and so forth. Fidelity to promises made to God is a sign of the respect owed to the divine majesty and of love for a faithful God."[111]

Vows are made for our own profit. They add nothing to God. He does not need them. However, vowing to do something makes our good acts even more meritorious. A vow confers to the will greater fixity on the good, which is the matter of the promise, beyond the here and now. Thereby, it brings the will closer to the perfection of virtue.

Moreover, a vow enhances the material good that is its object by reordering it toward divine worship. Furthermore, he who fulfills a vow subjects or gives himself more to God than he who does the same thing without the aforementioned vow. Definitely, one who gives to another a tree with its fruit gives more to him than the one who just gives the fruit. Similarly, by means of a vow, one not only gives a fruit to God (the performance of a good action), but also its "tree," as it were, because the person vowing relinquishes his willful power to do otherwise. In so doing, he offers to God, as in

---

110 For an interesting development of the notion of vows in Aquinas as applied to marriage, see Mary Catherine Sommers, "Marriage Vows and 'Taking Up a New State,'" *Nova et Vetera, English Edition* 7, no. 3 (2009): 679–95.

111 CCC 2101.

a holocaust, the very source or "tree" wherefrom the good action springs, namely, his will.

It would be very beneficial to look over the rite of ordination to the diaconate and to the priesthood and then meditate on the promises to God that are found there. Their devout fulfillment is one of the ways in which a priest grows in the virtue of religion. One could also make private and personal promises to God that gradually lead to the ones made at the day of ordination.

Tempting God, Idolatry, and Simony

Many of the obstacles to the virtue of religion discussed by Aquinas are completely absent from the life of the seminary. I will concentrate on the ones that I think are most relevant for a future priest: tempting God, idolatry, and simony. In fact, the obstacles to the virtue of religion can be divided into those by way of defect and those by way of excess.

The Obstacle of Irreligion

The first kind of obstacles corresponds to the contrary vice to religion, namely, irreligion. This vice is expressed, for example, when we tempt God, when we put him to the test, acting against the reverence that is due to him. In fact, to tempt God is to be irreverent to him inasmuch as "no one presumes to tempt one of whose excellence he is sure."[112] For this reason, to tempt God is a species of irreligion.[113]

One can tempt God by words in prayer and, sometimes, even by deeds. Moreover, one can tempt God explicitly or implicitly. A future priest "tempts God *explicitly* in his prayers when he asks

---

112 *ST* II–II, q. 97, a. 3, c.

113 See *ST* II–II, q. 97, a. 3, ad 1.

something of God *with the intention of probing God's knowledge, power or will.*"[114]

Moreover, a seminarian *explicitly* tempts God in his deeds "when he intends, by whatever he does, to experiment on God's power, good will or wisdom."[115] On the other hand, it is also possible to tempt God *implicitly* by words or deeds. A future priest falls into this sin "if, though he does not intend to make an experiment on God, yet he asks for or does something which has no other use than to prove God's power, goodness or knowledge."[116]

We do not put to the test something or someone unless we are uncertain about it or about him. The one doubting may be the tempter himself or his audience. When the one doubting is the tempter and the one tempted is God, there is always a sin: "It is a sin to be ignorant of or to doubt that which pertains to God's perfection. Wherefore it is evident that it is a sin to tempt God in order that the tempter himself may know God's power."[117] However, when there is a just motive, for example when it was necessary for the apostles to show God's power to others, there is no sin (see Acts 4:30).

The vices that oppose the virtue of religion by way of excess are manifold. They can be grouped under the vice of superstition: "Superstition is a vice contrary to religion by excess, not that it offers more to the divine worship than true religion, but because it offers divine worship either to whom it ought not, or in a manner it ought not."[118] Thomas Aquinas distinguishes the different kinds of superstition. Out of them, we should concentrate on idolatry.[119]

---

114 *ST* II–II, q. 97, a. 1, c. Emphasis added.

115 Ibid.

116 Ibid.

117 *ST* II–II, q. 97, a. 2, c.

118 *ST* II–II, q. 92, a. 1, c.

119 See *ST* II–II, q. 92, a. 2, c.

The Obstacle of Idolatry

We have already briefly discussed this vice. Idolatry consists in giving unduly divine honor to a creature. No creature is the Alpha and Omega. No creature can be sought as the ultimate source of our happiness. We need to purify ourselves from this kind of infidelity to the Lord.

Religion as *latria* is owed to God alone (see Dt 6:13). No human person and no other creature deserves it. No other being is our Creator. Hence, "man ought to return something special to God in acknowledgment of this special benefit."[120]

Were a seminarian or a priest to offer the cult and service of *latria* to any creature, he would be making an idol. He would be treating this creature as the Lord of lords. However, our own lordship over creation and over our own actions must always be in the Lord. When the human person rebels and does not bow to God in religion, he ends up becoming a slave to sin. He ends up bowing and subjecting his own greatness to many other realities inferior to him.

We are not to offer *latria* even to our own will. Only God deserves this total gift of self or total self-offering of our being: in religion, "our spirit [*mens*] offers itself to God as the principle of its creation, the author of its actions, the end of its happiness. These attributes are, in fact, appropriate to the highest principle of things only."[121]

Indeed, "the creative cause of the rational soul is the highest God alone; moreover, He alone is able to incline the will of man to whatever He wishes . . . man's ultimate felicity consists solely in the enjoyment of Him. Therefore, man ought to offer sacrifice and the cult of *latria* only to the highest God."[122]

---

120 *SCG* III. 120.

121 Ibid.

122 Ibid.

Money, power, pleasure, prestige, etc., are not what truly and ultimately make us happy. Not even our own will does. The virtue of religion fights against the idolatrous temptation of materially identifying the source of our happiness with any being other than God.

As Thomas explains, "Idolatry happens when the honor due God alone is given to creatures. Now there is a twofold honor due God; we must establish him as the goal of our life and we must put our trust of reaching the goal in him."[123]

Whenever we demand ultimate happiness in our life-project from any creature, even if this creature is a human person, we are directly acting against the virtue of religion. For instance, married people who demand from the other spouse ultimate happiness fall into this exact pit. In so doing, they resemble a covetous person: "Whoever places [ultimate happiness] 'in creatures is guilty of idolatry. A covetous person commits this when he fixes his end in a created reality as well as putting all his trust in it."[124] In this sense, the Scriptures warn us: "Cursed is the man who trusts in man" (Jer 17:5).

A seminarian should never fix his end and put all his trust in a human person, be it a priest, spiritual director, catechist, theologian, a bishop, or any other Church leader. Admiration and observance to them is always in order. However, none of them is God. Consequently, the virtue of religion helps the seminary community to be purified from the disordered phenomenon in which seminarians become fans of others, with a disordered and idolatrous love toward them.

---

123 *Super Eph.*, cap. 5, lect. 3.

124 Ibid.

The Obstacle of Sacrilege

Let us also say a brief word about sacrilege. It consists in the violation of a sacred thing deputed for divine worship by being irreverent: "Whatever pertains to irreverence for sacred things is an injury to God, and comes under the head of sacrilege."[125] There are different kinds of sacrilege, corresponding to the different kinds of sacred things.

The gravest sacrilege concerns the sacraments, especially that of the Eucharist. Undeniably, among the sacred things deputed for divine worship, "the highest place belongs to the sacraments whereby man is sanctified: chief of which is the sacrament of the Eucharist, for it contains Christ Himself. Wherefore the sacrilege that is committed against this sacrament is the gravest of all."[126] The life of a seminarian and that of a priest entail daily celebration of the Mass. It should be accompanied with frequent confession and with a growing awareness that grave matter and potential mortal sins are not only the ones concerning sexuality and against the sixth commandment.

The Obstacle of Simony

Another obstacle to the virtue of religion, which may appear in different degrees in the life of a priest, is simony: "By buying or selling a spiritual thing, a man treats God and divine things with irreverence, and consequently commits a sin of irreligion."[127] There is a fine distinction to be made here. Thomas describes simony as the action by which one receives "money for the spiritual grace of the sacraments."[128] No human custom can justify such an act, because

125 *ST* II–II, q. 99, a. 1, c.

126 *ST* II–II, q. 99, a. 3, c.

127 *ST* II–II, q. 100, a. 1, c.

128 *ST* II–II, q. 100, a. 2, c.

it goes against Divine Law. By money, Aquinas understands not only actual currency but also anything that has a pecuniary value.

Yet the Angelic doctor also clarifies that "to receive anything for the support of those who administer the sacraments, in accordance with the statutes of the Church and approved customs, is not simony, nor is it a sin."[129] In order to avoid simony, one needs to look at his own intention; he needs to make sure he does not have the willful aim of doing business. Thus, Aquinas explicitly offers the following advice in order to avoid simony: one needs to make sure that "there be *no intention of buying or selling*, and that *no pressure* be brought to bear on those who are unwilling to give, by withholding spiritual things that ought to be administered, for then there would be an appearance of simony."[130]

Honoring Our Parents

The human person is in debt first and foremost with God. The virtue of piety, properly distinguished from the virtue of religion, is directed to our parents insofar as they have given us life and an education in the virtues. By extension, the virtue of piety is also directed to the society in which we have been raised. Aquinas establishes a very strong comparison between religion and piety: "Just as it belongs to religion to give worship to God, so does it belong to piety, in the second place, to give worship to one's parents and one's country."[131]

One's parents and one's country are seen here as including our kindred and our fellow citizens. They have also contributed, in their own way, to the possibility of our conception and to our education. Therefore, "the worship due to our parents includes the

---

129 *ST* II–II, q. 100, a. 2, c.

130 *ST* II–II, q. 100, a. 3, c. Emphasis added.

131 *ST* II–II, q. 101, a. 1, c.

worship given to all our kindred," and "the worship given to our country includes the worship to all our fellow-citizens and to all the friends of our country."[132]

Piety is also an annexed virtue to justice. Like justice, piety is ordered to another, and it deals with a legal debt. Unlike justice, in piety, one cannot exactly repay what is received. There is no possibility for an equal return of what is owed to one's parents and country.[133] Even if our parents have not been the greatest parents ever, they have given us the gift of life, for which there is no equal return to them.

However, in most instances, our parents have done much more than just give us life and physical support or nourishment. Our parents have also helped us in the formation of our souls. They have been our first "formators."

Our fathers and mothers have also exercised a spiritual parenthood over us, for which we are greatly indebted to them. As Wojtyła explains, "Paternity and maternity in the world of persons are certainly not limited to the biological function of transmitting life. Their significance is much deeper, and must be so in as much as the transmitter of life, father or mother, is a person."[134]

Commenting on the act of piety consisting in honoring father and mother, Thomas explains that our parents give us "birth, nourishment, and instruction" (see Sir 7:29–30; Jb 1:21; Heb 12: 9; Sir 7:25).[135] Hence, human procreation is not to be confused with sheer animal reproduction. Although human procreation is generically animal, it is a specifically rational phenomenon.

Thus, "paternity and maternity in the world of persons are the mark of a certain spiritual perfection, the capacity for 'procreation'

---

132 *ST* II–II, q. 101, a. 1, c.

133 See Aristotle, *Nichomachean Ethics*, VIII. 14.

134 Wojtyła, *Love and Responsibility*, 260.

135 *In Duo Praec.*, a. 6.

in the spiritual sense, *the forming of souls*. So that spiritual paternity and maternity have a much wider significance than physical parenthood. *A father and mother who have given their children life in the merely biological sense must then supplement physical parenthood by spiritual parenthood, taking whatever pains are necessary for their education*."[136] Consequently, the contemplation of the gift of life, as well as the contemplation of the gift of the formation that we may have received in our families, should help us to understand the debt of piety that we owe to our parents.

The *Catechism* connects the debt of piety with the virtue of gratitude: "Respect for parents (*filial piety*) derives from *gratitude* toward those who, by the gift of life, their love and their work, have brought their children into the world and enabled them to grow in stature, wisdom, and grace."[137] We owe our parents *reverence* and *service* for the very fact of being our parents. Then, depending on their own circumstances, we owe them all sorts of "services": to visit them and to take care of them when they are ill, to help them financially when they are in need, etc.[138] Piety requires us to honor our parents. We do so not only by showing them reverence and service. Our good conduct also speaks well and gives glory to them insofar as it evidently clarifies and manifests their goodness.

---

136 Wojtyła, *Love and Responsibility*, 260.

137 CCC 2215.

138 "We owe something to our parents in two ways: that is to say, both essentially, and accidentally. *We owe them essentially* that which is due to a father as such: and since he is his son's superior through being the principle of his being, the latter owes him *reverence and service*. Accidentally, that is due to a father, which it befits him to receive in respect of something accidental to him, for instance, if he be ill, it is fitting that his children should visit him and see to his cure; if he be poor, it is fitting that they should support him; and so on in like instance, all of which come under the head of service due" (*ST* II–II, q. 101, a. 2, c.). Emphasis added.

When we are talking about piety for one's own country, we are really transported into the arena of *legal justice*, that kind of justice that concerns the common good. Piety directs the virtues of the individual toward it in accordance with the nature of true and authentic participation. However, piety concentrates on one particular aspect: since our country has been for us a principle of being, we owe it our service for its common good.[139]

Within the context of seminary formation, it is important to remember that our duties of religion do not conflict with our duties of piety toward our parents. Our Lord rebuked the Pharisees for teaching that there was such an opposition (see Mt 15:3–6). Religion and true piety do not mutually hinder one another. There is a proper order that must be respected, otherwise piety will cease to be such, and virtue will turn into vice. There can be no contradiction between religion and piety, because no *true* virtue can be opposed to another.

The act of one virtue never excludes the act of another: "The act of every virtue is limited by the circumstances due thereto, and if it oversteps them it will be an act no longer of virtue but of vice. Hence, it belongs to piety to pay duty and homage to one's parents *according to the due mode*. But it is not the due mode that man should tend to worship his father rather than God."[140] To worship one's parents to the point of not worshiping God is not an act of piety. However, if "by paying the services due to our parents, we are not withdrawn from the service of God, then will it be an act of piety, and there will be no need to set piety aside for the sake of religion."[141]

As I already mentioned, the seminary community should consider itself as a way of continuing or extending the family's

---

139 See *ST* II–II, q. 101, a. 3, ad 3.

140 *ST* II–II, q. 101, a. 4, c.

141 Ibid.

mission. The promotion of piety at the seminary is another way of promoting gratitude in future priests not only toward their physical parents but also toward those responsible for their priestly formation. Moreover, fostering the correct environment for the virtue of piety to grow in future priests entails a certain rediscovery of the father figure. Such a rediscovery is most beneficial for a proper relationship with the spiritual fathers responsible for priestly formation. Even more importantly, such a rediscovery aids and removes some potential obstacles in the seminarian's relationship with God as Father.

The Gift of Piety

From the perspective of charity, acquired human virtues could be considered as false counterfeit virtues, or as true but imperfect virtues.[142] The acquired virtue of religion is a true virtue inasmuch as it is directed to a true and honest good. It has a certain integrity of its own. It includes human reason's natural capacity to order the acts of religion to God as Creator and Supreme Provider.

Nevertheless, although true, acquired religion is an *imperfect* virtue. It does not lead to our supernatural end. Besides, its imperfection is also manifested in the fact that, wounded by original sin, the human person has great difficulty in naturally loving God above all things.[143]

Thanks be to God, seminary is not the Aristotelian Lyceum. Future priests have found healing in supernatural grace.[144] Within this supernatural elevation, faith and charity contribute to the seminarian's growth in the virtue of religion. Faith "makes clear the

142 See *ST* II–II, q. 23, a. 7; I–II, q. 65, a. 2, c. See Decomiso, *Ethics as a Work of Charity*, 106–38, 178–97; Hütter, "Happiness and Religion," 44–47.

143 See *ST* I–II, q. 119, a. 3, c.

144 See ibid.

one to whom *latria* is to be exhibited."[145] Charity, as friendship with God, "binds toward Him to whom religion is to be exhibited."[146]

Adopting our same perspective of charity, Thomas Aquinas explains: "It belongs immediately to charity that man should give himself to God, adhering to Him by a union of the spirit; but it belongs immediately to religion, and, through the medium of religion, to charity which is the principle of religion, that man should give himself to God for certain works of Divine worship."[147]

Future priests have been baptized. They have also received a sacramental character that enables them to partake of Christ's priest-hood. Thus, they can worship God with the *infused* virtue of religion.[148]

Nevertheless, the perspective of charity has to account for another perfection. Both the acquired and the infused virtue of religion as well as that of piety are further perfected by the gifts of the Holy Spirit, especially by the gift of piety.[149] Hence, in our spiritual exercises in religion and piety, we should pray to God for this particular gift.

Like Sails on a Boat

Isaiah prophesied about Christ as the shoot from the stump of Jesse when he said: "'The Spirit of the Lord shall rest upon him, / the spirit of wisdom and understanding, / the spirit of counsel and might, / the spirit of knowledge and the fear of the Lord [and

145 *In III Sent.*, d. 9, q. 1, a. 1, qc. 2, c.

146 Ibid.

147 *ST* II–II, q. 82, a. 2, ad 1.

148 See *ST* III, q. 63, a. 1, c.

149 See John of St. Thomas, *The Gifts of the Holy Ghost*, trans. Dominic Hughes (New York: Sheed and Ward, 1951), 175.

of piety]" (see Is 11:2).[150] These gifts are also present in God's adoptive children (see Rom 8:14; 5:5). They are to be distinguished from gratuitous graces, which do not conform us to Christ, are not meant for our profit but that of others, and do not depend either on our moral behavior or on our being in communion with God (see 1 Cor 12:7).[151]

Instead, the gifts of the Holy Spirit perfect our being created in God's image, they profit our own salvation, and depend on our living in the state of grace. They are gifts from the Triune God. They are said to be from the Spirit, because, since the Holy Spirit proceeds from the Father and the Son as Love, he is God's first gift by which all other gifts are given to us.[152]

These gifts are habits, but not virtues. In fact, they perfect the virtues. As we know, they perfect the acquired virtues because the latter are essentially natural, whereas the ultimate end of the human person is essentially supernatural.

Also, the infused moral virtues have an imperfection that belongs to them *per se* insofar as they are ordered to creatures, to created goods. Even the theological virtues like faith and hope are also in need of being perfected inasmuch as they imply a certain distance from God as their proper object (see 1 Cor 13:9, 13). On this earth, even charity participates in this essential imperfection, insofar as it is adjacent to faith and hope.

---

150 The Vulgate and the Greek Septuagint add the gift of piety. For a greater explanation, see Ramírez, *Los Dones Del Espíritu Santo*, 114. John of St. Thomas also noted this same point: see John of St. Thomas, *The Gifts of the Holy Ghost*, 176. Other helpful and more contemporary treatises on the Holy Spirit's gifts are: Walter Farrell, *Swift Victory: Essays on the Gifts of the Holy Spirit* (New York: Sheed and Ward, 1955); Michael-Marie Philipon, *Les Dons Du Saint–Esprit* (Bruges: Desclée De Brouwer, 1964); Antonio Royo Marín, *El Gran Desconocido: El Espíritu Santo y Sus Dones* (Madrid: BAC, 1987).

151 Farrell, *Swift Victory*, 12.

152 See *ST* I, q. 27, a. 4; q. 37, a. 1; q. 43, a. 5, ad 1; *Super Is.,* cap. 11.

All these imperfections are aided by the Holy Spirit's gifts because they move the human person by a superior principle that exceeds the *human* mode of acting. The gifts surpass the perfection of the virtues "as regards the manner of working, in respect of man being moved by a higher principle."[153] Isaiah calls them spirits because, through them, the Holy Spirit moves us. He is the guide of this *divine* mode of acting, in which we are more passive and thus docile recipients of the movement. For this reason, while virtues perfect us to act in a *human* mode, the gifts dispose us with docility to act in a *divine* or ultra-human mode.[154]

The classic metaphor is that of the soul as a boat. The virtues would correspond with rowing, while the gifts would resemble the sail that captures the wind (*ruah*) of the Spirit, moving us to our supernatural end. Extending this metaphor, we can think of each of the gifts as a small spiritual sail in one of the soul's faculties whereby we are habitually receptive to the promptings of the Spirit. They allow us to catch the wind of his motions, as it were.

This metaphor is quite pertinent in order to illustrate the distinct mode of acting present in the virtues and in the gifts. In the virtues, human reason, as perfected by acquired and infused prudence, is the moving principle, rule, and measure. One's soul moves toward God like a boat advances by rowing.

Instead, in the gifts, it is Divine Providence moving, ruling, and measuring our actions by, as it were, a connatural instinct. In this other case, one's soul moves toward God much faster. It assumes the power of rowing and adds to it the power of the divine wind/ Spirit (*ruah*).

---

153 *ST* I–II, q. 68, a. 2, ad 1. See Ramírez, *Los Dones Del Espíritu Santo*, 94.

154 See *ST* I–II, q. 68, a. 1, ad 1. See Aristotle, *Nichomachean Ethics*, VII. 1.

Clearly, Divine Providence is superior to any human providence or prudence. The gifts make us docile to follow the instinct of the Holy Spirit. They are necessary for salvation because the instinct of human reason is not enough to reach it, not even when perfected by the infused and theological virtues, since we always possess the latter in an *imperfect manner*. Salvation is a long journey. Without the gifts as sails and the Spirit as wind, we do not get there.

What do I mean when I say that we possess the theological virtues in an imperfect manner? Consider the following example. A physician who perfectly possesses the science of medicine is capable of moving himself to perform a medical procedure, even if he usually has help. Likewise, the human person can move himself to his *natural* end, even if God in his great mercy also aids him in this regard.

In turn, when we are talking about our supernatural end, even if we are perfected by the infused and theological virtues, we are more like the student of medicine. We possess the science imperfectly. We do not know and love God as he knows and loves himself.

Hence, with respect to our supernatural end, we are like students of medicine that cannot perform the medical procedure without being moved by the physician. For this reason, we are in need to follow the divine instinct in order to be saved. And the gifts of the Holy Spirit allow us to do so.[155]

The Sail of Piety

The gift of piety perfects all the virtues within the province of justice.[156] It permeates our relationship with others at the seminary and with God. It is like a spiritual sail in our will, whereby we capture the movement of the Holy Spirit to act as brothers in Christ and as God's children, as members of one household.[157] This

---

155 See *ST* I–II, q. 68, a. 2, c.

156 See *In III Sent.*, d. 34, q. 3, a. 2, qc. 2, ad 1.

157 See John of St. Thomas, *The Gifts of the Holy Ghost*, 187–88.

gift disposes us to receive the Spirit's motions to have a certain filial affection for God similar to that of Christ's. For this reason, Aquinas explains that "since it belongs properly to piety to pay duty and worship to one's father, it follows that piety, whereby, at the Holy Ghost's instigation, we pay worship and duty to God as our Father, is a gift of the Holy Ghost."[158]

Moreover, the gift of piety also impacts our relationship with others on account of their being children of the same Father. "As by the virtue of piety man pays duty and worship not only to his father in the flesh, but also to all his kindred on account of their being related to his father so by the gift of piety he pays worship and duty not only to God, but also to all men on account of their relationship to God."[159] As Paul says, "You are no longer strangers and sojourners, but you are fellow citizens with the saints and members of the household of God" (Eph 2:19; see Rom 8:15).

By the acquired virtue of religion, we worship God as our Alpha and Omega. By the infused virtue of religion, we worship him as our Father. In that sense, Thomas reasons: "To pay worship to God as Father is yet more excellent than to pay worship to God as Creator and Lord. Wherefore religion is greater than the virtue of piety."[160]

Yet the infused virtue of religion still operates in a human mode, like rowing, according to our metaphor. For this reason, "the gift of piety is greater than religion."[161] The gift of piety has a divine mode of acting in which we are receptive recipients of the Spirit's promptings, especially to his promptings to be grateful, just, affable, truthful, observant, obedient, religious, reverent toward our parents, generous, merciful, etc. Consequently, it would

158 *ST* II–II, q. 121, a. 1, c.

159 *ST* II–II, q. 121, a. 1, ad 3.

160 *ST* II–II, q. 121, a. 1, ad 2.

161 Ibid.

be very unwise for a seminarian to exercise spiritually in the virtues of the province of justice without asking God for the gift of piety.

Nevertheless, the gift of piety plays a special role in our life of prayer as it perfects the acquired and the infused virtue of religion. Faith reveals the God we worship. Hope directs us to him, loving everything from him that we need to reach salvation. In charity, we live with God as with a friend.

These theological virtues work in unison with the infused virtue of religion. Yet piety brings all of them to a higher level insofar as this gift makes us receptive to the Holy Spirit, moving our wills to be devout. Thereby, in conjunction with the intellectual gifts, it fosters the intellectual life of the future priest.

Piety also fosters the Spirit's active participation in the liturgies we celebrate. Thereby, we are receptive to his intercession in our own prayer: "The Spirit helps us in our weakness; for we do not know how to pray as we ought, but the Spirit himself intercedes for us with sighs too deep for words" (Rom 8:26). By the gift of piety, we honor the saints as well.[162] It helps us to develop a fraternal friendship with them.

Especially, piety makes us receptive to the Holy Spirit. He moves our wills to participate actively in the Holy Sacrifice of the Mass. This participation is essential for every Christian.

However, for a priest it is of the utmost importance. The gift of piety helps the priest to bring to fulfillment the words the bishop addresses to him the day of his ordination, when the paten and the chalice with bread and wine are given to him: "Understand what you do, imitate what you celebrate, and conform your life to the mystery of the Lord's Cross." That conformation is true and active participation in the Eucharist. For a priest, this is especially true when pronouncing the words of consecration.

---

162 See *ST* II–II, q. 121, a. 1, ad 3.

The gift of piety moves the priest's will to a filial devotion to the Father. It confers on the priest Christ's filial reverence and obedience. It allows the priest to bring about his greatest act of devotion in his active participation in Christ's sacrificial self-gift on the cross.

Spiritual Exercises in Piety and Religion

After providing the essential knowledge to understand religion and piety, we will conclude our reflections, offering some spiritual exercises in them. As usual, these spiritual exercises are to be done within the context of the Examen prayer. Moreover, we should also bring them up in spiritual direction and *mutatis mutandis* in formation meetings.

	I have a good awareness of the place of honor and dignity that belongs to me within the universe as hierarchically ordered by God.
	I am convinced that the following advice will have a beneficial impact on my priesthood: be a good son in order to be a good spouse and a better father.
	I have meditated on how much I have received from God and from my parents.
	I am fully convinced that I am not autonomous, but rather a dependent rational animal.
	I have called God to mind in my daily activities, ordering them for his greater glory.
	I have been doing a morning offering of all my good deeds as a spiritual sacrifice of worship to God.
	Mutatis Mutandis, I understand my priestly formation as a sort of continuation or extension of my family's mission.
	My experience of fatherhood in my own family helps me to relate to God as Father.

	My experience of fatherhood in my own family helps me to relate to those responsible for my priestly formation as spiritual fathers.
	I experience my prayer as a participation in Jesus's filial dialogue with the Father.
	I am eager to prepare myself to become a teacher of prayer by being trained at seminary, attending Jesus's school of prayer.
	I experience that my human and spiritual formation are integrated.
	My intellectual formation is animated by my life of prayer and the latter is also nourished by my studies.
	I have prayed, meditating on Psalm 100:3: "Know that the Lord is God! / It is he that made us, and we are his; / we are his people, and the sheep of his pasture."
	I desire to worship and serve the Lord by giving myself totally to him, thereby making of my life a spiritual host and imitating Jesus's sacrificial self-gift on the cross.
	I have prayed, meditating on Psalm 116:12: "What shall I render to the Lord / for all his bounty to me?"
	I have prayed for the gift of the fear of the Lord in order to better reverence God in the contemplation of his perfection and my imperfections.
	I experience the need that I have to worship and serve God daily and not to fall in the sin of idolatry.
	While knowing that the most important acts of religion are internal, I also value the importance of external signs and good liturgy as an aid to foster true devotion and prayer.
	I experience devotion not as a sentimental array of warm and fuzzy feelings, but as a serious and radical claim of love to offer my entire self as a sacrificial offering to God (Rom 12:1), and the prompt will to give myself in that way to God's service.
	I have asked God in prayer to increase my devotion.
	I have exercised acts of other virtues with devotion.

	My devotion springs from my love for God and, at the same time, nourishes such a love.
	I have grown in my devotion by cultivating the virtue of humility.
	I have meditated on God's goodness so as to increase the intensity of my devotion. I have paid special attention to those difficult moments of suffering in my life where God seemed to be absent.
	I have meditated on my own shortcomings and sins in light of God's love so as to increase the intensity of my devotion and combat the proud presumption that leads me to rely on my own strength.
	I find myself spending my days too busy to meditate on God.
	I have meditated on my conscience as a place where I can hear God's voice and submit to him by subordinating my intellect and will to the truth about the good.
	I desire to increase in my devotion so as to participate more fully in Christ's priesthood.
	My desire to pray originates in my devotion toward God.
	I experience prayer as a sheer emotional phenomenon.
	I value prayer as a sign of my dignity before God.
	I experience my prayer as a dialogue with God.
	I experience that there is real causality in my petitionary prayers. God counts on them.
	My prayer is animated by the fervor of love, the truth of faith, a rectitude of intention, and a constant desire to be in union with God. It makes me aware of my radical dependency on God as the Alpha and Omega.
	My experience of prayer corresponds to that intimate conversation and *communicatio* of spirits between friends, to a certain concord between God and me.
	I have experienced in my prayer that when God is my delight, he grants me my heart's desire (see Ps 37:4).

	Through my life of prayer, I have developed intimate friendships with the saints in heaven, with the Virgin Mary, with my guardian angel, and with other saintly people as well.
	My habit of prayer is developing with greater intensity at the seminary. My times of vacation demonstrate such a growth.
	My external acts of adoration are informed by devotion and prayer.
	I offer acts of abstinence and continence as sacrifice to the Lord.
	I offer the giving away of my material possessions as a sacrifice to God.
	I have looked over the rites of ordination to the diaconate and to the priesthood. Meditating on the promises therein contained, I have made a plan of life (or formation goals) by which to grow gradually in my future fulfillment of these same promises. Hence, I have devised a series of doable and smaller private and personal promises to God, which I intend to fulfill during this year.
	I have had difficulties by tempting God explicitly or implicitly in my prayers or in my deeds.
	I still find some idolatries within my own heart.
	I strive to participate in the Eucharist in a reverent and worthy manner.
	I have been irreverent to God by intending to buy or sell "spiritual things" such as sacraments, prayers of intercession, spiritual talks, etc.
	I acknowledge the debt that I have with my parents for their giving me life and an education in the virtues. Consequently, I honor them, by offering them assistance and by my good conduct.
	I have prayed for the gift of piety to perfect all the virtues within the province of justice in which I have been spiritually exercising, especially the virtue of religion.

CHAPTER 7

LIBERALITY'S FREEDOM

THE VALUE OF LIBERALITY

THE Latin word *liberalitas* refers to the peculiar frame of mind characteristic of free men.[1] This virtue, also called "generosity," has to do with a kind of attitude and mindset, as it affects our use of money or material goods, chiefly our internal disposition to give them away. For this reason, Aristotle noted that the liberal man is praised "with regard to the giving and taking of wealth, and especially in respect of giving."[2]

Like Aristotle, Aquinas also prefers the word *liberalitas* to the term *generositas*. In fact, rescinding its contemporary political connotations, the word "liberality" is most appropriate to describe the reality signified by this virtue, because it accurately refers to a certain *interior freedom* with respect to material goods.[3] During this chapter, I will speak about the liberal priest or the liberal seminarian. Yet, by this adjective, I will imply neither a political affiliation nor a tendency to be lax in matters of faith and morals, but only the possession of this particular virtue.

---

1 Roy J. Deferrari, *A Lexicon of Saint Thomas Aquinas* (Fitzwilliam, NH: Loreto Publications, 2004), 635.

2 *Nichomachean Ethics*, IV. 1. 119b20–25.

3 See José Francisco Nolla, "La Virtud de La Generosidad Según Santo Tomás de Aquino," 384–85 (Universidad de Navarra, 2010).

God's Liberality

Liberality belongs to the province of justice. However, precisely because of its inherent internal freedom, liberality resides on the border, as it were, between the provinces of justice and temperance. Liberality does not have dual citizenship in these two provinces. Nevertheless, like temperance, liberality entails a certain *moderation* of our love and desires: "As temperance moderates the desire of tactile pleasures, so liberality moderates the desire of acquiring or possessing external goods."[4] Thus, it is most appropriate that we deal with this virtue at the end of this book, right before our next volume dedicated to the priest as a man of temperance.

Thomas Aquinas believes that *no one is more liberal than God.* The Lord distributes the goods of the universe with maximum liberality. Indeed, "to act from need belongs only to an imperfect agent, which by its nature is both agent and patient. But this does not belong to God, and therefore He alone is the most perfectly liberal giver [*ipse solus est maxime liberalis*], because He does not act for His own profit, but only for His own goodness."[5]

Of course, virtues can be said to be in God only in a certain and most eminent way. God is just or merciful differently from any creature. Likewise, God is liberal without his liberality implying any imperfection pertaining to the creatural manner in which this divine perfection is reflected in intellectual creatures.[6]

Nevertheless, to become a liberal priest is to resemble God. The Lord is the exemplar of liberality. To acquire this virtue is to grow in one's being created in God's image and likeness. For this reason, St. Paul counsels those who have possessions in this world "to do good, to be rich in good deeds, liberal and generous" (1 Tm

---

4 *In IV Ethic.,* lect. 1, no. 650.

5 *ST* I, q. 44, a. 4, ad 1. See also I, q. 21, a. 1, ad 1; *SCG* I. 93.

6 See *SCG* I. 92–93.

6:18). Our Lord also refers to this virtue when he tells us: "Give to him who asks from you, and do not refuse him who would borrow from you" (Mt 5:42).

A priest or a seminarian is not to be enslaved to his own material goods. On the contrary, he should be able to be generous with them. The liberal priest is liberal because he is free to part with them.[7]

Illiberality as Covetousness and Idolatry

Conversely, the illiberal priest or seminarian is in great spiritual danger. God's revelation is unequivocal. Since the love for money is the root of all evil, the absence of the virtue of liberality can lead the candidate to the priesthood to commit all kinds of evils out of avarice (see 1 Tm 6:10).

What makes covetousness such a desirable sin is the usefulness of riches, "for with riches men believe they can buy anything."[8] People think that they can buy material possessions, respect, prestige, friends, other people, etc., as if everything and everyone had a price tag. As a result, one could do anything evil in order to obtain that kind of power. Instead, we cannot conform to the mentality of this world: "All material things obey money, so far as the multitude of fools is concerned, who know no other than material goods, which can be obtained for money."[9] We need to renew our minds and "take our estimation of human goods not from the foolish but from the wise: just as it is for a person whose sense of taste is in good order, to judge whether a thing is palatable."[10]

---

7 See *ST* II–II, q, 117, a. 2, c.

8 *Super I Tim.*, cap. 6, lect. 2, no. 251.

9 *ST* I–II, q. 2, a. 1, ad 1. See Rom 12:2.

10 *ST* I–II, q. 2, a. 1, ad 1.

Wealth cannot buy authentic spiritual goods (see Prv 17:16). Material goods are always instrumental. But they are not the true end of man's existence.

No wonder Paul lists avarice, greed, or covetousness as one of the sins that belong to those who rejected the truth about God (see Rom 1:29). He goes so far as to say: "Be sure of this, that no immoral or impure man, or one who is *covetous* (that is, an idolater), has any inheritance in the kingdom of Christ and of God" (Eph 5:5; emphasis added). Furthermore, our Lord clearly teaches that one cannot serve two masters (see Mt 6:24; Lk 16:13). Consequently, lack of liberality greatly impacts a future priest's relationship with God. It makes the candidate to the priesthood regrettably rich, precisely in that way to which Jesus refers when he says that it is very hard for the rich to enter God's kingdom (see Mk 10:23; Lk 18:24).

Additionally, according to the parable of the sower, lack of liberality is one of the impediments that does not allow God's word to give fruit in one's own life (see Mt 13:22; Lk 8:14; Mk 4:19). Thus, a seminarian or future priest who lacks liberality and is afflicted by avarice would be immune to the healing action of God's word.

The Ties That Bind

St. John of the Cross explains that it does not matter what it is that hinders one from being in union with God. If that which ties a seminarian here below is big or small, it makes no difference as long as it binds him here below, not allowing him to be in communion with God. Disordered attachments do not allow us to become holy, to be happy. "As long as this attachment remains, it is impossible to make progress in perfection, even though the imperfection be very small."[11]

---

11 John of the Cross, *Ascent of Mount Carmel*, I. 11. 4.

The Spanish mystic invites us to consider the following example: "It makes little difference whether a bird is tied by a thin thread or by a cord. Even if it is tied by a thread, the bird will be held bound [...] it will be impeded from flying as long as it does not break the thread."[12]

The virtue of liberality, therefore, has great value. It breaks threads that do not allow us to be in union with God. It orders our love for money and wealth.

Moreover, it also allows us to live, concentrated on the needs of others, for the liberal man spends more on others than on himself.[13] The virtue of liberality allows us to treasure what is truly important, namely, our salvation. As our Lord says, what is the point of gaining the whole world if one loses his own soul? (see Mt 16:26).

Aquinas evidences liberality's value explaining that "by reason of his not being a lover of money, it follows that a man readily makes use of it, whether for himself, or for the good of others, or for God's glory."[14] Consequently, let us follow the command that we find in St. Paul: "Put to death therefore what is earthly in you: immorality, impurity, passion, evil desire, and *covetousness*, which is idolatry" (Col 3:5; emphasis added). The best and more positive way of following this command is to grow in the virtue of liberality in conjunction with that of religion, since the latter directly opposes idolatry.

Embracing Voluntary Poverty

Vatican II has emphasized liberality's value for priests. The Council deals with it within the context of its discussion on the priest's relationship to the world, to temporal goods, and on voluntary

---

12 John of the Cross, *Ascent of Mount Carmel*, I. 11. 4.

13 See *ST* II–II, q. 117, a. 1, ad 2.

14 *ST* II–II, q. 117, a. 6, c.

poverty. In a sense, priests are to use the world without using it, that is, enjoying internal freedom from it.

In this way, *Presbyterorum Ordinis* explains that priests are to "achieve that freedom [*libertatem*] whereby they are free [*liberati*] from every inordinate concern and become docile to the voice of God in their daily life. From this freedom [*libertate*] and docility grows spiritual discretion in which is found the right relationship to the world and earthly goods. Such a right relationship is of *great importance to priests*, because the mission of the Church is fulfilled in the midst of the world and because created goods are altogether necessary for the personal development of man."[15] In this context, for the liberal priest, the Lord is his portion and heritage (see Nm 18:20). He uses temporal goods "only toward ends which are licit according to the doctrine of Christ and the direction of the Church."[16]

Therefore, it is of the utmost importance for priests to grow in the virtue of liberality: "In no way placing their heart in treasures, they should avoid all greediness and carefully abstain from every appearance of business."[17] The council reminds us that poverty is not something only for those consecrated to the religious life. As Thomas says, "Poverty is praiseworthy according *as it frees man* from the vices in which some are involved through riches."[18]

Presbyterorum Ordinis invites diocesan priests to this same freedom, to liberality's freedom, "to embrace voluntary poverty by which they are more manifestly conformed to Christ and become eager in the sacred ministry."[19] Thus, a priest should be careful so that his way of life does not throw people off. "Before the other

---

15 PO, 17. Emphasis added.

16 Ibid. See OT, 9.

17 Ibid.

18 *SCG* III. 133. Emphasis added.

19 PO, 17.

followers of Christ, let priests set aside every appearance of vanity in their possessions. Let them arrange their homes so that they might not appear unapproachable to anyone, lest anyone, even the most humble, fear to visit them."[20]

John Paul II also deals with the value of liberality within the context of a priest's vocation to foster a life of evangelical poverty.[21] As the pope notes, "Only the person who contemplates and lives the mystery of God as the one and supreme good, as the *true and definitive treasure*, can understand and practice poverty, which is certainly not a matter of despising or rejecting material goods but of a loving and responsible use of these goods and at the same time an ability to renounce them *with great interior freedom*—that is, with reference to God and his plan."[22]

To be free from attachments to money and to material possessions allows a priest to fulfill his vocation. In that sense, voluntary poverty is good: "Poverty in itself is not good, but only in so far as it *liberates* from those things whereby a man is hindered from intending spiritual things."[23] This kind of poverty is extremely good for a priest, as it frees him to do God's will, because it "ensures that the priest remains available to be sent wherever his work will be most useful and needed even at the cost of personal sacrifice."[24] By doing so, a priest is benefitting his people much more profoundly than by working another job and giving them his salary.

Priests who live out liberality and this kind of voluntary poverty incite others to virtue by their own example. As Thomas Aquinas would say, "Those who profit by their examples become

---

20 PO, 17.

21 See PDV, 27.

22 Ibid., 30. Emphasis added.

23 *SCG* III. 133. Emphasis added.

24 PDV, 30.

less attached to riches when they observe other people completely abandoning their wealth for the sake of perfection in life. But the less a man loves riches, and the more intent on virtue he is, the more readily, also, does he distribute his wealth for the needs of others."[25]

Consequently, it is true that when diocesan priests live out the virtue of liberality and the kind of voluntary poverty that is appropriate to their own state of life, "rather than causing loss to the poor by taking the benefactions which would support the lives of others, [these priests] become more beneficial to other poor people, because they by words and examples stimulate other men to works of mercy."[26]

The Preferential Option for the Poor

Moreover, we should never forget that a priest should also have *a preferential option for the poor*.[27] Liberality is the virtue that essentially accompanies this preferential option. Liberality frees the priest to be able to make such an option, to adopt such a lifestyle. Thus, the pope explains that "the *interior freedom* which is safeguarded and nourished by evangelical poverty *will help* the priest to stand beside the underprivileged; to practice solidarity with their efforts to create a more just society; to be more sensitive and capable of understanding and discerning realities involving the economic and social aspects of life; and *to promote a preferential option for the poor*."[28]

Obviously, such a preferential option is inseparable from the proclamation of the Gospel. It is actually a needed imitation of

---

25 *SCG* III. 135.

26 Ibid.

27 See RMis, 60.

28 PDV, 30. Emphasis added.

Christ's own priesthood. A priest can *never* forget it, for such an option leads one's ministerial priesthood toward "the poor, sinners and all those on the margins of society, following the model given by Jesus in carrying out his prophetic and priestly ministry."[29]

An Integral View of Man and the World

Additionally, the promotion of the virtue of liberality or of its contrary vices presupposes a certain view of the human person and of the world. For instance, consumerism presupposes a reductive anthropology because, in order to create a constant need to get new things, it appeals to the human person's instincts "while *ignoring* in various ways the reality of the person as intelligent and free."[30] Not considering the spirituality of the human person, "consumer attitudes and life-styles can be created which are objectively improper and often damaging to his physical and spiritual health."[31]

Instead, the virtue of liberality presupposes an integral view of the human person or adequate anthropology that is not reductionistic. Consequently, "in singling out new needs and new means to meet them, one must be guided by an integral view of man [*integra hominis imagine dirigi*] which respects all the dimensions of his being and which subordinates his material and instinctive dimensions to his interior and spiritual ones."[32] Material goods should be at the service of the spiritual goods of the human person, not the other way around.

---

29 PDV, 30.

30 CA, 36. Emphasis added.

31 Ibid.

32 Ibid. Translation altered in view of the original Latin. I have dealt with John Paul's philosophical integral view of the human person in my *De la experiencia.* I have studied his adequate theological anthropology, instead, in my *Procreation and the Spousal Meaning of the Body.*

Our spirit should not be enslaved by material goods. We should enjoy liberality's freedom. When one has it, he truly enjoys material goods, because then these goods are used in accordance to their true purpose, that is, they "are used to attain to the enjoyment of God."[33] Indubitably, in the order of importance, as Thomas explains, "We should seek temporal things not in the first but in the second place."[34]

On the other hand, the virtue of liberality and its contrary vices also entail diverse metaphysical and religious worldviews. It certainly belongs to the human condition to worry in some measure and be solicitous for temporal and material goods. We need them for our own existence. Nevertheless, there is an axial line of demarcation between the pagan and the Christian attitude toward material goods. Because of their ignorance of Divine Providence, "the gentiles are solicitous in seeking temporal goods *before all others*."[35]

In turn, the metaphysics of liberality includes Divine Providence. Such a metaphysical worldview is the exact context of Jesus's sermon on the mount. Therein, the Lord calls us to live day by day, trusting in God. His providence takes care of irrational beings, such as lilies in the field or birds. How much more will he take care of us! (see Mt 6:26–30).[36]

In this manner, Jesus concludes: "Therefore I tell you, do not be anxious about your life, what you shall eat or what you shall drink, nor about your body, what you shall put on. Is not life more than food, and the body more than clothing?" (Mt 6:25).[37] Our

---

33 *Super I Tim.*, cap. 6, lect. 4, no. 276.

34 *ST* II–II, q. 83, a. 6, ad 1.

35 *ST* II–II, q. 55, a. 6, c. Emphasis added. See also *SCG* III. 135.

36 *ST* II–II, q. 55, a. 6, c.

37 See *Super Matt.*, cap. 6, lect. 5.

Lord remarks that, "the Gentiles seek all these things" (Mt 6:32). Instead, to us who are his friends and who follow him, Jesus says, "Seek first his kingdom and his righteousness, and all these things shall be yours as well" (Mt 6:33).[38]

A lifestyle or vital project oriented toward material goods and the feeling one gets out of having more and new possessions betrays an adequate anthropology and an integral metaphysical view. Such a lifestyle ignores man's spirituality and Divine Providence. It falls back into idolatry and it frustrates our true happiness.

Keeping these brief reflections in mind, let us pause and discuss the following questions:

(1) What does lack of liberality do to my life?
(2) What does lack of liberality do to the life of the seminary?
(3) What will lack of liberality do in my future life as a priest?
(4) What will my incapacity to be an example of liberality mean for the life of my spiritual children?
(5) How will my growth in the virtue of liberality impact my life as a seminarian and as a future priest, as well as the life of those around me in the seminary, and in my future parish?

A Matter of the Heart and the Rich Young Man

The virtue of liberality is really a matter of the heart (*mens*). It is a virtue that chiefly perfects our will as it interacts with our intellect. It indirectly orders the sensible appetite.

Like all virtues residing in the will, liberality is ordered toward another. It mainly regulates the act of giving what is my own to another. However, in so doing, it impacts the giving subject without

38 See *ST* II–II, q. 83, a. 6, ad 1; q. 188, a. 7, c.

this impact necessarily being the main theme of our liberal action. In short, acts of liberality are also acts of self-determination.[39]

Thus, liberality ends up regulating the affections of the will such as spiritual love, hope, joy, or sadness. This virtue also directs the sensible appetite's passions pertaining to the concupiscible and irascible appetite. As a result, the virtue of liberality is not exactly about the size of one's bank account.

There are plenty of people who have riches and have this virtue as well. There are also plenty of poor people who are rich in a morally bad way. Many poor people have disordered desires of attachment to money. These desires are covetous and idolatrous. They are contrary to the virtues of liberality and religion.

Liberality and Freedom of the Heart

As a matter of the heart, liberality is all about its freedom. The very name of this virtue refers to a certain "open-handedness [*largitas*], because that which is open does not withhold things but parts of them."[40] Liberality's freedom of heart entails a certain internal disposition toward riches: "When a man quits hold of a thing he frees it [*liberat*], so to speak, from his keeping and ownership, and shows his heart to be free of attachment thereto [*animum suum ab eius affectu liberum esse ostendit*]."[41] One's possessions are, in a certain sense, part of us. The liberal man is free from attachment to them, because he can disengage from them: "A person giving what is his cuts himself away, so to speak, from what was a part of him."[42] It is clear by now that the virtue of liberality frees our heart,

---

39 See Wojtyła, *Person and Community*, 187–96; Wojtyła, *The Acting Person*, 105–88.

40 *ST* II–II, q, 117, a. 2, c.

41 Ibid. Translation altered.

42 *In IV Ethic.,* lect. 1, no. 663.

so that our treasure may be in heaven, and not in material goods (see Mt 6:21).

Although this virtue deals especially with money, we should expand its subject matter to include all material possessions, all wealth. Money is just a way to signify them, insofar as they can be valued in currency. Thomas offers an interesting etymology of the Latin word for money, *pecunia*, in order to explain this very point. He says that "everything whatsoever man has on earth, and whatsoever he owns, goes by the name of *pecunia*, because in olden times men's possessions consisted entirely of "*pecora*" [flocks]."[43]

Now, when one says that money or wealth is the matter of the virtue of liberality, one means that wealth is its *remote* matter. The same thing happens in the neighboring province of temperance, as food or sex are its remote matter. However, the latter has also a more proximate matter, namely, how we relate to food or sex. Likewise, liberality's proximate material object is not just wealth, but the desire or the love for money.[44] Since liberality is a matter of the heart (*mens*)—of our will as informed by our intellect—there is nothing evil about money in and of itself: "External riches are necessary for the good of virtue; since by them we support our body and give assistance to other people."[45]

Hence, Thomas clarifies that "whatever has any utility can be used well or badly. But riches are sought because they have some utility. Therefore, they can be used well or badly."[46]

The virtue of liberality orders our heart and regulates its use so that the latter becomes good. Through it, we avoid imprudent forms of voluntary poverty as well as disordered love for riches: "Since neither riches, nor poverty, nor any external thing is in itself man's

43 *ST* II–II, q. 117, a. 2, ad 2.

44 See *In IV Ethic.,* lect. 1, no. 652.

45 *SCG* III. 133.

46 *In IV Ethic.,* lect. 1, no. 658.

good, but they are only so as they are ordered to the good of reason, nothing prevents a vice from arising out of any of them, when they do not come within man's use in accord with the rule of reason. Yet they are not to be judged evil in themselves; rather, the use of them may be evil."[47] As a result, the virtue of liberality confers on us the *freedom* whereby we can live out the following maxim: "Riches are good, to the extent that they advance the practice of virtue, but if this measure is departed from, so that the practice of virtue is hindered by them, then they are not to be numbered among goods, but among evils."[48]

The Rich Young Man

In order to further illustrate the way in which liberality is a matter of the heart, it is important to briefly take a look at how Thomas comments on the Gospel passage about the rich (young) man who questions Jesus about what to do in order to inherit eternal life (see Mt 19:16–30). Thomas points out that while this man had good intentions to follow the Lord, his heart was sick and disordered: "He was hindered by the passion of avarice."[49] This man asks Christ about eternal life because, in the Old Law, he heard mostly about temporal rewards, like the promised land, numerous descendants, a long life, etc. The Lord questioned this man's address to him as "good," because, in reality, this man asked of Jesus "as though of a good man, but not as though of God."[50] Christ was "aware of his emotions, that his soul was not ready to submit to the good."[51]

Aquinas follows Jerome's interpretation, according to which, this man lied when he said that he had fulfilled all of the

47 *SCG* III. 134.

48 *SCG* III. 133.

49 *Super Matt.*, cap. 19, lect. 1, no. 1580.

50 *Super Matt.*, cap. 19, lect. 1, no. 1582.

51 Ibid.

commandments. Thomas argues that this man was not telling the truth, otherwise "he would not have gone away sad."[52] He surely desired excellence, but he could not follow the Lord, and as a result, he was downcast. As the Angelic Doctor puts it, "This man desired perfection, and heard what he should have through this. And *because he was greedy*, he went away sad."[53]

Jesus called this man to the perfection of following him, to imitate Christ, to the perfection of charity. Liberality was needed to follow this call, as it is needed in the priestly vocation as well. In fact, "abandonment of things is the way toward perfection," because "the growth of charity is the diminution of greed, and the perfection of charity is no greed."[54]

At this point in his commentary, Thomas appeals to the Augustine conception of ordered self-love as heavenly citizenship: "Whoever has perfect charity even to the contempt of himself and his things has perfection."[55] As I already explained, Thomas obviously means the contempt for ourselves and for our things, insofar as they separate us from God and from our union with him. Nevertheless, this man's heart was not in order. He was not liberal. He was enslaved by his disordered self-love and by his disordered love for his things or possessions.

A Matter of the Heart

Jesus takes advantage of this moment to give a foundational lesson to his disciples: "Truly, I say to you, it will be hard for a rich man to enter the kingdom of heaven" (Mt 19:23). Thomas makes very important distinctions while commenting on this last verse.

---

52 *Super Matt.*, cap. 19, lect. 1, no. 1587.

53 *Super Matt.*, cap. 19, lect. 1, no. 1599. Emphasis added.

54 *Super Matt.*, cap. 19, lect. 1, no. 1593.

55 Ibid. See *De Civitate Dei*, XIV. 28.

They are most pertinent to our spiritual exercises in the virtue of liberality. They continue to reveal that this virtue is really a matter of the heart.

Aquinas focuses on the fact that Jesus spoke of a rich man and not of a man who *has* riches. The distinction is relevant because "some men have riches and do not love them, while some have and love and place hope in them. These who have and do not love them can enter into the kingdom of heaven."[56]

Liberality is a matter of the heart, because it is all about orderly loving riches and not placing our hope in them to attain happiness. Usually, when someone places his heart and hope in wealth as the meaning of his life, he does not constantly think about it. More often, this is a habitual intention concerning his last end.

Nevertheless, such an intention permeates his daily actions. As Thomas would say, in the journey of one's life, one could be walking toward avarice without thinking constantly, every step of the way, about this final destination. "One need not always be thinking of the last end, whenever one desires or does something: but the virtue of the first intention, which was in respect of the last end, *remains in every desire directed to any object whatever*, even though one's thoughts be not actually directed to the last end."[57]

The virtue of liberality, in conjunction with religion, plays an important role in freeing our hearts from such an interior disorder. Again, this is not a matter of the size of your bank account. Seminarians and priests are not excluded from these considerations just because they are not making five or six figures.

As I mentioned, there are priests and seminarians who have no riches, but are rich in the sense of having a disordered love and placing their hope for happiness in them. They have an idolatrous heart. Indeed, "there are many poor men who are rich in

---

56 *Super Matt.*, cap. 19, lect. 1, no. 1601.

57 *ST* I–II, q. 1, a. 6, ad 3. Emphasis added.

desire."[58] Even if they do not have external possessions, their will is disordered.

However, we should remember that "one trusts in that from which he expects help; but help is obtained from the strong, whereas riches are fragile. Therefore, trust should not be placed in riches: "do not lay up to yourselves treasure on earth, where the rust and moth consume" (Mt 6:19); but in the living God, where true hope must be placed."[59] Without a doubt, "where your treasure is, there will your heart be also" (Mt 6:21).

The Good Use of External Possessions

Liberality has to do with the good *use* of external possessions, namely, the good use of the things of this world granted unto us for our livelihood. Additionally, this virtue also orders the necessary preparation so that this good use can take place. A virtuous seminarian is not only able to make good use of his material possessions, he is also capable of searching for opportunities for such good actions: "It belongs to liberality not only to use money, but also to keep it in preparation and safety in order to make fitting use of it."[60]

Like many of the virtues studied in this volume, the virtue of liberality is not a species of justice, but an annexed virtue to it. Liberality is somewhat similar to justice, and at the same time, it is also somewhat different. Both virtues are ordered toward others; both of them are concerned with external things, and both of them have to do with a certain debt.[61]

---

58 *Super Matt.*, cap. 19, lect. 1, no. 1604.

59 *Super I Tim.*, cap. 6, lect. 4, no. 276.

60 *ST* II-II, q. 117, a. 3, ad 2. See also *ST* I–II, q. 16, a. 3, c.

61 See *In IV Ethic.*, lect. 1, no. 649.

Liberality's Moral Debt

However, while justice gives another what is *their* own, liberality gives to others what is *our* own. Justice's debt is legal in nature, whereas liberality's debt is moral.[62] Although liberality is indeed concerned with external things, it is about them under the aspect of our spiritual and sensible affects for money and possessions.[63]

Any human act is morally good because of its object of choice, its intention, and if its circumstances are good. From the moral viewpoint, this teaching is expressed by saying that a good moral action is good *ex integra causa*.[64] It could not be otherwise with the act of liberality. It is not only concerned with giving, but also with giving in the right circumstances and with a good intention. In other words, there is no true virtue of liberality without discernment or prudence ordering and commanding the positive desire to give one's possessions away.[65]

It is easy to see the importance of this teaching. For instance, the Lord warns us against the attitude of the hypocrite. In this context, Jesus explained that giving money for the sake of being seen and honored by others is not something morally good (see Mt 6:2).

Hence, a seminarian or a priest is to give with rectitude of intention. Moreover, he is to do so prudently. Thus, the liberal priest also takes care of his own goods, while giving to others. He does not give to everyone, but to the right persons, at the right time, and in the right place.[66]

---

62 See *ST* II–II, q. 117, a. 5, ad 1.

63 See *In V Ethic.*, lect. 12, nos. 1016–17; *ST* II–II, q. 58, a. 9, c; q. 80, a. 1, c; q. 106, a. 1, ad 2 & a. 4, ad 1; q. 117, a. 5, c.

64 See *ST* I–II, q. 18, a. 4, c.

65 See *In IV Ethic.,* lect. 2, no. 666. See also *SCG* III. 134; *ST* II-II, q. 117, a. 4, ad 2.

66 See *In IV Ethic.,* lect. 2, no. 671.

The liberal seminarian is prompt to give eagerly and generously. He thinks not so much about himself but about others, giving more than what he retains. Yet "it does not belong to a liberal man so to give away his riches that nothing is left for his own support, nor the wherewithal to perform those acts of virtue whereby happiness is acquired."[67]

Virtuous Giving and Taking

Although the virtue of liberality is more concerned with giving than with receiving, the latter is also important: "Virtuous giving and taking that accompany one another are united in the liberal person."[68] The key in both instances is to love acting in accordance with right reason, doing what is right or what is good. The liberal seminarian or priest loves doing what is good more than money itself. Both his giving and receiving proceed from preferring "the reasonable good to the desire for wealth."[69]

As a result, such a priest or seminarian would not accept dishonorable money. Nevertheless, the virtue of liberality concentrates in a special way on one's internal attitude toward giving. But it does so under a very specific aspect.

Compare, for instance, the giving of money or possessions that belongs to beneficence or mercy as parts of charity, with the giving of money or possessions that is characteristic of liberality. A priest gives out of beneficence or mercy when he concentrates on his affection toward the person that is in need. In fact, mercy is that kind of benevolence toward others directed to eliminate their misery. That kind of love is often elicited and accompanied by compassion, in this instance, by feeling another's misery as one's own. As Aquinas explains, "The giving of beneficence and mercy

---

67 *ST* II–II, q. 117, a. 1, ad 2.

68 *In IV Ethic.,* lect. 3, no. 680.

69 Ibid.

proceeds from the fact that a man has a certain affection toward the person to whom he gives: wherefore this giving belongs to charity or friendship."[70]

However, all of this is not necessarily present in the giving away out of liberality. As was said, "Primarily and of its own nature it [liberality] tends to *set in order one's own affection* toward the possession or use of money."[71] Hence, "the giving of liberality arises from a person being affected in a certain way toward money, in that he desires it not nor loves it: so that when it is fitting he gives it not only to his friends but also to those whom he knows not. Hence it belongs not to charity, but to justice, which is about external things."[72]

All the same, it is important to describe well how an act of liberality affects the giving subject. It is crucial to clarify that one does *not* need to be thinking about that effect on one's personality at the very moment of giving away something to another. For the most part, the main direct object and theme of the act of liberality is the giving to another. The ordering of one's affections seems to be the indirect object.

For those of you who study Latin, the following example may illustrate best what I mean. The ordering of one's affects in the act of liberality seems to be something like a psychological dative. Along these lines, and inspired by Thomas Aquinas, Karol Wojtyła has explained that in every voluntary action we will two things: the action itself specified by its object and to become the kind of person who does that kind of action. For this reason, every free action is an act of self-determination.[73]

---

70 *ST* II–II, q. 117, a. 5, ad 3.

71 *ST* II–II, q. 117, a. 6, c. Emphasis added.

72 *ST* II–II, q. 117, a. 5, ad 3.

73 See Wojtyła, *The Acting Person*, 120–28.

Many times, we perform acts of liberality without aiming to grow in this specific virtue. Obviously, there is also the possibility of making more explicit one's intention to grow and spiritually exercise in this virtue. There is nothing wrong with that.

The reflexivity of the will allows that one wills to will this liberal act. In so doing, one also wills "indirectly" to become the kind of person who wills to will this liberal action. In short, one wills to grow in liberality. Thus, when we spiritually exercise so as to grow in this virtue, we are aiming at becoming, in our free actions, that kind of person who has such an ordered love for money and possessions that he can easily give them away.

Contrary to what one may think *prima facie*, it is quite probable that a seminarian who has experienced poverty or who has worked very hard for his own possessions would tend to have greater difficulties with the virtue of liberality. Such a person often tends to love his possessions more for two main reasons: "The first is that people who are given wealth by their parents have never felt the pinch of need. Consequently, they are not afraid to spend, as those are who have experienced poverty at one time."[74]

The second reason why a seminarian who has worked hard to obtain his possessions may find a greater difficulty with the virtue of liberality is that "all men naturally love their own works; parents love their children, and poets, their poems. Likewise, those who acquire riches by their labor look upon them as their own works and rather desire to keep them."[75]

---

74 *In IV Ethic.,* lect. 2, no. 674.

75 Ibid. Aquinas also echoes this position when he says: "Not infrequently, the fear of want that results from the experience of want hinders those who have acquired money from using it up by acting with liberality; as does likewise the love they have for it as being their own effect" (*ST* II–II, q. 117, a. 4, ad 1).

The Cheerful Giver

The liberal seminarian or priest is a *cheerful* giver (see 2 Cor 9:7).[76] The Scriptures are quite clear about it: "You shall give to him freely, and your heart shall not be grudging when you give to him" (Dt 15:10). Indeed, "a man who gives with sadness is not liberal. The reason is that the cheerless giver seems to prefer wealth to the virtuous action of honorable giving—which is not the case with a liberal person."[77]

A virtuous man finds joy and pleasure in the acts of the virtues. In these acts "there are two elements, namely, the species of the act and the manner of acting, which is taken on the side of the one acting. Hence, unless both are found in an act of virtue, that act is not said to be absolutely virtuous, just as a person is not said to be perfectly just according to the virtue, when he does works of justice, unless he acts with delight and with joy."[78]

Conversely, it belongs to the miser to be saddened by giving. Instead, "by the fact that he gives with pleasure," the liberal man "differs from the miser who is saddened by the giving away of his wealth."[79] Giving away with sadness entails a certain violence that goes against the spontaneity and willful character of virtuous actions.[80] God sees our heart. Thus, he requires us not merely to do acts of virtue, but also to do them virtuously, with delight and with joy.

---

76 See *Super I Tim.*, cap. 6, lect. 4, no. 277.

77 See *In IV Ethic.,* lect. 2, no. 668.

78 *Super II Cor.*, cap. 9, lect. 1, no. 332.

79 *In IV Ethic.,* lect. 3, no. 679.

80 See *Super II Cor.*, cap. 9, lect. 1, no. 331.

Not Caring is Not Virtuous

A seminarian may be tempted to think that the way to educate one's affections toward money is simply not to care about it. However, in this instance, not to care is not virtuous, but vicious. In fact, the vice of prodigality consists precisely in the giving away of money without caring, without the direction of right reason. Although it looks like liberality, in reality, it is not.[81]

Unfortunately, prodigality is *not* the most common of the two vices that oppose the virtue of liberality. Experience shows that the human person is more inclined *not* to give: "More lovers and custodians of money exist than donors."[82] There are way more people afflicted by greed than by prodigality.

While avarice entails an excess, prodigality implies a certain defect: the prodigal seminarian, for instance, does not care enough. As Thomas would say, he is "deficient, by *being less careful of them [material possessions] than he ought.*"[83] As a result, the prodigal priest or seminarian basically opts out of caring about money, as if that would be virtuous. However, this lack of care, in reality, is an internal defect that has a negative impact on one's external actions.

Prodigality lacks right reason in the ordering of the love and appreciation for riches. It also lacks rational order in giving them away. Both dimensions, the internal and the external, are important.

The Spendthrift and the Miser

The vice of prodigality also seems to connect to what Aristotle calls extravagance: "A man is truly called extravagant who dissipates his

81 See *In IV Ethic.,* lect. 5, no. 705.

82 *In IV Ethic.,* lect. 5, no. 698.

83 *ST* II–II, q. 119, a.1, c. Emphasis added.

riches precisely *because he does not have proper care of them.*"[84] Aristotle also refers to this kind of person as the spendthrift, as someone who spends his money irresponsibly: "He is called extravagant when he spends or gives beyond his means."[85]

Consider the opposite of the spendthrift man; that is, the miser: "It is precisely in expenditures that the spendthrift and the miser exceed and fall short in opposite things. The spendthrift is excessive in giving and not taking. But the miser, on the contrary, is deficient in giving and excessive in taking, except perhaps in trifling things that he gives and does not care to take."[86] To be a miser is far worse than to be a spendthrift.[87]

Virtues are the mean between extremes—*in medio virtus*. Often, the extreme by way of excess resembles the virtue more and tends to be a lesser evil than the other extreme. Of course, the trick is not to confuse, in oneself or in another, prodigality with liberality.

What is more, at the seminary, one should be very cautious to speak about *natural virtues*. Frequently, they are nothing but certain inclinations of one's temperament. Unless they are ordered by right reason, they end up turning into vices like prodigality, that is, vices that look like virtues. Ignorance of this fact can lead to a disastrous place. Priestly formation cannot foster in seminarians something as a virtue when, in reality, we are talking about a vice or a great occasion for vice.[88]

Nevertheless, as I mentioned, vices by way of excess tend to be less evil. Experience shows that the squanderer can heal more

---

84 *In IV Ethic.,* lect. 1, no. 657. Emphasis added.

85 *In IV Ethic.,* lect. 3, no. 678.

86 *In IV Ethic.,* lect. 3, no. 685.

87 See *In IV Ethic.,* lect. 4, no. 686.

88 See Marie I. George, "Aquinas on the Dangers of Natural Virtue and The Control of Natural Vice," *Tópicos* 40 (2011): 13–50.

easily. Age helps in this regard, as growing older increases the awareness of one's own needs.

Moreover, unless enabled by others, sooner rather than later, the spendthrift often ends up being poor. This resulting poverty is at least an initial remedy for his prodigality. But most essentially, what the spendthrift needs is a bit of right reason. His true remedy is a rational order inserted into his already existing inclination to give to others. He needs a little more common sense.[89] As a result, he can easily become liberal.

The Prodigal Sum

At first, the spendthrift may need the aid of another's rationality. In seminary, this may correspond to that of the spiritual director or the formation advisor. Consequently, prodigality, considered in itself, is a less grievous sin than covetousness. The latter is way more difficult to cure, because "giving, wherein the prodigal exceeds, belongs to liberality more than receiving or retaining, wherein the covetous man exceeds."[90] Additionally, while the prodigal future priest serves the many to whom he gives, the greedy seminarian is of use to no one, not even himself.

When I say that the prodigal priest or seminarian has an excess in giving and a defect in keeping and acquiring, I am not speaking about sheer fixed quantities.[91] Rather, I am talking about how much one ought to give and how much one actually gives. For this reason, one should never accuse someone of being prodigal when he or she, following Christ's words and wanting to become his disciple, sells *everything* he or she has and gives it away. Thomas

89 See *In IV Ethic.,* lect. 3, no. 689.

90 *ST* II–II, q. 119, a. 3, c.

91 See *ST* II–II, q. 119, a. 1 c.

explains it lucidly when he clarifies that "the excess in prodigality consists chiefly, not in the total amount given, but in the amount over and above what ought to be given."[92] As a result, it is perfectly possible that the liberal priest or seminarian gives more than the prodigal one.

Accordingly, Thomas clarifies that "those who give *all* their possessions with the intention of following Christ, and banish from their minds *all* solicitude for temporal things, are not prodigal but *perfectly liberal.*"[93] To be perfectly free to follow Christ is to be perfectly liberal. It is an important step in one's growth in charity, in loving God above everything and everyone else.

There is another obstacle to the virtue of liberality different from prodigality but related to it, inasmuch as it also involves a certain not caring. It has to do with a particular immoderation with respect to taking or receiving money from unlawful sources: "Certain illiberal persons are immoderate in taking, *not caring what or whence they take or profit.*"[94] A priest or a seminarian should not fall into this lack of care either. He should not accept money or profit from shameful or immoral works. Indeed, he should care very much.

Thomas Aquinas makes a point of warning clergy against these dangers. Other than their own personal money, often clergy "are dispensers of the Church's goods."[95] It is obvious that if the priest is a miser with these goods, he harms those for whom those goods are intended. On the other hand, Thomas Aquinas says that the vice of prodigality in clergy is also an offense against the poor. This is how he puts it: "This applies chiefly to the clergy, who are the

---

92 *ST* II–II, q. 119, a. 2, ad 3.

93 Ibid.

94 *In IV Ethic.,* lect. 5, no. 703.

95 *ST* II–II, q. 119, a. 3, ad 1.

dispensers of the Church's goods, that belong to the poor whom they defraud by their prodigal expenditure."[96]

The Heart of the Giver

A liberal seminarian may not be judged only by the amount of money or material possessions that he gives. Someone who gives a lesser amount may end up being more liberal: "There is no reason why someone who bestows smaller gifts may not be judged more liberal, if he gives from more moderate means."[97] As Thomas says elsewhere, "Nothing prevents a virtuous man from being liberal, although he may be poor."[98]

We may think that, since we are in seminary and we do not have much money or possessions, we cannot really exercise in the virtue of liberality. This is absolutely false. Liberality is above all a matter of the *heart* with which one gives. Although wealth or money is the remote matter of liberality, the proximate matter has to do with one's affections toward material goods.[99] It really "depends not on the quantity given, but on *the heart of the giver*."[100]

We can find a good biblical illustration of this thesis in the episode of the Gospel when Jesus is watching those who were giving money to the temple. At that time, Jesus saw a woman who did not give a huge amount of money; however, she gave *everything* that she had. "He looked up and saw the rich putting their gifts into the treasury; and he saw a poor widow put in two copper coins. And he said, 'Truly I tell you, this poor widow put in more

---

96 *ST* II–II, q. 119, a. 3, ad 1.

97 *In IV Ethic.,* lect. 2, no. 673.

98 *ST* II–II, q. 117, a. 1, ad 3.

99 Se *ST* II–II, q. 117, a. 5, ad 2; q. 118, a. 4, ad 2.

100 *ST* II–II, q. 117, a. 2, ad 1. Emphasis added.

than all of them; for they all contributed out of their abundance, but she out of her poverty put in all the living that she had'" (Lk 21:1–4).

Clearly, we see here how liberality has to do not so much with the quantity given, but with the heart with which one gives. This woman had no attachment to her possessions, and did not put her trust and security in them, but in God. Her internal passions were in order with respect to money and possessions. She was "solicitous most of all about spiritual goods, hoping that temporal goods also may be granted [to her] according to [her] needs, if [she] did what [she] ought to do."[101] Therefore, Jesus, who can see the heart of the human person, understood that she had given more than all the rest.

By contrast, when confronted with an apparent dispute between two brothers about an inheritance, Jesus warned against the dangers of covetousness: "Take heed, and beware of *all covetousness*; for man's life does not consist in the abundance of his possessions" (Lk 12:15; emphasis added). We could find here a warning against illiberality, against any *defect* in giving or in taking.[102] Yet, since liberality is most concerned with giving, we are more used to considering the main forms of illiberality as a defect in *giving*.

Sins in Avarice

Aristotle identified different shapes of this general covetousness, against which Jesus warns us. The philosopher clarifies that "some are called *stingy* who spend very little; others are called *grasping* who retain nearly everything from a defect in giving. Still others are called *closefisted*, or cumin seed splitters from an excessive

101 *ST* II–II, q. 55, a. 6, c.

102 *In IV Ethic.,* lect. 5, no. 699.

tenacity they manifest in refusing to give the smallest thing without a return."[103]

These sins are not daughters of the capital vice of avarice or covetousness. They are not different sins that spring from this capital vice as from their head, as it were. Instead, being stingy, grasping, or closefisted are species or kinds of illiberality. They are different ways in which one sins in avarice.[104]

John Cassian explains that this vice consists in a very peculiar disordered love for money, a vice contracted "from without"—that is to say, without a natural inclination for it.[105] It is a vice with which we are not born, but that can have extreme catastrophic consequences in our lives. The covetousness against which Jesus warns "arrives later and comes upon the soul from without. As easily as it can be watched out for and rejected, it becomes that much more dangerous than all the others and is that much more difficult to get rid of once there has been neglect and it has been let into the heart. For it turns into 'the root of all evils,' sprouting the shoots of many vices."[106]

In a very broad sense, covetousness or avarice refers to any immoderate desire for having something. It could mean "a genus under which all sins fall, inasmuch as it implies the inordinate desire for a temporal thing—and this is involved in every sin."[107]

---

103 *In IV Ethic.,* lect. 5, no. 700.

104 See *ST* I–II, q. 118, a. 8, ad 4.

105 "Certain vices, however, we say take shape without any antecedent natural impulse but by the decision of a corrupt and evil will alone, as is the case with envy and also with avarice itself. Inasmuch as these do not have their source in a natural movement within us, they are contracted from without." [John Cassian, *The Institutes*, trans. Boniface Ramsey (New York: Newman Press, 2000), VII. 5].

106 Ibid., VII. 1–2.

107 *Super I Tim.*, cap. 6, lect. 2, no. 251.

This is not the way in which we are speaking here about avarice or greed as an obstacle to the virtue of liberality.

We are referring to something more specific. We are talking about covetousness or avarice as a special sin that directly opposes the virtue we are dealing with. In this more restrictive meaning, "covetousness is a special sin, forasmuch as it is an immoderate love of having possessions, which are comprised under the name of money."[108] It is an *immoderatus amor habendi*—an immoderate love of possessing: "Not to be satisfied with money and to love it inordinately are opposed to liberality, which observes the mean in the desire of riches."[109]

We are not so much concerned with the form of avarice, which is immediately about the acquisition and keeping of riches beyond one's due, stealing or retaining another's property. This kind of avarice is directly opposed to justice. Instead, we are concerned with the kind of avarice or greed that directly opposes the virtue of liberality. Thomas Aquinas describes it as an "immoderation in the interior affections for riches; for instance, when a man loves or desires riches too much, or takes too much pleasure in them, even if he be unwilling to steal."[110]

The Covetous Fool and the Love of Riches

The way Jesus continues in the episode we are commenting on illustrates this exact form of covetousness directly opposed to liberality. Within the parable the Lord tells, there is a moment in which the rich man who stores the crops in his new large barns falls into covetousness. Obviously, his sin cannot consist in building the

108 *ST* II–II, q. 118, a. 2, c.

109 *ST* II–II, q. 118, a. 3, sc.

110 *ST* II–II, q. 118, a. 3, c.

large barns. Neither can his sin consist in storing the crops therein. What seems to be the fault of this rich man is found in the following words: "And I will say to my soul, Soul, you have ample goods laid up for many years; take your ease, eat, drink, be merry" (Lk 12:19). In fact, it is after these words that, according to the parable, God rebukes him saying: "Fool! This night your soul is required of you" (Lk 12:20).

What is actually immoderate and sinful in the attitude of the rich man is his love of his possessions. This rich man was not stealing; they were his own crops that he was storing. However, his internal affections were immoderate.

As we know, "external riches must be a good for man; not, of course, the principal one, but as a secondary good."[111] It seems that this man, however, was giving a certain priority to his own possessions. He was directly disobeying what we read in Psalm 62: "If riches increase, set not your heart on them" (Ps 62:10).

The man in Jesus's parable loved those crops too much. Into them, he deposited all of his security and trust. His idolatrous heart was therein at rest.[112]

The rich fool placed his hope for happiness in his own possessions, thinking that "money answers everything" (Eccl 10:19; see Mt 6:19–21). He took too much spiritual pleasure in knowing himself as their owner. In this way, the man commits a spiritual sin: "The covetous man takes pleasure in the consideration of himself as a possessor of riches. Therefore, covetousness is a spiritual sin."[113]

In a certain sense, we could say that avarice causes us to be blinded by a mirage that we experience in our consciousness when

---

111 *SCG* III. 133.

112 See *Super Eph.*, cap. 5, lect. 3; *SCG* III. 120.

113 *ST* II–II, q. 118, a. 6, c.

we possess something. Namely, we think our life is ours and that we can do with it what we want. Avarice blinds us to the fact that we cannot add one cubit to the span of our lives (see Mt 6:27).

As a matter of fact, "riches give great promise of self-sufficiency."[114] However, as we know, this is only a delusion, an empty promise. Our self-sufficiency cannot be absolute. We depend on God. "He made us; we belong to him" (Ps 100:3).

For this reason, the "thirst" for experiencing those feelings of possessing something, experienced by someone who is covetous, have no end. In reality, they can never be satisfied. This is what we read in the Scriptures: "He who loves money will not be satisfied with money; nor he who loves wealth with gain" (Eccl 5:10).

In fact, there is a great difference between the infinite character of our desire for the good as our true final end or sovereign good and the certain infinity experienced by the covetous person.[115] The more we lead a life of virtue and get to know and love God, the more we love him and the less we need *other* things. To know and to love God is the "water" that quenches our deepest thirsts. When we truly drink it, we do not thirst again. By contrast, the thirst experienced in avarice has no end.

I think that we can identify two main reasons as to why God calls the man "fool" in this parable. The first has to do with the following phenomenon: this sort of lust for riches brings about a certain darkness in the soul; it puts out the light of charity.[116] Thereby, one prefers this inordinate desire or love for riches rather than the love of God. In this case, avarice becomes a mortal sin. "If the love of riches becomes so great as to be preferred to charity, in

---

114 *ST* II–II, q. 118, a. 7, c.

115 See *ST* I–II, q. 2, a. 1, ad 3; Jn 4:13.

116 *ST* II–II, q. 118, a. 4, ad 2.

such wise that a man, through love of riches, fear not to act counter to the love of God and his neighbor, covetousness will then be a mortal sin."[117]

The Deformity of the Sin of Avarice

It seems that this man is sinning mortally by placing his final end in riches and possessions. Now, perhaps the second reason why this man is called a fool has to do with the way in which the sin of avarice deforms us. In every sin, there is a twofold aspect.

First, every sin implies a certain privation or corruption of some good. Second, every sin also implies a desire for something that is good. Considering this second aspect, the sin of avarice unites us with a good that is the lowest of the human goods. It does not unite us with the divine good, nor with the good of the soul, or that of the body, but with something even lower, namely, an external good.[118] This is where I find the second reason why the man of the parable is also called a fool: while he is loving inordinately his external possessions, God reveals to him that that very night, he will die.

So, the widow and the covetous fool have two opposing views of the human person and of the world. The widow operates within the context of an integral view of the human person. She loves herself for whom she truly is, not reducing the meaning of her existence to material goods.

Divergently, the covetous fool adopts in practicality a reductionistic and inadequate anthropology. He loves himself

117 *ST* II–II, q. 118, a. 4, c. On the other hand, Thomas clarifies that if "the inordinate nature of his love stops short of this, so that although he loves riches too much, yet he does not prefer the love of them to the love of God, and is unwilling for the sake of riches to do anything in opposition to God or his neighbor, then covetousness is a venial sin" (II–II, q. 118, a. 4, c.).

118 See *ST* II–II, q. 118, a. 5, c.

disorderedly, according to a false view of man that leads him to estimate himself wrongly. In fact, he values his exterior man above his interiority. In turn, the widow operates within a sound metaphysics of finite and eternal being. Thus, she trusts in God's providence.

In contrast, the fool's metaphysical worldview includes no such a thing; it is very materialistic. It is closed to the transcendent and eternal being of God. As a result, this fool has charged himself with being the sole provider for his own existence. However, as Jesus points out, although some people can live their lives adopting this reductionistic anthropology and metaphysics, no one will be able to hold to these as true, once they meet their Maker. The reality of death will finally wake this fool up from his injudicious and imprudent slumbers.

Spiritual Exercises in Liberality

After providing the essential knowledge to understand the virtue of liberality, a knowledge needed not only to better grow in this virtue but also to teach others and equip those who will teach about liberality, we will conclude our reflections by offering a practical tool to exercise spiritually in this same virtue.

	I desire to imitate God's liberality in my own life.
	I understand and desire to avoid the great spiritual danger inherent in the lack of liberality and covetousness.
	I often behave as if everything and everyone had a price tag.
	I desire and have asked God that I not conform to this world's mentality, but to renew my mind in Christ in order to judge well about human goods (see Rom 12:2).
	I have renewed in my heart my desire to serve the Lord as my only master (see Mt 6:24).
	I have experienced that lack of liberality has impeded God's word to give fruit in my own life.

	My growth in liberality has helped me to concentrate on the needs of others.
	My growth in liberality has helped me to treasure what is truly important.
	I have used my material possessions for God's greater glory.
	I asked God to help me and I have taken concrete actions to put to death covetousness within me (see Col 3:5).
	As a future priest, I want to be able to use the world with internal freedom, having God as my true portion and heritage (Nm 18:20; PO 17).
	I understand that voluntary poverty is not something exclusive to the members of religious orders.
	I value poverty not in and of itself, but only insofar as it frees me from the vices involved through riches.
	My life as a seminarian throws some people off, being too ostentatious.
	I want to grow in liberality in order to be ready to go wherever my bishop will send me as a priest, even at the cost of personal sacrifice.
	I have been an example of liberality, which incites others to works of mercy.
	I want my future priestly ministry to be configured to Christ's and to his preferential option for the poor, especially those afflicted by sin and living, as it were, in the peripheries or margins of society.
	I have been influenced by the view of the human person and of the world inherent in consumerism, but I am working to purify those erroneous opinions and practical convictions, especially by growing in my awareness of God's providential care.
	I understand that liberality is not a matter of the size of my bank account, but of the disposition of my heart toward money, wealth, or material possessions. I may not have riches but can be rich as discussed in Mt 19:23.
	I experience a certain ease in disengaging from or cutting myself off from my personal possessions.

	I find ease and pleasure in giving money away.
	When I give money away, I think more about others and their needs than about myself and my needs.
	When I give money away, I give it to the proper person, in a fitting manner, with a good intention, and in the right circumstances.
	I find ease and pleasure in giving money away not only to my friends and people for whom I have a certain affection, but also to anyone in need that I can help.
	Since I have worked hard to earn the money that I have, it is difficult for me to give to others like a liberal man would.
	I am a cheerful giver.
	The virtue of liberality is freeing my heart so that my treasure is in heaven.
	I experience that riches are not bad in themselves and that they should be an instrument to foster virtue.
	I have prayed for the grace of infused liberality while meditating on Mt 19:16–30.
	I have experienced that my growth in charity has entailed a diminution of greed.
	I have grown in proper self-love as a consequence of my spiritual exercises in liberality.
	I have examined my heart to eradicate and mortify any habitual intention toward greed and idolatry.
	I have faked the virtue of liberality in order to be seen well by others (Mt 6:2).
	My position regarding material possessions has always been not to care too much about them.
	I spend my money irresponsibly.
	Since I tend toward prodigality, I have sought the advice and rational judgment of my spiritual director or formation advisor in matters concerning giving money or material possessions away.

	As a future administrator of the Church's material goods, I want to avoid being a miser and a spendthrift.
	I do care about the sources wherefrom people give me money.
	I have difficulties with the vice of covetousness.
	I am stingy because I spend very little.
	I am *grasping* because I retain nearly everything from a defect in giving.
	I am *closefisted* because I tend to refuse to give the smallest thing without a return.
	I think that to receive money or valuable things from others is dishonorable.
	I have experienced perfect liberality in giving away my possessions in order to follow Christ.
	I have asked God for the virtue of liberality, meditating on Lk 21:1–4.
	I have asked God for the virtue of liberality, meditating on Lk 12:15–20.
	I often meditate on the shortness of my own life and my own death in order to acquire wisdom of heart (see Ps 90: 12).

Works Cited

Ambrose of Milan. "On the Duties of the Clergy. In *St. Ambrose: Select Works and Letters*. Edited by P. Schaff and H. Wace. Translated by H. De Romestin and H. Duckworth, Vol. 10. A Select Library of the Nicene and Post-Nicene Fathers of the Christian Church, Second Series. Christian Literature, 1896.

Annas, Julia. *The Morality of Happiness*. New York: Oxford University Press, 1993.

Aquila, Samuel J. "The Priest as a Man of Charity: Integrating Human and Spiritual Priestly Formation." In *Christ as the Foundation of Seminary Formation*. Edited by James Keating. Omaha: IPF Publications, 2016.

Aquinas, Thomas. "Collatio 6 Super Credo in Deum." In *The Liturgy of the Hours*, vol. 3. New York: Catholic Book Publishing, 1975.

———. *Comentum in Quartum Librum Sententiarum Magistri Petri Lombardi*. Vol. 7/2, Opera Omnia, 872–1259. Parma: Typis Petri Fiaccadori, 1858.

———. *Commentary on Aristotle's Metaphysics*. Translated by J. P. Rowan. Notre Dame, IN: Dumb Ox Books, 1999.

———. *Commentary on the Gospel of John*. Latin/English Edition of the Works of St. Thomas Aquinas. Vols. 35–36. Translated by F. R. Larcher. Lander: Aquinas Institute, 2013.

———. *Commentary on the Gospel of Matthew.* Latin/English Edition of the Works of St. Thomas Aquinas. Vols. 33–34. Translated by Jeremy Holmes and Beth Mortensen. Lander, WY: The Aquinas Institute, 2013.

———. *Commentary on the Letter of Saint Paul to the Hebrews.* Latin/English Edition of the Works of St. Thomas Aquinas. Vol. 41. Translated by F. R. Larcher. Edited by J. Mortensen and E. Alarcón. Lander, WY: Aquinas Institute, 2012.

———. *Commentary on the Letters of Saint Paul to the Corinthians*. Latin/English Edition of the Works of St. Thomas Aquinas. Vol. 38. Translated by F. R. Larcher, B. Mortensen, and D. Keating. Edited by J. Mortensen and E. Alarcón. Lander, WY: Aquinas Institute, 2012.

———. *Commentary on the Letters of Saint Paul to the Galatians and Ephesians*. Latin/English Edition of the Works of St. Thomas Aquinas. Vol. 39. Translated by F. R. Larcher and M. L. Lamb. Edited by J. Mortensen and E. Alarcón. Lander, WY: Aquinas Institute, 2012.

———. *Commentary on the Letters of Saint Paul to the Philippians, Colossians, Thessalonians, Timothy, Titus, and Philemon.* Latin/English Edition of the Works of St. Thomas Aquinas. Vol. 40. Translated by F. R. Larcher. Edited by J. Mortensen and E. Alarcón. Lander, WY: Aquinas Institute, 2012.

———. *Commentary on the Letter of Saint Paul to the Romans.* Latin/English Edition of the Works of St. Thomas Aquinas. Vol. 37. Translated by F. R. Larcher. Edited by J. Mortensen and E. Alarcón. Lander, WY: Aquinas Institute, 2012.

———. *Commentary on the Nichomachean Ethics*. Translated by C. I. Lintzinger. Notre Dame, IN: Dumb Ox Books, 1993.

———. *De Principis Naturae Ad Fratrem Sylvestrum*. Vol. 43, Opera Omnia Iussu Leonis XIII P. M. Edita. Roma: Editori di San Tommaso, 1976.

———. *De Veritate. On Truth*. Translated by R. Schmidt. Chicago: Henry Regnery, 1954.

———. *Disputed Questions on Virtue*. Translated by Jeffrey Hause. Indianapolis: Hackett, 2010.

———. *In Duo Praecepta Caritatis et in Decem Legis Praecepta Exposition*. In *Opuscula Theologica*. Vol. 1. Turin: Marietti, 1975.

———. *On Evil*. Edited by Brian Davies. Translated by Richard Regan. New York: Oxford University Press, 2003.

———. *On the Power of God.* Translated by English Dominican Province. Westminster, MD: Newman, 1952.

———. *Scriptum Super Libros Sententiarum Magistri Petri Lombardi Episcopi Parisiensis*. Edited by M. F. Moos. Vol 3. Paris: P. Lethielleux, 1956.

———. *Summa Contra Gentiles: Liber de Veritatae Catholicae Fidei Contra Errores Infidelium*. Edited by P. Marc, C. Pera, and P. Caramello. Taurini-Rome: Marietti, 1961.

———. *Summa Theologiae.* Latin/English Edition of the Works of St. Thomas Aquinas. Vols. 13–20. Edited by J. Mortensen and E. Alarcón. Lander, WY: Aquinas Institute, 2012.

———. *Super Boetium De Trinitate*. Vol. 50. Opera Omnia Iussu Leonis XIII. P. M. Edita. Rome: Editori di San Tommaso, 1992.

Aristotle. *The Basic Works of Aristotle*. Edited by R. McKeon. New York: Random House, 1941.

Armitage, Mark. "Obedient unto Death, Even Death on a Cross: Christ's Obedience in the Soteriology of St. Thomas Aquinas." *Nova et Vetera, English Edition* 8, no. 3 (2010): 505–26.

Augustine of Hippo. *The City of God.* In *St. Augustine's City of God and Christian Doctrine*. Edited by P. Schaff. Translated by M. Dods. Vol. 2. Buffalo, NY: Christian Literature, 1887.

———. *On the Morals of the Catholic Church*. In *St. Augustine: The Writings against the Manichaeans and against the Donatists* Vol. 4. Edited by P. Schaff. Translated by R. Stohert. Buffalo, NY: Christian Literature, 1887.

———. *Sermons 151-183 (III/5)*. Edited by John E. Rotelle. Translated by Edmund Hill. New York: New City Press, 1992.

———. *The Trinity*. Edited by John E. Rotelle. Translated by Edmund Hill. Vol. 5. The Works of Saint Augustine. A Translation for the 21st Century, I. New York: New City Press, 1991.

Badhwar, Neera. "Introduction: The Nature and Significance of Friendship." In *Friendship: A Philosophical Reader*, 1–38. Ithaca: Cornell University Press, 1993.

Bejczy, Istvan P. *The Cardinal Virtues in the Middle Ages; A Study in Moral Thought from the Fourth to the Fourteenth Century*. Edited by Han Van Ruler. Boston: Brill, 2011.

Benedict. *The Rule of St. Benedict*. Translated by Anthony C. Meisel and M. L. Del Mastro. New York: Image Books, 1975.

Benedict, Joseph. *The Virtue of Observance According to St. Thomas Aquinas*. Washington: Thomist Press, 1954.

Bergamino, Federica. *La Razionalità Della Libertà Della Scelta in Tommaso d'Aquino*. Roma: EDUSC, 2002.

Bernard of Clairvaux. *The Steps of Humility*. Notre Dame, IN: University of Notre Dame Press, 1963.

Biolo, Salvino. *L'autoconscienza in S. Agostino*. Roma: Editrice Pontificia Università Gregoriana, 2000.

Bobik, J. "Aquinas on Communicatio, The Foundation on Friendship and Caritas." *The Modern Schoolman*, no. 64 (1986): 1–18.

Borgonovo, Graziano. *Soggetto Morale e Chiesa: Lutero, Erasmo, Newman, e Guardini a Confronto*. Casale: Edizioni Piemme, 2000.

Brock, Stephen. "On the Causality of Petitionary Prayer: C. S. Lewis, Peter Geach, and Thomas Aquinas." *Living Faith* 12, no. 2 (2012): 11–22.

Bunge, Gabriel. *Dragon's Wine and Angel's Bread: The Teaching of Evagrius Ponticus on Anger and Meekness*. Crestwood: St Vladimir's Seminary Press, 2009.

Burt, Donald X. *Friendship and Society: An Introduction to Augustine's Practical Philosophy*. Grand Rapids, MI: William B. Eerdmans, 1999.

Cantalamessa, Raniero. *Virginity: A Positive Approach to Celibacy for the Sake of the Kingdom of Heaven*. Translated by Charles Serignat. New York: St. Pauls, 2011.

Carlson, Sebastian. *The Virtue of Humility*. River Forest, Illinois: Studium Generale S. Thomae Aquinatis, 1949.

Cassian, John. *The Institutes*. Translated by Boniface Ramsey. New York: Newman Press, 2000.

Catechism of the Catholic Church. New York: Doubleday, 1997.

Cessario, Romanus. *The Moral Virtues and Theological Ethics*. Notre Dame, IN: University of Notre Dame Press, 2013.

Cole, Basil. *The Hidden Enemies of the Priesthood: The Contributions of St. Thomas Aquinas*. New York: St. Pauls, 2005.

Collegii Salmaticiensis Fr. Discalceatorum. *Cursus Theologicus Summan Theologicam Angelici Doctoris D. Thomae Complectens*. Vol. 6. 20 vols. Parisiis: Apud Victorem Palme, 1878.

Crespo, Mariano. *El Perdón. Una Investigación Filosófica*. Madrid: Ediciones Encuentro, 2004.

Decomiso, David. *Ethics as a Work of Charity: Thomas Aquinas and Pagan Virtue*. Stanford: Stanford University Press, 2014.

Deferrari, Roy J. *A Lexicon of Saint Thomas Aquinas*. Fitzwilliam, NH: Loreto Publications, 2004.

De Marchi, Carlo. *L'affabilitas Nei Rapporti Sociali: Studio Comparativo Sulla Socievolezza e il Buonumore in Tommaso d'Aquino, Thomas More e Francesco Di Sales*. Rome: EDUSC, 2010.

De Sales, Francis. *An Introduction to the Devout Life*. Dublin: M. H. Gill and Son, 1885.

Dewan, Lawrence. *Wisdom and Law: Essays in Thomistic Ethics*. New York: Fordham University Press, 2008.

Estrada, Bernardo. "La Giustizia in Matteo: Presenza Del Rengo." *Rivista Biblica*, no. 59 (2011): 373–403.

Farrell, Walter. *Swift Victory: Essays on the Gifts of the Holy Spirit*. New York: Sheed and Ward, 1955.

———. *The Fullness of Life: A Companion to the Summa*. Vol. 3. New York: Sheed and Ward, 1940.

Gallagher, Timothy M. *The Discernment of Spirits: An Ignatian Guide for Everyday Living*. New York: Crossroad, 2005.

———. *The Examen Prayer*. New York: Crossroad, 2006.

Galot, Jean. *Who Is Christ? A Theology of Incarnation*. Chicago: Franciscan Herald Press, 1989.

García López, Jesús. "El Amor Humano." *Persona y Derecho* 1 (1974): 267–82.

———. *Metafísica Tomista: Ontología, Gnoseología y Teología Natural*. Navarra: EUNSA, 2001.

———. *Tomás de Aquino: Maestro Del Orden*. Madrid: Ediciones Pedagógicas, 1996.

———. *Virtud y Personalidad Según Tomás de Aquino*. Pamplona: EUNSA, 2003.

Garrigou-Lagrange, Reginald. *The Three Ages of the Interior Life: Prelude of Eternal Life*. Translated by Timothea Doyle. 2 vols. Rockford, IL: TAN Books and Publishers, 1989.

George, Marie I. "Aquinas on the Dangers of Natural Virtue and The Control of Natural Vice." *Tópicos* 40 (2011): 13–50.

Gilson, Étienne. *Wisdom and Love in Saint Thomas Aquinas*. Milwaukee: Marquette University Press, 1951.

Giuseppe Butera. "On Reason's Control of the Passions in Aquinas's Theory of Temperance." *Medieval Studies* 68 (2006): 133–60.

Gomez, José H. *Men of Brave Heart: The Virtue of Courage in the Priestly Life*. Huntington, IN: Our Sunday Visitor, 2009.

Grundmann, Walter. "ταπεινός." In *Theological Dictionary of the New Testament*. Edited by Kittel Gerhard and Friedrich Gerhard, VIII:1–26. Grand Rapids, MI: William B. Eerdmans, 1972.

Guardini, Romano. *Learning the Virtues That Lead You to God*. Translated by Stella Lange. Manchester, NH: Sophia Institute Press, 1998.

———. *The End of the Modern World: A Search for Orientation*. Translated by J. Theman and H. Burke. London: Sheed and Ward, 1957.

Hoeck, Andreas. "From Kénosis to Tapeínosis: A Case Study on the Relationship between ἐκένωσεν and ἐταπείνωσεν in Phil 2:7-8." *Estudios Biblicos* 68, no. 2 (2010): 173–83.

———. "Holy Communion: Sharing in the Threefold Munus of the Divine Gladiator." *Homiletic and Pastoral Review* (2013), http://www.hprweb.com/2013/06/holy-communion-sharing-in-the-threefold-munus-of-the-divine-gladiator/.

Hütter, Reinhard. "Happiness and Religion: Why the Virtue of Religion Is Indispensable for Attaining the Final End. A Re-Lecture of Thomas Aquinas with an Eye to His Contemporary Relevance." *Nova et Vetera, English Edition* 14, no. 1 (2016): 15–60.

Ignatius of Loyola. *The Spiritual Exercises of St. Ignatius*. Translated by Louis J. Puhl. New York: Vintage Books, 2000.

Jensen, Steven. *Knowing the Natural Law: From Precepts and Inclinations to Deriving Oughts*. Washington, DC: Catholic University of America Press, 2015.

———. *Living the Good Life: A Beginner's Thomistic Ethics*. Washington, DC: Catholic University of America Press, 2013.

John of the Cross. *The Collected Works of St. John of the Cross*. Translated by Kieran Kavanaugh and Otilio Rodriguez. Washington, DC: ICS Publications, 1991.

John Paul II. *Man and Woman He Created Them: A Theology of the Body*. Edited by Michael Waldstein. Boston: Pauline Books & Media, 2006.

John of St. Thomas. *The Gifts of the Holy Ghost*. Translated by Dominic Hughes. New York: Sheed and Ward, 1951.

Kant, Immanuel. *Lectures on Ethics*. Translated by Louis Infield. Indianapolis: Hackett, 1984.

———. "What is Enlightenment." In *On History*, 3–10. Edited and translated by L. White Beck. New York: Bobbs-Merrill, 1963.

Kauth, Matthew. *Charity as Divine and Human Friendship: A Metaphysical and Scriptural Explanation According to the Thought of St. Thomas Aquinas*. Charlotte, NC: Saint Benedict Press, 2012.

Kierkegaard, Søren. *Christian Discourses*. Translated by Walter Lowrie. Princeton University Press, 1971.

———. *Works of Love*. Translated by Howard Hong. New York: Harper Torchbooks, 1962.

Linacre Institute. *After Asceticism: Sex, Prayer, and Deviant Priests*. Bloomington, IN: AuthorHouse, 2006.

Lovasik, Lawrence G. *The Hidden Power of Kindness: A Practical Handbook for Souls Who Dare to Transform the World, One Deed at a Time*. Manchester, NH: Sophia Institute Press, 1999.

MacIntyre, Alasdair. *Dependent Rational Animals: Why Human Beings Need the Virtues*. Chicago: Open Court, 2001.

Malo, Antonio. *Io e Gli Altri: Dall'identità Alla Relazione*. Roma: EDUSC, 2010.

Manzanedo, Marcos. "La Amistad En La Filosofia Greco-Romana." *Angelicum* 70 (1993): 329–61.

Maritain, Jacques. *Education at the Crossroads*. New Haven: Yale University Press, 1943.

Melina, Livio, José Noriega, and Juan José Pérez-Soba. *Caminar a la Luz del Amor: Los Fumdamentos de la Moral Cristiana*. Madrid: Ediciones Palabra, 2007.

Migne, Jacques Paul, ed. *Patrologia Latina*. Paris: 1844–1864.

Millán-Puelles, Antonio. *El Valor de La Libertad*. Madrid: Ediciones Rialp, 1995.

———. "La Formación de La Personalidad Humana." In *Obras Completas*, III:193–366. Madrid: Ediciones Rialp, 2013.

———. *La Libre Afirmación de Nuestro Ser: Una Fundamentación de La Ética Realista*. Madrid: Ediciones Rialp, 1994.

———. "Las dimensiones morales del interes por la verdad." *Anuario Filosófi* co 62, no. 3 (2009): 532.

Mondin, Baptista. "Affabilità/Cortesia." In *Dizionario Enciclopedico Del Pensiero Di San Tommaso d'Aquino*, 25–26. Bologna: ESD, 1991.

Nolla, José Francisco. "La Virtud de La Generosidad Según Santo Tomás de Aquino." Universidad de Navarra, 2010.

Ocáriz Braña, Fernando. *Hijos de Dios En Cristo: Introducción a Una Teología de La Participación Sobrenatural*. Pamplona: EUNSA, 1972.

O'Mahoney, Christopher. *St. Thérèse of Lisieux by Those Who Knew Her: Testimonies from the Process of Beatification*. Huntington, IN: Our Sunday Visitor, 1975.

Pérez-López, Ángel. *De La Experiencia de La Integración a La Visión Integral de La Persona: Estudio Histórico-Analítico de La Integración En "Persona Y Acción" de Karol Wojtyła.* Valencia: Edicep, 2012.

———. "Karol Wojtyła's Thomistic Understanding of Consciousness." *The Thomist* 79, no. 3 (2015): 407–37.

———. *Procreation and the Spousal Meaning of the Body: A Thomistic Argument Grounded in Vatican II.* Eugene, OR: Pickwick, 2017.

Phelan, Gerald B. "Justicia y Amistad." *Finisterre* 1 (1948): 221–45.

Philipon, Michael-Marie. *Les Dons Du Saint–Esprit.* Bruges: Desclée De Brouwer, 1964.

Pieper, Josef. *A Brief Reader on the Virtues of the Human Heart.* Translated by Paul C. Duggan. San Francisco: Ignatius Press, 1991.

———. *The Four Cardinal Virtues: Prudence, Justice, Fortitude, Temperance.* Notre Dame, IN: University of Notre Dame Press, 1966.

———. *Living the Truth: The Truth of All Things and Reality and the Good.* Translated by Lothar Krauth. San Francisco: Ignatius Press, 1989.

Polo, Leonardo. "La Amistad En Aristóteles." *Anuario Filosófico* 32 (1999): 477–85.

Ramírez, Jacobus. *De Caritate.* In *II-II Summae Theologiae Divi Thomae Expositio (QQ. XXIII-XLIV).* Vol. 12. Opera Omnia. Salamanca: Editorial San Esteban, 1998.

———. *De Fide Divina.* In *II-II Summae Theologiae Divi Thomae Expositio (QQ. I-VII).* Edited by Victorino Rodriguez. Vol. 10. Opera Omnia. Salamanca: Editorial San Esteban, 1994.

———. *De Passionibus Animae*. In *I-II Summae Theologiae Divi Thomae Expositio (QQ. XXII-XLVIII)*. Vol. V. Opera Omnia. Madrid: Instituto de Filosofia Luis Vives, 1973.

———. *Los Dones del Espíritu Santo*. Madrid: Editorial San Esteban, 1978.

Ratzinger, Joseph. *A New Song for the Lord: Faith in Christ and Liturgy Today*. Translated by Martha Matesich. New York: Crossroad, 1996.

Rhonheimer, Martin. *Natural Law and Practical Reason: A Thomist View of Moral Autonomy*. Translated by Gerald Malsbary. New York: Fordham University Press, 2000.

———. *The Perspective of Morality: Philosophical Foundations of Thomistic Virtue Ethics*. Translated by Gerald Malsbary. Washington, DC: Catholic University of America Press, 2011.

Richardson, John. "The Virtue of Gratitude According to the Mind of Saint Thomas Aquinas." Washington, DC: Pontificium Institutum Angelicum de Urbe, 1954.

Rivera, Abelardo. "El Amor de Amistad en Santo Tomás de Aquino." Facultad de Teología de la Universidad de Navarra, 2008.

Rodríguez Luño, Angel. *Ética General*. Pamplona: EUNSA, 2001.

———. *Scelti in Cristo Per Essere Santi: Morale Speciale*. Vol. 3. Sussidi Di Teologia. Roma: EDUSC, 2008.

Romera Oñate, Luis. *El Hombre Ante El Misterio de Dios: Curso de Teología Natural*. Madrid: Ediciones Palabra, 2007.

Roqueñí, José Manuel. *Educación En La Afectividad: Una Propuesta Desde El Pensamiento de Santo Tomás de Aquino*. Pamplona: EUNSA, 2005.

Royo Marín, Antonio. *El Gran Desconocido: El Espíritu Santo y Sus Dones*. Madrid: BAC, 1987.

———. *Teología Moral Para Seglares: Moral Fundamental*. Vol. 1. 2 vols. Madrid: BAC, 1986.

Scheler, Max. *Formalism in Ethics and Non-Formal Ethics of Values: A New Attempt toward the Foundation of an Ethical Personalism*. Evanston: Northwestern University Press, 1973.

———. *The Nature of Sympathy*. New Jersey: Transaction Publishers, 2008.

———. "On the Rehabilitation of Virtue." *American Catholic Philosophical Quarterly* 79 (2005): 21–37.

———. *Ressentiment*. Translated by Lewis Coser and William Holdheim. Milwaukee: Marquette University Press, 2010.

———. *Selected Philosophical Essays*. Translated by David Lachterman. Evanston: Northwestern University Press, 1973.

Schwartz, Daniel. *Aquinas on Friendship*. Oxford: Clarendon Press, 2007.

———. "Friendship and the Circumstances of Justice According to Aquinas." *The Review of Politics* 66, no. 1 (2004) 35–54.

Senovilla García, José Antonio. "La Virtud de La Piedad En Santo Tomás de Aquino. Fuentes Y Análisis Textual." Universidad de Navarra, 2004.

Sertillanges, Antonin-Gilbert. *The Intellectual Life. Its Spirit, Conditions, Methods*. Translated by Mary Ryan. Washington, DC: Catholic University of America Press, 1998.

Smith, Janet E. *The Right of Privacy*. San Francisco: Ignatius Press, 2008.

Sommers, Mary Catherine. "Marriage Vows and 'Taking Up a New State.'" *Nova et Vetera, English Edition* 7, no. 3 (2009): 679–95.

Staudt, Robert Jared. "Religion as a Virtue: Thomas Aquinas on Worship Through Justice, Law, and Charity." Ave Maria University, 2008.

Stern-Gillet, Suzanne. *Aristotle's Philosophy of Friendship*. Albany: State University of New York Press, 1995.

Teresa of Avila. *The Collected Works of Saint Teresa of Avila*. Translated by Kieran Kavanaugh and Otilio Rodriguez. Washington, DC: ICS Publications, 2012.

———. *The Interior Castle or the Mansions*. Charlotte, NC: TAN Books and Publishers, 2011.

Thérèse of Lisieux. *Story of a Soul: The Autobiography of Saint Thérèse of Lisieux*. Translated by John Clarke. Washington, DC: ICS Publications, 1996.

Vázquez de Prada, Andrés. *Estudio Sobre La Amistad*. Madrid: Ediciones Rialp, 1975.

Von Hildebrand, Dietrich. *The Art of Living*. Manchester, NH: Sophia Institute Press, 1994.

———. *The Heart: An Analysis of Human and Divine Affectivity*. Edited by John Henry Crosby. South Bend, IN: Saint Augustine's Press, 2007.

———. *Transformation in Christ: On the Christian Attitude*. San Francisco: Ignatius Press, 2001.

Wadell, Paul J. *Friendship & the Moral Life*. Notre Dame, IN: University of Notre Dame Press, 1991.

Westberg, Daniel. *Right Practical Reason: Aristotle, Action, and Prudence in Aquinas*. Oxford: Clarendon Press, 1994.

White, Kevin. "The Virtues of the 'Animal Sociale': Affabilitas and Veritas in Aquinas." *The Thomist* 57, no. 4 (1993): 641–53.

Wojtyła, Karol. *Love and Responsibility*. Translated by H. Willets. San Francisco: Ignatius Press, 1993.

———. *Max Scheler y la Etica Cristiana*. Madrid: BAC, 1980.

———. "On the Meaning of Spousal Love." In *Love and Responsibility*, translated by Grzegorz Ignatik, 275–94. Boston: Pauline Books & Media, 2013.

———. *Osoba i Czyn-Persona e Atto*. Edited by Tadeusz Styczen. Santarcangelo: Rusconi Libri, 1999.

———. *Person and Community: Selected essays*. New York: Peter Lang, 1993.

———. *Sources of Renewal: The Implementation of the Second Vatican Council*. Translated by P. S. Falla. San Francisco: Harper & Row, 1980.

———. *The Acting Person*. Edited by Anna-Teresa Tymieniecka. Dordrecht: D. Reidel, 1979.

Yarza, Ignacio. *La Racionalidad de La Ética de Aristóteles: Un Estudio Sobre Ética a Nicómaco I*. EUNSA, 2001.